TRANSACTIONS

of the

American Philosophical Society

Held at Philadelphia for Promoting Useful Knowledge

VOLUME 80, Part 1, 1990

Paradise Restored

The Mechanical Arts from Antiquity through the Thirteenth Century

ELSPETH WHITNEY

Division of Human Studies, Alfred University

THE AMERICAN PHILOSOPHICAL SOCIETY

Independence Square, Philadelphia

1990

Library of Congress Catalog
Card Number 88-82930
International Standard Book Number 0-87169-801-3
US ISSN 0065-9746

Table of Contents

Acknowledgments

Any project such as this one draws inspiration from many sources. I owe much to my teachers at the Graduate School of the City University of New York, including Howard Adelson, Richard Lemay and, especially, Nancy G. Siraisi, who introduced me to the adventure, as well as the rigors of scholarship. The spirited conversation of my friends and colleagues, in particular Irving Kelter, Janice Gordon-Kelter, Tom Peterson, Vicki Eaklor, William Dibrell and John H. Phillips, has helped me to understand both myself and my ideas better. I wish to thank my editors, Carole Le Faivre and Susan M. Babbitt, for their care and patience. My brother, Peter Nichols, gave encouragement when it was most needed. I thank my parents, Elliott and Sally Nichols, not only for their love and support, but for their continuing dialogue about the relationship of matter and spirit which is one reason this book came to be written. Most of all I thank my husband Charles for his unfailing liveliness of mind and for the love "which also makes meaning" and all else.

I received grants for research and writing from the Graduate School of the City of New York, the Center for European Studies, CUNY and the NEH Summer Seminar Program.

Chapter III previously appeared in *Annals of Scholarship* 4 (1987): 11–27.

Trans. Amer. Phil. Soc.
Vol. 80 Pt. 1, 1990

I. Introduction: The History of the Problem

At least since the Renaissance, historians, philosophers, and other critics have attempted to judge the positive and negative contributions of the Middle Ages to the development of Western civilization. In particular, these writers have assessed the extent to which medieval culture and institutions may have either hindered or fostered scientific and technological progress.[1] Until the present century such assessments have tended to be overwhelmingly negative: both scholastic habits of thought and medieval religiosity have been thought to be incompatible with the development of a true scientific method and the rational application of human intelligence to the natural world. Over the past fifty years, however, this view has been substantially revised. Historians have not only recognized the Middle Ages as a critical period in the development of Western technology but have re-evaluated the whole relationship of religious ideas and attitudes to science and technology. These new views, further, have had a continuous impact on interpretations of medieval society and culture.

Research focused first on medieval innovations in the use of animal, wind and water power; subsequently attention was paid to how these inventions may have been an element in social change, including the development of feudalism and the emergence of a more vital society in the eleventh century. Most recently, historians have centered on how religious and intellectual attitudes and institutions reflected technological growth and how these and other aspects of medieval culture may have helped create a technologically dynamic society.

The provocative and often insightful body of work produced since the early twentieth century has contributed to a deeper understanding of medieval attitudes toward manual labor and a more precise conception of how medieval thinkers conceived the proper relationship between human actions and the natural world. It has not, however, yet resulted in a detailed and coherent assessment of what might properly be called the philosophy of technology in the Middle Ages, that is, the metaphysical and ontological status accorded to craftsmanship and the process of invention in medieval thought. Indeed, much of this research has tended to obscure crucial distinctions between attitudes toward labor, which might be considered as mere physical drudgery yet still be

[1] For a summary and discussion of evaluations of the Middle Ages and concepts of progress since the sixteenth century, see George Ovitt, Jr., *The Restoration of Perfection: Labor and Technology in Medieval Culture* (New Brunswick, N.J.: Rutgers University Press, 1987), 19–47.

valued as a form of penance, attitudes toward the products of such labor, which were liable to moral judgments as to their use and abuse, and attitudes toward the physical and intellectual activity necessary to produce technological change. Whether technological innovation should be considered as a form of physical labor or as a category of rational thought was of course an issue deeply influenced by social class, yet it was also a philosophical question with its roots in a tradition deeply imbued with the classical dichotomy of mind and body. The present study examines the intellectual process by which medieval philosophers and theologians revised classical concepts of technology and its place in classifications of the arts and sciences in order to redefine technological invention as a full-fledged category of knowledge. If this process of rethinking was fully complete only in the seventeenth century, when the Scientific Revolution provided a new ontological basis for the manipulation of the physical world, medieval thinkers established a framework upon which these new ideas could be developed.

The impact of technological change and innovation on medieval society was first suggested by Richard Lefebvre des Noëttes in 1924. Lefebvre des Noëttes argued that the invention of the modern rigid horse collar in the early Middle Ages and the adoption of stirrups and iron horseshoes provided medieval society with a far more efficient use of animal power than had been available in antiquity.[2] His work was quickly followed by the research of Marc Bloch and others on medieval agricultural practices, the use of water and wind mills, and improved ship design and building techniques.[3] Much of this information was collected, commented upon and brought to the attention of American medievalists in 1940 by Lynn White, jr., who concluded that "the chief glory of the later Middle Ages was not its cathedrals or its epics or its scholasticism: it was the building for the first time in history of a complex civilization which rested not on the backs of sweating slaves or coolies but primarily on non-human power."[4]

It is now possible to speak of a medieval industrial revolution. Medieval society is often pictured as one in which industry was increasingly mechanized and in which human beings found themselves increasingly

---

[2] Richard Lefebvre des Noëttes, *La force motrice animale à travers les âges* (Paris: Berger-Levrault, 1924), 94–118; see also Lefebvre des Noëttes, "La force motrice animale et le rôle des inventions techniques," *Revue de synthèse historique* 43 (1927): 83–91 and *L'attelage et le cheval de selle à travers les âges* (Paris: A. Picard, 1939). For an engaging history of the history of medieval technology, see Lynn White, jr., "The Study of Medieval Technology, 1924–1974: Personal Reflections," in *Medieval Religion and Technology: Collected Essays* (Berkeley, Los Angeles and London: University of California Press, 1978), xi–xxiv.

[3] Marc Bloch, "Avènement et conquêtes du moulin à eau," *Annales d'histoire économique et sociale* 7 (1935): 538–563 and "Les 'inventions' médiévales," *Annales d'histoire économique et sociale* 7 (1935): 634–643. These essays are translated in *Land and Work in Mediaeval Europe: Selected Papers by Marc Bloch,* trans. J. E. Anderson (London: Routledge and Kegan Paul, 1967; rpt. New York: Harper and Row, 1969), 136–185.

[4] White, "Technology and Invention," 156.

surrounded by machines.[5] Not only were the conditions of agricultural and industrial work transformed by more efficient uses of power and the invention of new techniques and devices, such as tidal mills, water-driven bellows, iron-casting and the compound crank, but people's lives were affected by the introduction and spread of mechanical clocks, eyeglasses, chimneys and other innovations.[6] In the phrase of a historian of twelfth-century theology, medieval man began to live in a "mechanism-minded world."[7]

The widespread acceptance of the view that the Middle Ages, more than any earlier or contemporary society, used newly invented, borrowed and adapted devices and machines to transform society has naturally led to an examination of the extent to which technological change could be identified as a cause of specific forms of social change. In the 1930s, Lefebvre des Noëttes and Bloch argued the question whether the disappearance of slavery in the medieval West was a consequence (as Bloch thought) or a cause (as Lefebvre des Noëttes claimed) of technological advance.[8] More recently, in 1962 Lynn White attempted to explain the development of feudalism and the economic and intellectual revival of the eleventh and twelfth centuries as direct results of the use of the stirrup and new agricultural techniques.[9] Although almost every detail of White's thesis has come under attack, the overall thrust of his work—that technological change was a crucial element in the formation of medieval society—has been virtually universally accepted.[10] Today,

---

[5] See, for example, E. M. Carus-Wilson, "An Industrial Revolution in the Thirteenth Century," *Economic History Review* 7 (1941): 39–55; A. C. Crombie, *Medieval and Early Modern Science* (Garden City, N.Y.: Doubleday, Anchor Books, 1959) 1: 199 and Jean Gimpel, *The Medieval Machine: The Industrial Revolution of the Middle Ages* (New York: Holt, Rinehart and Winston, 1976; rpt. New York and London: Penguin Books, 1980).

[6] For a good overview of medieval technology and its effects on medieval life, see, especially, Crombie, *Medieval and Early Modern Science* 1: 175–238; Gimpel, *The Medieval Machine*; Friedrich Klemm, *A History of Western Technology*, trans. Dorothea Waley Singer (Cambridge, Mass.: The Massachusetts Institute of Technology Press, 1964), 55–107 and LeRoy Dresbeck, "*Techne, Labor et Natura*: Ideas and Active Life in the Medieval Winter," *Studies in Medieval and Renaissance History* n. s. 2 (1979): 83–119. For more specialized information on medieval technology, see Charles Singer, E. J. Holmyard, and A. R. Hall, eds., *A History of Technology* (Oxford: Clarendon Press, 1965), vol. 2; Maurice Daumas, ed., *Histoire générale des techniques* (Paris: Presses Universitaires de France, 1962), 1: 429–598 and Lynn White, *Medieval Technology and Social Change* (London: Oxford University Press, 1964). On eyeglasses, see Edward Rosen, "The Invention of Eyeglasses," *Journal of the History of Medicine and Allied Sciences* 11 (1956): 13–46, 183–218. For bibliography on the mechanical clock, see White, *Medieval Technology* 119–124.

[7] M.-D. Chenu, *Nature, Man, and Society in the Twelfth Century: Essays on New Theological Perspectives in the Latin West*, ed. and trans. Jerome Taylor and Lester K. Little (Chicago: University of Chicago Press, 1968), 43.

[8] Bloch presents his case against Lefebvre des Noëttes in "Les 'inventions' medievales," 634–643. See also the discussion in William Carroll Bark, *Origins of the Medieval World* (Stanford, Calif.: Stanford University Press, 1958), 95–96.

[9] White, *Medieval Technology*, 1–78.

[10] For criticism of White's methodology, see R. H. Hilton and P. H. Sawyer, "Technical Determinism: The Stirrup and the Plough," *Past and Present* 24 (1963): 90–100 and Bernard S. Bachrach, "Charles Martel, Mounted Shock Combat, the Stirrup and Feudalism," *Studies in Medieval and Renaissance History* 7 (1970): 49–75.

the social history of medieval technology is one of the more lively areas of medieval studies.[11]

The recognition of the importance of technology for economic growth and social change in the Middle Ages has also increasingly prompted investigation into the cultural environment in which technological development took place. Historians have, especially, attempted to define the cultural and intellectual meaning technology had for the medieval world. Although it had sometimes been suggested that the Middle Ages possessed certain qualities which encouraged the development of technology,[12] it is only in the last thirty years that detailed studies have appeared relating technological growth to medieval religion, science, philosophy and attitudes toward craftsmanship and manual labor. In part an aspect of the far broader movement initiated by Pierre Duhem, Lynn Thorndike and others to claim for the Middle Ages a decisive role in the formation of modern Western society and values,[13] these studies have added a new dimension to medieval intellectual history and, in many ways, have profoundly changed our image of the tone and tenor of medieval life.

The thrust of much of the work on medieval technology and ideas about technology has been to suggest that the medieval world, or significant groups within it, took a consciously active, practical and even aggressive stance toward nature. In a survey of medieval technology and ideas connected to the problem of overcoming the effects of the winter climate, for example, LeRoy Dresbeck remarks that "in the central Middle Ages, many philosophers and theologians were abandoning as

---

[11] See the argument for a social history of technology in Dresbeck, "*Techne, Labor et Natura*," 83–84, 117–118. See also Pamela O. Long, ed., *Science and Technology in Medieval Society* (New York: New York Academy of Science, 1985).

[12] Lewis Mumford, *Technics and Civilization* (New York: Harcourt, Brace and Company, 1934), 12–17, 33–37 briefly argued that the institutions of the medieval Church "prepared the way for the machine" through encouragement of an orderly, disciplined, punctual life and contempt for the body. Alfred North Whitehead, *Science and the Modern World* (New York: The Macmillan Company, 1925; rpt. New York: The Free Press, 1967),15 suggested that "the alliance of science with technology . . . owes much to the practical bent of the early Benedictines."

[13] Lynn Thorndike, "Renaissance or Prenaissance?" *Journal of the History of Ideas* 4 (1943): 65–74 and Pierre Duhem, *Le système du monde: Histoire des doctrines cosmologiques de Platon à Copernic* (Paris: Hermann, 1913–54) argue for the medieval origins of modern science; C. H. McIlwain, "Mediaeval Institutions in the Modern World," *Speculum* 16 (1943): 275–283 makes a comparable argument for the medieval origins of modern government. For a review of the historiography and issues connected with the relationship of medieval and early modern science see Edward Rosen, "Renaissance Science as Seen by Burckhardt and His Successors," in *The Renaissance: A Reconsideration of the Theories and Interpretations of the Age*, ed. T. Helton (Madison, Wisc.: University of Wisconsin Press, 1961), 77–103. The tendency for some enthusiasts for medieval technology to identify medieval technology with the genesis of the more cherished virtues of Western civilization, including freedom, humanitarianism, democracy and world-domination, is especially evident in Bark, *Origins of the Medieval World*, 100–112; Gimpel, *The Medieval Machine*, vii–xi, 1; White, "Technology and Invention," 141, 156 and "The Historical Roots of our Ecologic Crisis," in *Western Man and Environmental Ethics: Attitudes toward Nature and Technology*, ed. Ian G. Barbour (Reading, Mass.: Addison-Wesley Publishing Company, 1973), 21.

an heretical notion the idea of mere survival in a hostile world as they began to understand the role of technology and labor as transformers of things and objects which ultimately could create a better society."[14] Most recently George Ovitt has suggested that medieval attitudes toward labor, while "neither univocal or even consistent," were nevertheless seminal in the development of Western institutionalization of labor.[15] It is now often acknowledged that many of the attitudes long associated with the Middle Ages and considered to be inimical to an appreciation of technology, including an emphasis on theoretical over practical knowledge, intellectual over manual labor, and a concern with inner spiritual and moral needs rather than material progress, were more flexible than had been assumed and were held neither absolutely nor without modification. Some scholars have carried this viewpoint further and identified the Middle Ages as the historical source of many of the values we now associate with modern technological practice.[16] Among the values recently attributed to the medieval period, for example, are a belief in the moral goodness of labor and technology, a sense of radical separation between man and his natural environment, and the view that man's relationship to nature is properly utilitarian and exploitative.[17] This new perspective, which contrasts so strongly with older views of the Middle Ages as largely indifferent, passive or antagonistic toward the physical world, has had a far-reaching, if often indirect, influence on interpretations of medieval culture.

On the one hand, historians have turned to the question of attitudes toward technology and labor as a focus for examining the interaction of intellectual and social patterns in the Middle Ages. Jacques Le Goff, for example, has approached the study of medieval society through an analysis of scholastic and popular cultural attitudes toward work and time.[18] Similarly, LeRoy Dresbeck has suggested that it is only through the synthesis of the history of technological devices and techniques in the Middle Ages with an examination of how technological innovation influenced people's imagination, thought and values that the historian can fully understand many aspects of social change.[19] These scholars, like Lynn White and others, see attitudes toward labor, nature and crafts as vital clues to the ways in which medieval society functioned. On the other hand, students of medieval intellectual history have increasingly

[14] Dresbeck, "*Techne, Labor et Natura*," 91.

[15] Ovitt, *Restoration of Perfection*, 199–204.

[16] White, "Historical Roots of Our Ecologic Crisis," 21–27. For an example of the older view, see Robert K. Merton, *Science, Technology and Society in Seventeenth-Century England* (New York: Howard Fertig, 1970), 76, originally published in 1938, who remarks that to see technological discoveries as pleasing to God in themselves "would have been simply unthinkable in the medieval period."

[17] See below, pp. 13–15.

[18] Jacques Le Goff, *Time, Work, and Culture in the Middle Ages*, trans. Arthur Goldhammer (Chicago and London: The University of Chicago Press, 1980).

[19] Dresbeck, "*Techne, Labor et Natura*," 83.

integrated technology into their picture of medieval scientific and theological thought. When, for example, Charles Homer Haskins described in 1927 the salient characteristics and historical background of the cultural and intellectual movement still known as the Twelfth-Century Renaissance, he made no mention of either technology or the mechanical arts; neither term appears in the index of Haskins's otherwise still important work.[20] Today, however, it is difficult to assess the intellectual world of the High Middle Ages without taking some account of contemporary statements about the worth of crafts, the mechanical arts or manual labor.[21] Without claiming an identity between the attitudes of artisans, merchants, monastic craftsmen and others who produced or used new techniques and the views of philosophers and theologians who articulated systems of thought or belief relevant to a concept of technology, scholars such as M.-D. Chenu, A. C. Crombie, Brian Stock, Winthrop Wetherbee, Franco Alessio, Maurice de Gandillac, John Van Engen and Olaf Pedersen have explored how technological development may have been reflected in contemporary thought.

The scholarly effort to define medieval cultural attitudes toward labor and technology, however, has raised several important questions about medieval concepts of technology which remain largely unresolved. First, the history of ideas relating to the mechanical arts is still unclear. Although historians have begun to examine ideas about crafts, labor and the mechanical arts as they appear in isolated texts, for the most part, this work has proceeded without any overall historical and philosophical perspective. It is not surprising, therefore, that scholars have presented strikingly different views of the relationship of medieval ideas about technology to medieval science, to medieval theology and to the classical philosophical tradition. Whereas, for example, Crombie, Bertrand Gille, Pedersen, and Guy Beaujouan have considered the genesis of a more positive view of technology in the Middle Ages as a product of changing contemporary conceptions of the nature and purpose of scientific knowledge, Alessio, de Gandillac and others have seen this development in terms of a broad "religious or natural anthropology" with its roots in antiquity.[22] Still other historians, including Chenu, Stock, Van Engen, Le Goff, Ovitt and White have found the source of new attitudes toward technology in specifically Christian ideas about work, art and nature; yet, as we shall see, these scholars differ markedly among themselves in their analysis of the interplay between religion, social conditions and the mechanical arts.

---

[20] Charles Homer Haskins, *The Renaissance of the Twelfth Century* (Cambridge, Mass.: Harvard University Press, 1927).

[21] See, for example, in the recent up-dating of Haskins's work, Robert L. Benson, Giles Constable and Carol D. Lanham, eds., *Renaissance and Renewal in the Twelfth Century* (Cambridge, Mass.: Harvard University Press, 1982), the article by Gerhart B. Ladner, "Terms and Ideas of Renewal," 21: "We may note the new esteem shown in the early twelfth century to the mechanical arts. . . ."

[22] The work of these historians is discussed in detail below.

Nor have philosophers of technology fully assimilated this research. Until recently, discussion of the development of Western philosophical ideas on technology has typically focused on the differences between classical and modern conceptions of knowledge with a view to explaining why the latter led to a metaphysical and scientific basis for technology and the former could not.[23] Medieval philosophy, often assumed to be merely restating classical ideas on crafts, was for the most part subsumed under the umbrella of ancient thought. Hans Jonas, for example, in his well-known essay, "The Practical Uses of Theory" (1959), on how modern conceptions of the practical use of knowledge and science differed from the classical contemplative ideal, refers to only one medieval author, Aquinas, "who of course speaks for Aristotle."[24] Similarly, Paolo Rossi's *Philosophy, Technology, and the Arts in the Early Modern Era* (1970) and Carl Mitcham's study, "Philosophy and the History of Technology" (1979), contrast classical and modern ideas of technology with only a few passing comments on medieval works.[25] Although new insights into both classical and medieval thought have begun to alter this perspective, a balanced view of the historical development of Western thinking on technology is still to be achieved.

Second, the current focus of many historians upon social rather than intellectual history has sometimes tended to obscure the significance of medieval perceptions of technology as a branch of knowledge. Several recent studies, among them articles by Lynn White and Guy Allard, have suggested that medieval philosophers and scientists, individually and as a group, did not share in the cultural receptiveness to technology otherwise characteristic of the Middle Ages; instead, it is argued that medieval intellectuals were influenced by a system of thought inherited from antiquity which encapsulated philosophical and social values strongly antagonistic to the appreciation of the mechanical arts.[26] This exclusion of the philosophical tradition from relevance to the problem of attitudes toward technology in the Middle Ages in a sense revives or perpetuates in a new guise the older view of the Middle Ages as intel-

---

[23] For an overview of philosophical theories about the origins of modern technology, see Carl Mitcham, "The Religious and Political Origins of Modern Technology," in *Philosophy and Technology*, ed. Paul T. Durbin and Friedrich Rapp (Boston: D. Reidel, 1983), 267–273 and Langdon Winner, *Autonomous Technology: Technics-out-of-Control as a Theme in Political Thought* (Cambridge, Mass. and London: The MIT Press, 1971), 109–122.

[24] Hans Jonas, "The Practical Uses of Theory," in *The Phenomenon of Life: Toward a Philosophical Biology* (New York: Dell Publishing Co., Delta Books, 1966), 189.

[25] Paolo Rossi, *Philosophy, Technology, and the Arts in the Early Modern Era*, trans. Salvator Attanasio and ed. Benjamin Nelson (New York, Evanston, and London: Harper and Row, Harper Torchbooks, 1970), 32–33 and 138, denies medieval thinkers any "theory" of technology and briefly cites Hugh of St. Victor as a representative of Aristotelian thought on the relationship of nature and art; Carl Mitcham, "Philosophy and the History of Technology," in *The History and Philosophy of Technology*, ed. George Bugliarello and Dean B. Doner. (Urbana, Chicago and London: University of Illinois Press, 1979), 178 mentions no medieval thinkers except Aquinas.

[26] See below, pp. 17, 19–20.

lectually indifferent to technological development. Although philosophers of technology have widely criticized what they see as an oversimplification of the classical Western philosophical tradition, this aspect of recent historiography has been tacitly accepted by medievalists.[27]

Western attitudes toward technology have often been tinged with ambivalence. Neither classical nor medieval thinkers were entirely free of negative attitudes toward the practice of crafts or their products. As I shall demonstrate in this study, however, ancient thought on technology was flexible and ambiguous enough to allow creative, positive revision and development by medieval writers. Thus from classical and patristic sources many twelfth- and thirteenth-century writers developed positive frameworks—both religious and scientific—for integrating technology as a category of knowledge into their thought. Although social history has rightly challenged the assumption that a culture can be understood largely in terms of its philosophy, medieval discussions of technology do not bear out the opposite view, that medieval philosophy is marginal to the understanding of Western cultural attitudes toward technology. A full reassessment of the relation of technology and philosophy in medieval culture, toward which this study builds, should therefore give due allowance to both the constraints and possibilities presented by the contemporary framework of thought.

Scholarship on medieval technology and culture does provide a setting for the problem of how medieval philosophers defined the mechanical arts. M.-D. Chenu, the eminent historian of twelfth-century theology, wrote, for example, in 1957 that "the rise of new techniques both betokened and promoted a true discovery, an active discovery of nature, and man advanced toward self-discovery as he came thus to master nature."[28] This sensibility, Chenu suggests, was expressed in a new concern for the mechanical arts and, especially, in an awareness of the power of human art *vis-à-vis* nature.[29] Chenu's assessment was echoed by other scholars writing about the same time. Olaf Pedersen, seeming to characterize the evolution of medieval science, remarked that "we discern throughout the Middle Ages an always growing interest in the mechanical arts. Manual labor, if little esteemed in antiquity, was rehabilitated."[30] Maurice de Gandillac reached a similar conclusion. Drawing attention to the existence of a continuous metaphysical-theo-

---

[27] For discussion of the issues involved, see below, pp. 15–16. To my knowledge, the only medieval historian to comment on White's dismissal of philosophy is Brian Stock, "Science, Technology, and Economic Progress in the Early Middle Ages," in *Science in the Middle Ages*, ed. David C. Lindberg (Chicago and London: The University of Chicago Press, 1978), 1.

[28] Chenu, *Nature, Man, and Society*, 39.

[29] Ibid., 39–48.

[30] Olaf Pedersen, "Du quadrivium à la physique: Quelques aperçus de l'évolution scientifique au Moyen Âge," in *Artes Liberales von der Antiken Bildung zur Wissenschaft des Mittelalters*, ed. Josef Koch, Studien und Texte zur Geistesgeschichte des Mittelalters, no. 5 (Leiden: E. J. Brill, 1959), 113.

logical tradition from antiquity through the Renaissance which defined man as *homo faber*, de Gandillac noted, "Far from despising the *artes mechanicae*, medieval man was already far along the way which made his sons the masters and possessors of nature."[31]

These studies, and, for the most part, those which followed, however, did not attempt to deal systematically with the specific problem of how medieval philosophers defined the mechanical arts. Rather, they began the important task of elaborating how general attitudes toward crafts and manual labor fed into the larger picture of medieval culture.

What, for example, was the relationship between the practical achievements of medieval craftsmen and the development of medieval scientific theory and method? Such a problem, of course, is not unrelated to the larger issue of the relationship of medieval to modern science and several of those medievalists especially concerned with demonstrating the medieval roots of early modern scientific ideas have also emphasized the interrelationship between the craft tradition and natural philosophy in the Middle Ages. The interest of medieval thinkers in the mechanical arts was thus made an aspect of the broader rehabilitation of medieval science earlier set in motion by Pierre Duhem, Lynn Thorndike, Marshall Clagett and Anneliese Maier.[32]

Although they recognized that artisans and scientists for the most part remained distinct groups in the Middle Ages (and for long after), A. C. Crombie and others suggested that the two activities of science and technology need not have been completely divorced. In both *Robert Grossesteste and the Origins of Experimental Science* (1953) and *Augustine to Galileo* (1953), revised as *Medieval and Early Modern Science* (1959), Crombie pointed to a long-standing and lively concern with technical problems and methods on the part of medieval scientists, which, in his view, ultimately both influenced education and contributed to the formation of a concept of experimental science.[33] Crombie, along with other historians of medieval science and medicine, including Pedersen, Bertrand Gille and Guy Beaujouan, argued that the work of medieval craftsmen

---

[31] Maurice de Gandillac, "Place et signification de la technique dans le monde médiéval," in *Tecnica e casistica*, ed. Enrico Castelli (Padua: Casa Editrice Dott. Antonio Milani, 1964), 271.

[32] For the historiographical issues and bibliography relating the craft tradition and the genesis of modern science, see Lynn White, "Natural Science and Naturalistic Art in the Middle Ages," *American Historical Review* 52 (1947): 422–423; Pedersen, "Du quadrivium à la physique," 107–109; Rupert Hall, "The Scholar and the Craftsman in the Scientific Revolution," in *Critical Problems in the History of Science*, ed. Marshall Clagett (Madison, Wisc.: University of Wisconsin Press, 1959), 3–22 and A. C. Crombie, "The Significance of Medieval Discussions of Scientific Method for the Scientific Revolution," in *Critical Problems*, 79–101. For a bibliographic introduction to works by Duhem, Maier, Alexandre Koyré, John H. Randall and others on the general relationship of medieval science to the Scientific Revolution, see Edward Grant, *Physical Science in the Middle Ages* (Cambridge, England: Cambridge University Press, 1977), 114–115.

[33] A. C. Crombie, *Robert Grosseteste and the Origins of Experimental Science, 1100–1700* (Oxford: Clarendon Press, 1953), 16–43 and *Medieval and Early Modern Science*, 1: 175–189.

was not entirely devoid of a theoretical basis, and, conversely, that some medieval thinkers acknowledged, at least theoretically, the importance of practical applications of scientific knowledge.[34]

Following the lead of Lynn Thorndike, scholars have also investigated the role of magic and the so-called occult sciences of astrology and alchemy in fostering an empirical and manipulative approach to nature.[35] Bert Hansen and A. C. Crombie, for example, have emphasized that magic and technology share the same goal of exerting power over nature and they and others have pointed to the technical content of many books of "secrets."[36] Lynn White, despite his insistence on the general absence of interplay between science and technology in the Middle Ages, has singled out fourteenth- and fifteenth-century medical astrologers as a notable exception; in White's view this group developed a strong interest in machine design and construction arising out of their professional need for instruments and accurate astronomical observations.[37]

Although, in a further turn of the revisionist screw, much recent scholarship has tended to de-emphasize the impact of medieval technological practice on scientific method, the issue itself has remained part of the continuing debate on the character of medieval science. Thus, for example, George Ovitt, who in some respects returns to the view set forth in William Whewell's *History of the Inductive Sciences* (1837) that in the Middle Ages "the division between scientific theory and mechanical practice was unequivocal," nevertheless also concludes that a "first step" in resolving this disjunction was taken by the thirteenth-century thinker, Robert Kilwardby.[38] Even Guy Allard's vigorous attack on those scholars who he feels have distorted medieval scientific and philosophical ideas through an overemphasis on positive statements on the mechanical arts (a group in which he includes Crombie, Pedersen, and

---

[34] Crombie, *Robert Grosseteste*, 16–43; Pedersen, "Du quadrivium à la physique," 107–123; Bertrand Gille, "Le Moyen Âge en Occident," in *Histoire générale des techniques*, ed. Daumas, 1: 594–597; Guy Beaujouan, "Reflexions sur les rapports entre théorie et pratique au Moyen Âge," in *The Cultural Context of Medieval Learning*, ed. J. E. Murdoch and E. D. Sylla (Dordrecht and Boston: D. Reidel, 1975), 437–484 and "The Transformation of the Quadrivium," in *Renaissance and Renewal*, ed. Benson, Constable and Lanham, 463–487. However, cf. Rupert Hall, "The Scholar and the Craftsman," in *Critical Problems*, 3–22, who emphasizes the distance between craftsmen and theoretical scientists and Lon R. Shelby, "The Geometrical Knowledge of Mediaeval Master Masons," *Speculum* 47 (1972): 395–421 who shows that medieval masons, at least, had little knowledge of theoretical Euclidean geometry. See also John M. Riddle, "Theory and Practice in Medieval Medicine," *Viator* 5 (1974): 161–184.

[35] Lynn Thorndike, *A History of Magic and Experimental Science*, 8 vols. (New York and London: Columbia University Press, 1923–1958).

[36] Bert Hansen, "Science and Magic," in *Science in the Middle Ages*, ed. Lindberg, 483–506; Crombie, *Medieval and Early Modern Science*, 1: 52–53.

[37] Lynn White, "Medical Astrologers and Late Medieval Technology," *Viator* 6 (1975): 295–308, reprinted in *Medieval Religion*, 297–316.

[38] George Ovitt, Jr., "The Status of the Mechanical Arts in Medieval Classifications of Learning," *Viator* 14 (1983): 89–105.

Beaujouan) is itself a reflection of the importance which medieval attitudes toward technology are now accorded.[39]

A second area of interpretation is the relationship of medieval technology and religion. Historians and philosophers of technology at least since Weber have considered how Christian theology influenced Western attitudes toward nature, labor and wealth and, therefore, technology.[40] The recent emphasis on medieval technological dynamism has, on the one hand, focused much of this discussion on the Middle Ages and, on the other hand, drawn the attention of medievalists to the interaction of religious ideas, beliefs and institutions with attitudes toward technology.

Students of medieval thought, including Pedersen, de Gandillac, Chenu and Alessio, for example, have observed that medieval religious sensibilities sometimes appeared to support an interest in the mechanical arts, which could be viewed as an expression of human productivity in relationship to that of God and nature.[41] More often, however, historians have turned to the social context of religious attitudes toward labor and technology. Monasticism, for example, has long been an obvious focus for exploring attitudes about the value of work. Both Mumford and Whitehead had in the 1920s and 1930s identified monasteries as prime movers in the development of technology in the West.[42] For

---

[39] Guy Allard, "Les arts mécaniques aux yeux de l'idéologie médiévale," in *Les arts mécaniques au moyen âge*, Cahiers d'études médiévales 7 (Montreal: Bellarmin; Paris: J. Vrin, 1982), 13–32. For a discussion of the relationship between written texts on techniques in the Middle Ages and actual technological development, see Bert Hall, "Production et diffusion de certains traités de techniques au moyen âge," in *Les arts mécaniques*, 147–170.

[40] For a review of Max Weber's ideas as they apply to theological conceptions of technology in his *Die protestantisch Ethik und der Geist des Kapitalismus* (1904–1905), see, especially Carl Mitcham, "The Religious and Political Origins of Modern Technology," 267–270. For an excellent guide to past and present theological perspectives on technology, see Carl Mitcham and Jim Grote, "Aspects of Christian Exegesis: Hermeneutics, the Theological Virtues, and Technology," in *Theology and Technology: Essays in Christian Analysis and Exegesis*, ed. Carl Mitcham and Jim Grote (Lanham, New York and London: University Press of America, 1984), 3–20 and, in the same volume, Carl Mitcham's annotated "Selected Bibliography of Theology and Technology," 325–502.

[41] Pedersen, "Du quadrivium à la physique," 109; de Gandillac, "Place et signification de la technique dans le monde médiéval," 272; Franco Alessio, "La filosofia e le 'artes mechanicae' nel secolo XII," *Studi Medievali* 3rd series 6 (1965): 71–155 and Chenu, *Nature, Man, and Society*, 37–48. For discussion of Alessio's work, see below, 18. Chenu, *Nature, Man, and Society*, 40 finds "a religious metaphysics" which defined man as artisan to be an important part of twelfth-century theology: "The relationship to God's creative work conferred a religious significance upon human productive activity; the relationship to the work of nature provided such activity with its earthly standard of truth."

[42] Mumford, *Technics and Civilization*, 12–17; Whitehead, *Science and the Modern World*, 15. For an updated version of Mumford's thesis that monasticism encouraged technology by fostering a mechanistic approach to time, see David Landes, *Revolution in Time: Clocks and the Making of the Modern World* (Cambridge, Mass.: Harvard University Press, 1984), 53–84. Cf. Derek J. de Solla Price, "Clockwork before the Clock," *Horological Journal* 97 (1955): 27–35 and J. Needham, L. Wang and Derek J. de Solla Price, eds., *Heavenly Clockwork: The Great Astronomical Clock of Medieval China* (Cambridge: Cambridge University Press, 1959) who argue that the mechanical clock was invented not because of an interest in time-keeping but as a byproduct of the construction of astronomical models.

them, and other historians such as Clarence Glacken and Lynn White, the monastic life bridged the gap between practical experience of manual labor and theological notions of work and man's relationship to nature, creating in Glacken's works, "a chain from theology to manuring."[43] As Brian Stock, Christopher Holdsworth and John Van Engen have shown, the spiritual value of work was very much an intellectual issue in monastic circles from the late eleventh century on. Van Engen has drawn attention to a Benedictine tradition probably originating with Rupert of Deutz and explicated in Theophilus Presbyter's *De diversis artibus*, dated by Van Engen to the early twelfth century, which defined man's image-likeness to God in terms of skill in all the arts, including crafts.[44] In Holdsworth's view, however, the Cistercian justification of work as a spiritual exercise, developed in reaction to what had become the more common view of manual labor as servile and unnecessary to the monastic life, was most influential in the twelfth century. Holdsworth's examination of the debate between Cistercians and other monastic orders and Stock's analysis of Bernard of Clairvaux's sermons demonstrate that it was possible to turn traditional ideals of poverty, humility and social reform to the defense of human labor as an aspect of spiritual progress.[45]

The interplay of medieval religion and attitudes toward labor, time and technology has become a major interpretative tool in the hands of Jacques Le Goff and Lynn White, who, however, differ profoundly in their approach to the material. Le Goff sees the growth of what he calls a "positive theology of labor" as a result of social change and the interaction of "high" and "low" culture.[46] An approving evaluation of

---

[43] Clarence Glacken, *Traces on the Rhodian Shore: Nature and Culture in Western Thought from Ancient Time to the End of the Eighteenth Century* (Berkeley, Los Angeles, and London: University of California Press, 1967), 351. For White's thesis on the connection between monasticism and medieval technology, see below, p. 15.

[44] John Van Engen, "Theophilus Presbyter and Rupert of Deutz: The Manual Arts and Benedictine Theology in the Early Twelfth Century," *Viator* 11 (1980): 147–163.

[45] Christopher Holdsworth, "The Blessings of Work: the Cistercian View," in *Sanctity and Secularity: The Church and the World*, ed. Derek Baker, *Studies in Church History*, 10 (New York: Harper and Row, 1973), 59–76; Brian Stock, "Experience, Praxis, Work and Planning in Bernard of Clairvaux: Observations on the *Sermones in Cantica*," in *The Cultural Context of Medieval Learning*, Boston Studies in the Philosophy of Science, 24 (Dordrecht and Boston: D. Reidel, 1974), 219–259. However, cf. M.-D. Chenu, "Civilisation urbaine et théologie: L'Ecole de Saint-Victor au XIIe siècle," *Annales: Economies, Sociétés, Civilisations* 29 (1974): 1263, who contrasts St. Bernard with Hugh of St. Victor, author of the *Didascalicon* and one of the most important monastic writers on the mechanical arts: "The *Didascalicon* was unthinkable at Cluny or at Clairvaux; it was composed at the gates of Paris."

For religious thought in the twelfth century, see Giles Constable, "Renewal and Reform in Religious Life: Concepts and Realities," in *Renaissance and Renewal*, 37–67 and Jean Leclercq, "The Renewal of Theology," in *Renaissance and Renewal*, 68–87.

[46] Le Goff, "Licit and Illicit Trades in the Medieval West," in *Time, Work and Culture*, 58–70; "Labor, Techniques, and Craftsmen in the Value Systems of the Early Middle Ages (Fifth to Tenth Centuries)," ibid., 71–86 and "Trades and Professions as Represented in Medieval Confessors' Manuals," ibid., 107–121. For Le Goff's discussion of his method and philosophy of history, see ibid., preface, vii–xv.

labor, originally a "merely latent and undeveloped possibility in Christianity," emerged because of the growing economic and social pressure exerted by artisans, merchants and laborers beginning in the twelfth century.[47] The medieval Church's initial hostility and contempt for manual labor and trade were reflected, according to Le Goff, in the Benedictine definition of manual labor as a penitential instrument for the expiation of sin and the condemnation of commerce and related trades as illicit and immoral.[48] Twelfth- and thirteenth-century theologians and scholastics, however, responded to social pressure by modifying the traditional position of the Church, recasting labor as a positive means of salvation and greatly enlarging the number and types of professions regarded as legitimate and morally praiseworthy.[49] Like Georges Duby, John Baldwin and other historians of the social history of the High Middle Ages, Le Goff notes the preoccupation of theologians of the period with the ethical and social implications of wealth, commerce and the merchant's role in society.[50] "With the beginning of the thirteenth century," Le Goff concludes, "the working saint was losing ground, giving way to the saintly worker."[51] This movement, however, took a theological form only partly because the Bible and the writings of the Church Fathers contained elements of a spiritual approach to labor; rather, the emerging ideology of work was expressed theologically because "nothing could become an object of conscious reflection in the Middle Ages except by way of religion."[52]

In contrast, Lynn White argues that Latin Christianity was inherently sympathetic to technological advance and created in medieval Europe a cultural climate which encouraged an aggressive and exploitative at-

---

[47] Le Goff, "Trades and Professions," 110–112.

[48] Ibid., "Licit and Illicit Trades," 58–62. Le Goff argues that "there should be no mistaking the position of Saint Benedict and Benedictine spirituality with regard to labor. . . . In the Benedictine mind during the early Middle Ages, both labor's spirituality, which was merely a penitential instrument, and its theology, according to which labor was a consequence of original sin, had only negative value, as it were" (pp. 110–111). However, he also acknowledges that "there is no question about the important role played—from the beginning—by Benedictines in the areas both of manual labor and of intellectual labor. In practice, somewhat contrary to Saint Benedict's idea, they were exemplary" (p. 317, n. 10). Le Goff emphasizes the "ambiguity of the legacies" on labor inherited by the medieval world from classical, Germanic, and Judeo-Christian sources, "Labor, Techniques, and Craftsmen," 73–77.

[49] Le Goff, "Licit and Illicit Trades," 62–70; "Trades and Professions," 116–121.

[50] Georges Duby, *The Three Orders: Feudal Society Imagined,* trans. Arthur Goldhammer (Chicago and London: The University of Chicago Press, 1980) documents the impact of a changing society and economy on twelfth-century ideas of an ordered society; John W. Baldwin, "The Medieval Theories of the Just Price: Romanists, Canonists, and Theologians in the Twelfth and Thirteenth Centuries," *Transactions of the American Philosophical Society,* n. s. 49, pt. 4 (Philadelphia: The American Philosophical Society, 1959), reprinted in *Pre-Capitalist Economic Thought: Three Modern Interpretations,* ed. Leonard Silk (New York: Arno Press, 1972) and *Masters, Princes, and Merchants: The Social Views of Peter the Chanter and his Circle,* 2 vols. (Princeton, New Jersey: Princeton University Press, 1970), 1: 261–311 discusses scholastic and theological views of usury and the merchant.

[51] Le Goff, "Trades and Professions," 115.

[52] Ibid., 109.

titude toward nature. In a series of articles published between 1940 and 1975, White refers to many elements within Christianity which have long been associated by historians with the development of Western science and technology, including charity and compassion for the individual soul, the Judaic respect for work, a linear concept of history, a creator-god and the Biblical injunction to rule the earth.[53] In particular, following Robert Forbes and Ernst Benz, White suggests that Christianity, by replacing pagan animism with a view of matter as inert material created for a spiritual purpose, encouraged man to see himself as the master and exploiter of nature.[54] White's distinctive contribution, however, is the argument that the medieval West's unique technological dynamism (far more developed, for example, than equally Christian Byzantium) can be explained by the voluntaristic and activist character of Latin piety.

Historians of spirituality have long been aware of a basic contrast of tonality between the two great segments of Christendom which surely affected the development of their respective technologies. The Greeks have generally held that sin is ignorance and that salvation comes by illumination. The Latins have asserted that sin is vice, and that rebirth comes by disciplining the will to do good works. The Greek saint is normally a contemplative; the Western saint, an activist.[55]

The slight but significant differences between Greek and Latin piety in this pe-

---

[53] White's first article on medieval technology, "Technology and Invention in the Middle Ages," (1940), 157 concludes, "The labor-saving power-machines of the later Middle Ages were produced by the implicit theological assumptions of the infinite worth of even the most degraded human personality, by an instinctive repugnance towards subjecting any man to a monotonous drudgery which seems less than human in that it requires the exercise neither of intelligence nor of choice." White expanded and modified his thesis that Christianity was the cause of technological development in the West in "What Accelerated Technological Progress in the Western Middle Ages?" in *Scientific Change*, ed. A. C. Crombie (New York: Basic Books, 1963), 272–291; "The Iconography of *Temperantia* and the Virtuousness of Technology," in *Action and Conviction in Early Modern Europe: Essays in Memory of E. Harris Harbison*, ed. T. K. Rabb and J. E. Seigel (Princeton, New Jersey: Princeton University Press, 1969), 197–219; "Cultural Climates and Technological Advance in the Middle Ages," *Viator* 2 (1971): 171–201; "Medieval Engineering and the Sociology of Knowledge," *Pacific Historical Review* 44 (1975): 1–21 and "The Historical Roots of Our Ecologic Crisis," *Science* 155, whole no. 3767 (March 10, 1967): 1203–1207. With the exception of "What Accelerated Technological Progress in the Middle Ages?" and "The Historical Roots of Our Ecologic Crisis," these articles have been reprinted in *Medieval Religion*. "The Historical Roots of Our Ecologic Crisis," has been widely reprinted; see Carl Mitcham, "Select Bibliography of Theology and Technology," 396 for a partial list. In part perhaps because this article, unlike White's other work, presents the influence of Christianity in a negative light, it has become a focus of controversy; see below, n. 64.

[54] Robert J. Forbes, *Studies in Ancient Technology* (Leiden: E. J. Brill, 1965) 2: 103–105 and *Man the Maker: A History of Technology and Engineering* (New York: Schuman, 1950), 107–109; Ernst Benz, "Fundamenti cristiani della tecnica occidentale," in *Tecnica e casistica*, 241–265 and "The Christian Expectation of the End of Time and the Ideal of Technical Progress," in *Evolution and Christian Hope: Man's Concept of the Future from the Early Fathers to Teilhard de Chardin* (Garden City, N.Y.: Doubleday, 1966), 121–141; White, "Cultural Climates," 186–189 (*Medieval Religion*, 236–238).

[55] White, "Cultural Climates," 189 (*Medieval Religion*, 238).

riod help not only to make historically intelligible the accomplishment of the medieval West in technology but likewise to explain the psychic foundations of our modern technology which rests on that achievement.[56]

White's concern is focused on medieval Western monasticism, which "asserted the originally Jewish thesis that work . . . is an essential kind of worship."[57] The equation of work with prayer together with an ideal of active reform led European monks, according to White, to believe that advancing technology was both pleasing to God and morally salvatory, a belief expressed in manuscript illuminations and put into practice by the monks themselves.[58] Since this attitude toward technology, in White's view, was not shared, for the most part, by scientists and philosophers, it is primarily to the religious beliefs of monks that medieval Europe owed not only its technological supremacy but also its unique conception of technology as a divinely sanctioned activity.[59]

White's provocative presentation of his thesis that Latin Christianity was the cause of medieval technological dynamism raises several issues which are at the heart of the latent confusion over the history and significance of medieval thought on technology. On the one hand, White's insistence on religion as the primary shaper of culture invites him to overemphasize classical contempt for labor and technological arts as a contrast to Western monastic approval of them.[60] On this point, he has been questioned by Carl Mitcham, John Passmore and other philosophers of technology who have referred to a Greek, especially Stoic, and Roman tradition which valued work and man as controller of his physical environment.[61] On the other hand, although White himself points to the danger of regarding Christianity as a monolithic set of attitudes and ideas, he also may have neglected the variety of attitudes toward work

---

[56] Ibid., 201 (*Medieval Religion*, 253).

[57] Ibid., 191 (*Medieval Religion*, 241). See also, "Medieval Engineering," 2–3 (*Medieval Religion*, 319–320) and "Iconography of *Temperantia*," 198–199 (*Medieval Religion*, 182–184). White consistently emphasizes the absolute difference between classical contempt for labor and monastic approval of it.

[58] White, "Iconography of *Temperantia*," 201–202, 213–217 (*Medieval Religion*, 185–187, 192–203); "Cultural Climates," 197–199 (*Medieval Religion*, 248–251).

[59] White, "Medieval Engineering," 11–14 (*Medieval Religion*, 328–331).

[60] White, "Continuing the Conversation," in *Western Man and Environmental Ethics*, 57 (this is a reply to critics of White's article, "The Historical Roots of Our Ecologic Crisis"): "Every culture, whether it is overtly religious or not, is shaped primarily by its religion. . . . I have more and more converged upon religion, including cryptoreligion, as a source for historical explanations."

[61] Mitcham, "Religious and Political Origins of Modern Technology," 271–272; John Passmore, *Man's Responsibility for Nature: Ecological Problems and Western Traditions* (New York: Charles Scribner's Sons, 1974), 4–5, 28–40. Glacken, *Traces on the Rhodian Shore*, 35–149; de Gandillac, "Place et signification de la technique dans le monde médiéval," and Alessio, "La filosofia e la 'artes mechanicae' nel secolo XII," 114–117 also support this view. Cf. Moses I. Finley, "Technical Innovation and Economic Progress in the Ancient World," *Economic History Review* 2nd. series 18 (1965): 29–45 for the view that economic dependence on slavery in antiquity resulted in a contempt for technology and labor.

and technology within Latin Christianity.[62] White's position that "[technological] aggression is the normal Western Christian attitude toward nature,"[63] for example, has been challenged by scholars who argue for the presence of a second, if minority, Christian tradition of stewardship toward nature in the patristic, medieval and later periods.[64] The work of Crombie, Pedersen, and Beaujouan on the relationship of theory and practice in medieval science, and Le Goff, Holdsworth and others on theological perspectives on labor suggests a wider range of views about the value of manual labor and technology than White acknowledges.

The interpretations of both White and Le Goff have been substantially modified by George Ovitt. Ovitt, who has provided a valuable and much-needed overview of medieval concepts of progress, God as craftsman and monastic rules as they relate to attitudes toward labor and technology, suggests that while some medieval writers believed manual work to be redemptive, theologians more consistently subordinated manual work to spiritual ends and aspirations. He concludes, against White, that religious values in the Middle Ages produced a strongly ambivalent attitude toward labor and technology.[65] And, although Ovitt agrees with Le Goff that it is more accurate to see medieval theologians as merely responding to social and economic changes (rather than as White argues, that medieval theology itself produced these changes), Ovitt describes this response in far more negative terms than does Le Goff. If for Le Goff the twelfth and thirteenth centuries saw the triumph of a "theology of labor," for Ovitt it is precisely in this period that the Church disassociated itself from its earlier ideal of cooperative labor and initiated what Ovitt calls the "secularization of labor." Henceforth, he argues, manual labor was relegated to the separate (and inferior) sphere of workers and both labor and technology were divorced from moral and spiritual goals.[66]

---

[62] White, "Cultural Climates," 188 (*Medieval Religion*, 237).

[63] Ibid., 199 (*Medieval Religion*, 251).

[64] Passmore, *Man's Responsibility for Nature*, 4–5, 28–40; Keith Thomas, *Man and the Natural World: A History of the Modern Sensibility* (New York: Pantheon Books, 1983), 17–25 and, especially, Robin Attfield, "Christian Attitudes to Nature," *Journal of the History of Ideas* 44 (1983): 369–386 and *The Ethics of Environmental Concern* (New York: Columbia University Press, 1983), 20–33. See also Ovitt, *Restoration of Perfection*, 70–87.

White states his argument that Latin Christianity is the source of medieval and present Western exploitative attitudes toward nature most uncompromisingly in "The Historical Roots of Our Ecologic Crisis." This article, which has been widely reprinted as part of the current interest in environmental studies, has aroused considerable response among contemporary philosophers and theologians of technology. See, especially, Winner, *Autonomous Technology*, 112–118; Lewis W. Moncrief, "The Cultural Basis of Our Environmental Crisis," in *Western Man and Environmental Ethics*, 31–42; René Dubos, "A Theology of the Earth," in *Western Man and Environmental Ethics*, 43–54; and Thomas Seiger Derr, "Religious Responsibility for Ecological Crisis: An Argument Run Amok," *Worldview* 18, no. 1 (January, 1975): 39–45. For further examples see Mitcham, "Select Bibliography of Theology and Technology," 380–381.

[65] Ovitt, *Restoration of Perfection*, 164–165, 200–201.

[66] Ibid., 137–163, 200–201.

A less obvious corollary of White's emphasis on religion is his dismissal of medieval philosophy. For Le Goff, for example, the emergent approval of labor was expressed in philosophical and scholastic works of "high" culture no less than in types of evidence which reflected "low" culture: indeed, his argument in part turns on his view that medieval intellectuals responded to social change by adopting new views of manual labor. A peculiarity of White's presentation, however, as suggested above is that although it purports to connect theology and technology, it excludes the body of medieval philosophical and theological thought from any significant role in forming medieval response to technological progress. White sees the attempt by some medieval thinkers, such as Theophilus and Hugh of St. Victor to give technology a new philosophical status, as an "abject failure," not only because of the "old nonmonastic upper-class prejudice against manual labor," but also because of the pervasive contempt for the mechanical arts inherited from antiquity.[67] If religious feeling supported technology, the medieval philosophical tradition, in White's view, merely perpetuated "ancient perversities."[68] It is symptomatic of the gap created by White between "religion" and "philosophy" that his evidence for medieval conceptions of technology and labor is almost entirely iconographical or circumstantial (that is, evidence that Western churches unlike Byzantine churches, in fact used mechanical devices such as clocks and organs)[69] and that, by his own account, the values in Latin Christianity which made the pursuit of technology morally virtuous existed "below the level of verbal expression," "so deep that they are not often verbalized explicitly," and "so taken for granted, so axiomatic, that they largely elude expression in writing."[70]

These several questions—the relationship of medieval attitudes toward labor and technological arts to those of classical antiquity, the influence of contemporary conceptions of the nature and purpose of scientific knowledge, and the impact of religious ideas of human virtue on attitudes toward technological progress—are among those which a comprehensive study of the concept of the mechanical arts in the Middle Ages might help to answer. Such a study would contribute toward es-

---

[67] White, "Medieval Engineering," 11–12 (*Medieval Religion*, 328).

[68] Ibid., 12 (*Medieval Religion*, 328).

[69] White, "Cultural Climates," 197–198 (*Medieval Religion*, 248–250); "Iconography of *Temperantia*," 201–202 (*Medieval Religion*, 185–187). Although White's iconographical analysis is persuasive, he offers only two examples directly concerned with technology, one from the ninth century, the second from the fifteenth. White discusses only two treatises on crafts or the mechanical arts, Theophilus's *De diversis artibus* and Hugh of St. Victor's *Didascalicon*, "Cultural Climates," 195–197 (*Medieval Religion*, 246–248). As Winner, *Autonomous Technology*, 115 points out, White, as well as Weber, sees the West's preoccupation with technological domination as stemming from "the very identity of Western man."

[70] White, "Iconography of *Temperantia*," 216 (*Medieval Religion*, 201): "Cultural Climates," 190 (*Medieval Religion*, 239); "Medieval Engineering," 2 (*Medieval Religion*, 318). Mitcham, "Religious and Political Origins of Modern Technology," 272 and Stock, "Science, Technology, and Economic Progress," 1 briefly refer to this point.

tablishing the extent to which medieval thinkers articulated explicit justifications of technology as a human activity and category of knowledge. Although these issues have begun to be examined by the comparatively few scholars to deal directly and systematically with the medieval mechanical arts, in many ways these works have reproduced the fragmented perspective of more general studies of medieval culture and technology.

Peter Sternagel's *Die Artes Mechanicae im Mittelalter* (1966) collected for the first time most of the explicit references to the *artes mechanicae* or mechanical arts in the period from the early Middle Ages through the thirteenth century.[71] The work remains an invaluable bibliographic reference for the relevant primary source material and demonstrates the important point that the term *artes mechanicae* was coined in the ninth century and acquired further substance and meaning in the twelfth and thirteenth centuries when it became the usual rubric for technological arts in classifications of the arts and sciences.[72] As Sternagel himself acknowledges, however, his analysis is primarily linguistic and neither deals with the issues raised by the texts, nor puts them within a tradition or context of thought.[73] The limitations of Sternagel's focus are illustrated by his failure to discuss Roger Bacon, despite Bacon's well-known interest in technological devices and experimental science, because Bacon's classification of the sciences does not name technological arts as "mechanical" arts. Insofar as Sternagel goes beyond the collection and description of texts, he suggests that medieval views of the mechanical arts were fundamentally disordered by attitudes which, on the one hand, valued religious poverty and the "pure" labor of the farmer and, on the other hand, recognized the social prestige accorded the merchant and the owner of goods.[74]

Franco Alessio, in contrast, places twelfth-century views of the mechanical arts within a broad philosophical setting.[75] Arguing that the twelfth century was a pivotal period in the development of ideas about technology, Alessio analyzes the work of Hugh of St. Victor and Dominicus Gundisalvo as a "religious or natural anthropology" which had its ultimate origins in antiquity.[76] Specifically, he suggests that Hugh of St. Victor's positive conception of the mechanical arts was inspired by a passage in Augustine's *City of God,* which in turn reflects the views of Cicero and, beyond Cicero, Posidonius and Panaetius.[77] According to Alessio, the medieval conception of the *artes mechanicae* is best under-

[71] Peter Sternagel, *Die Artes Mechanicae im Mittelalter. Begriffs- und Bedeutungsgeschichte bis zum Ende des 13. Jahrhunderts* (Kallmung über Regensburg: Lassleben, 1966).

[72] Ibid., 30–36, 77–78.

[73] Ibid., 123–124.

[74] Ibid.

[75] Alessio's "Filosofia e le 'artes mechanicae'" appeared independently of Sternagel's work and does not refer to it.

[76] Ibid., 83.

[77] Ibid., 114–117.

stood not, as Crombie and Pedersen saw it, as a chapter in the history of science but rather as a conflation and enrichment of traditions about art, nature and man as *homo faber*.[78]

The framework set up by Alessio and Sternagel, however, was rejected in 1982 by Guy Allard.[79] According to Allard, those historians of philosophy and science who have followed the example of Pierre Duhem and sought the origins of modern science in the Middle Ages, a group in which he explicitly includes Sternagel and Alessio, have failed properly to distinguish between the statements of certain artisans, monks, preachers, and merchants and the philosophical thought of medieval intellectuals.[80] Whereas the former are, in Allard's phrase, "optimistic and favorable" toward technology, the latter are characterized by an "ideological blockage" which inevitably resulted in the devaluation of the mechanical arts.[81] The hierarchical system of thought used by Augustine and the medieval scholastics depended upon defining the interior, spiritual side of man as more important than the exterior, material man and theoretical knowledge as more valuable than the production of artifacts.[82] In support of his view that this system necessitated the inferiority of the mechanical arts, Allard marshals evidence that the mechanical arts were commonly referred to as "servile," "adulterate," "exterior," or "lesser," and suggests that the literary or rhetorical function often accorded them only further led to their occultation.[83]

Underlying this rejection of the mechanical arts was a "reflex of defense and fear" against the perceived threat of social change which in the twelfth and thirteenth centuries was occasioned by the new social mobility and access to moneymaking professions.[84] Allard recognizes only two exceptions to this general pattern: Roger Bacon, who expresses a "strange and new" appreciation for technological arts, and Dante, whose work, Allard suggests, reflects the political power of merchants and artisans in contemporary Florence.[85]

Yet another perspective is offered by George Ovitt's *The Restoration of Perfection*. Although largely concerned with the broader questions of attitudes toward work, Ovitt devotes a chapter to the place of the mechanical arts in classifications of knowledge. Like Allard, Ovitt finds medieval philosophy organized according to hierarchical principles

[78] Ibid., 82–83.

[79] Allard, "Artes mécaniques," 13–14 specifically discusses Alessio and Sternagel as the two pioneers in the study of the medieval mechanical arts.

[80] Ibid., 13–15.

[81] Ibid., 15.

[82] Ibid., 15–19.

[83] Ibid., 17–24. Allard gives Hugh of St. Victor, who is cited by Alessio and Lynn White as demonstrating a very positive view of technology (Alessio, "Filosofia e le 'artes mechanicae,'" 119–120; White, "Cultural Climates," 196–197 [*Medieval Religion* 246–248]), as an important example of the occultation of the mechanical arts.

[84] Allard, "Arts mécaniques," 15, 24–29.

[85] Ibid., 29–31.

which placed the mechanical arts on the lowest rung of knowledge. Unlike Allard, however, he does not see social or class relationships as sufficient to explain this low status; rather, he argues that the classificatory scheme used by medieval authors was the primary reason for the devaluing of the mechanical arts because it was based on "the metaphysical effects of the science [on the student] rather than on either their methods or products."[86] This "metaphysical" approach to knowledge necessarily limited the extent to which the mechanical arts could be considered as practical mechanics and brought into relationship with theoretical science. Although for example, Hugh of St. Victor includes the mechanical arts among the necessary parts of knowledge, they appear as the least valued category because they deal with the body and serve merely as a preliminary step toward salvation. A more modern idea of the relationship of theoretical and applied science, therefore, could only come about through the abandonment of what Ovitt calls the "metaphysical" or "salvationary" conception of knowledge. One important step in this direction occurs in Robert Kilwardby's *De ortu scientiarum* which, Ovitt points out, modifies Aristotelian principles in order to show that the theoretical sciences of mathematics and physics make use of the mechanical arts and *vice versa*.[87] Another important text is Raymond Lull's *Arbor scientiae* in which relationships among scientific disciplines are more crucial than the hierarchical subordination of the physical to the spiritual.[88] Although he emphasizes the overall limitations of medieval classifications of learning, therefore, Ovitt, like Allard, finds significant exceptions.

Scholars have thus far provided valuable insights into medieval ideas about technology but as yet no coherent overall picture of the contempory concept of the mechanical arts. The present study will seek to add clarity and completeness to scholarly assessments of the medieval mechanical arts and thereby contribute to further understanding of the cultural and intellectual context of medieval technology. The diverse interpretations offered by Le Goff, White, Crombie, Alessio, Allard, Ovitt and others reflect not only differences in scholarly emphasis but, more importantly, the complexity and ambiguity of the intellectual tradition itself. We cannot, in my view, hope to understand the history of medieval ideas about the value of technology or the significance of individual figures such as Hugh of St. Victor, Roger Bacon and Robert Kilwardby unless we apply a perspective at once broader and more precise than has heretofore been used. On the one hand, the often elusive statements of medieval authors on the mechanical arts must be seen as part of a continuing tradition on the nature and purpose of knowledge

---

[86] Ovitt, "Status of the Mechanical Arts," 93–94. See also *Restoration of Perfection*, 119–120, 136.

[87] Ibid., 127–130.

[88] Ibid., 133–135.

going back to antiquity at least as far as the time of Plato and Aristotle. It is perhaps difficult today to appreciate the logical and historical weight of classical philosophical principles which defined knowledge as truth sought for its own sake; yet, it is within this system of thought, inherited by the Middle Ages and absorbed by medieval Christianity, that medieval thinkers attempted to assimilate the impact of technological development. At the same time, as we shall see, this philosophical structure was not inflexible but could be modified and developed in various ways so as to give technology both moral and intellectual sanction. On the other hand, the reworking of ideas in new directions did not take place in a historical vacuum but reflected changing circumstances and intellectual currents. We must, therefore, also consider in more detail the history of Aristotelianism and Platonism in the Middle Ages, the impact of the availability or loss of specific texts, and the changing demands made on philosophy as an intellectual tool. Medieval definitions and evaluations of the mechanical arts reflected in varying degrees the subtle responses of thinkers to the social circumstances in which they found themselves, to a long-lived and respected, but still malleable, classical philosophical tradition, and to their individual intellectual concerns. If we look more closely at these responses through the focus of how crafts appeared in classifications of knowledge, a fuller view of medieval ideas about the nature and value of technology should emerge.

TRANS. AMER. PHIL. SOC.
VOL. 80 PT. 1, 1990

II. Liberal and Illiberal Arts: The Classification of Technical Arts in Antiquity

The Middle Ages were the philosophical heirs of classical antiquity. Medieval writers on the arts, although profoundly and deeply affected by contemporary conditions and the moral and spiritual demands of Christianity, wrote within an intellectual framework first set out in Greek thought. In particular, new attitudes toward technical arts, or crafts, developed with reference to classical ideas about the relationship of art to nature, physical to mental labor, craft to philosophy.[1] Many ancient statements of these ideas were unknown to the medieval world; others were known only in part, or through a series of intermediaries. Nevertheless, a study of the attitudes of antiquity as a whole toward the classification of technical arts as a part of knowledge provides a valuable basis for the examination of the mechanical arts in the twelfth and thirteenth centuries. Not only were the thinkers of the high Middle Ages engaged in a rediscovery of classical thought, but classical views on the nature of craftsmanship, in their most diffuse and general form, had become part of the medieval tradition. The ideas expressed in ancient classifications of the arts, although strongly modified by medieval thinkers, were also consistently referred to, either implicitly or explicitly, by them and provided the framework within which they developed their own thought on craft.

The complexity of classical ideas about technology has become increasingly apparent in the last thirty years. Whereas earlier historians of science saw only a pervasive contempt for manual labor and crafts, since the 1950s scholars have challenged the idea that antiquity as a whole possessed an anti-technological prejudice. The work of Ludwig Edelstein on the history of the idea of progress and on Greek technology, Rudolfo Mondolfo on Greek attitudes toward manual labor, Arthur D. Kahn on the Greek tragedians, Derek J. de Solla Price on the technical achievement of the ancients, and Clarence Glacken on environmental ideas, among others, have in various ways shown that there was a positive as well as a negative element in ancient attitudes toward work,

[1] Hugh of St. Victor's *Didascalicon* (c. 1127), one of the most important medieval texts on technology's place among the divisions of knowledge, exemplifies this point. Hugh's defense of craft, while in many respects original, is also in large part built upon classical and patristic ideas (see Chapter IV). Other twelfth- and thirteenth-century thinkers used ideas developed from Aristotle to support schema of the arts and sciences which included technology as the practical aspect of theoretical science (see Chapter V).

craftsmanship and technical invention.[2] One area which has tended to be overlooked in this reassessment is how crafts figure in classifications of the arts and sciences. Major studies have been done on the classification of the fine arts, the liberal arts and the parts of philosophy but these have treated technical arts only incidentally.[3] Yet the ways in which thinkers organize knowledge are extremely revealing of fundamental attitudes about the nature and value of the different arts and sciences which together make up the sum total of that knowledge. Much can be elucidated, for example, about the history of aesthetics, from the study of how painting, sculpture, and architecture have appeared in classifications of the arts.[4] The place of technical arts in overall schemes of knowledge similarly provides a valuable locus for the implicit expression of basic attitudes toward craft.

The classification of technical arts seems to have provided an especially complex philosophical problem for ancient thinkers.[5] Technology

---

[2] Ludwig Edelstein, *The Idea of Classical Antiquity* (Baltimore: Johns Hopkins, 1967) and "Recent Interpretations of Ancient Science," *Journal of the History of Ideas* 13 (1952):579–585; Rodolfo Mondolfo, "The Greek Attitude toward Manual Labor," *Past and Present* 6 (1954):1–5; Arthur D. Kahn, "'Every Art Possessed by Man Comes from Prometheus': The Greek Tragedians and Science and Technology," *Technology and Culture* 11 (1970):133–162; Derek J. de Solla Price, *Gears from the Greeks: The Antikythera Mechanism* (New York: Science History Publications, 1975); Clarence Glacken, *Traces on the Rhodian Shore* (Berkeley: University of California Press, 1967); J. Donald Hughes, *Ecology in Ancient Civilizations* (Albuquerque, N.M.: University of New Mexico Press, 1975). John Passmore, *Man's Responsibility for Nature: Ecological Problems and Western Traditions* (New York: Charles Scribner's Sons, 1974), 4–5, 28–40, has recently argued for a Stoic concept of stewardship toward nature; see also Robin Attfield, "Christian Attitudes to Nature," *Journal of the History of Ideas* 44 (1983):369–386 and *The Ethics of Environmental Concern* (New York: Columbia University Press, 1983), 1–66 for discussion of Passmore's thesis. For the argument that classical culture was unsympathetic toward technology see, especially, Moses I. Finley, "Technical Innovation and Economic Progess in the Ancient World," *Economic History Review* 2d series 18 (1965):29–45.

[3] For an excellent discussion and bibliography on art in antiquity see Paul Oskar Kristeller, "The Modern System of the Arts," *Journal of the History of Ideas* 12 (1951):496–527; rpt. in *Renaissance Thought II: Papers on Humanism and the Arts* (New York: Harper, 1965), 163–227. On the liberal arts see Henri Irénée Marrou, "Les arts libéraux dans l'antiquité classique," in *Arts libéraux et philosophie au Moyen Âge: Actes du Quatrième Congrès International de Philosophie Médiévale* (Montreal: Institut d'Études Médiévales, 1969; Paris: Libraire Philosophique J. Vrin, 1969), 5–27 and Marrou, *Saint Augustin et la fin de la culture antique*, Bibliothèque des Écoles Françaises d'Athènes et de Rome, Fasc. 145 (Paris: Boccard, 1938). Major studies on classification of the arts and sciences in antiquity which at least touch on the position of the crafts beside the above include Joseph Mariétan, *Problème de la classification des sciences d'Aristote à s. Thomas* (Paris: F. Alcan, 1901); W. Tatkiewicz, "Classification of the Arts in Antiquity," *Journal of the History of Ideas* 24 (1963):231–240; Robert Flint, *Philosophy as Scientia Scientiarum, and A History of Classification of the Sciences* (Edinburgh: W. Blackwood, 1904), which however concentrates on the period after the seventeenth century; the introductory material in Friedrich Marx, ed. *Corpus medicorum latinorum*, 1 (Leipzig: B. G. Teubner, 1915), and Julius Jünthner, introduction to his translation of *Über Gymnastik* by Philostratus (Leipzig and Berlin: Teubner, 1909), 127–133. For a discussion of ideas about art in general see Margherita Isnardi Parente, *Techne: Momenti del pensiero greco da Platone ad Epicuro* (Florence: La Nuova Italia, 1966).

[4] See, for example, Kristeller, "Modern System," 163–174.

[5] Two recent studies dealing with this problem, and reaching somewhat different conclusions, are Carl Mitcham, "Philosophy and the History of Technology," in *The History*

is in many respects a unique meeting place between mind and matter; the tendency of much of classical thought to emphasize the distinct and separate nature of these two realms led to a basic ambivalence in the treatment of technical arts as a kind of knowledge. On the one hand, technical invention and practice were frequently regarded as requiring physical rather than mental effort. When Democritus compares architecture and weaving with the building of nests by birds and webs by spiders, he came close to reducing technology to an instinct shared with animals.[6] Craftsmanship was often represented as a kind of unthinking experience (ἐμπειρία), a mere knack for manual dexterity, substantially different from the rational processes involved in the liberal arts and scientific knowledge. Regarded in this light, technical arts or crafts were not true knowledge at all. On the other hand, most ancient thinkers (including many, such as Plato and Aristotle who subscribe to the above view in some contexts) also assume craft to be a product of man's reason and, therefore, part of knowledge in a broad sense. Crafts were arts and, like all arts, achieved their purposes by the use of an orderly and rational method; unlike activities based entirely upon inspiration or physical exertion, the arts, including crafts, followed rules.[7] Because of this rational character, crafts were linked, however distantly, with higher types of knowledge.

These opposing conceptions of craft underlie much of ancient discussion on the value of technical arts. The Hippocratic doctors defended medicine on the grounds that it was an art, that is, based on knowledge.[8] Plato's paradoxical use of technical illustrations or imagery is another example. In the *Republic* and elsewhere, the artisan provides the model for the true statesman because it is the artisan who, unlike the poet, can give a clear account of his work, works competently toward a well-defined goal and produces work that can be judged objectively.[9] As has

---

and Philosophy of Technology, ed. George Bugliarello and Dean B. Doner (Urbana: University of Illinois Press, 1979), 163–201 and Wolfgang Schadewaldt, "The Concepts of Nature and Technique according to the Greeks," *Research in Philosophy and Technology* 2 (1979):159–171.

[6] Democritus, Fragment 154 in M. Diehls and W. Kranz, eds., *Die Fragmente der Vorsokratiker*, 6th ed. (Berlin: Weidmann, 1954), 2:173.

[7] The Greek term for art (τέχνη) and its Latin equivalent (*ars*) were used broadly to apply to virtually all human activities which were in some sense rational, including what we would now distinguish as science, fine art and technology; see Kristeller, "Modern System," 166–167. Irrational or nonrational activities, however, were not arts. Plato excludes poetry from the arts because it followed no fixed rules and, therefore, could not give a rational account of itself (*Ion* 533d) and Aristotle contrasts the experience of the manual laborer with the art of the master-worker because the latter knows the "why" and cause of things but the former acts without understanding what he does like an animal or inanimate object (*Metaphysics* 1.1, 981a25–981b9). On the other hand, even sex could be regarded as an art if sufficiently systematized, as, for example, in the classical sex manual *Dodecatechnon*; see Peter Caws, "Praxis and Techne," in *The History and Philosophy of Technology*, ed. G. Bubliarello and D. Doner, 228, 247 n. 5.

[8] Hippocrates, *The Art*, Loeb Classical Library (London: Heinemann, 1931), 2:191–217.

[9] Plato, *Republic* 488a–489, Loeb Classical Library (London: Heinemann, 1935), 2:16–22; *Politicus* 297e–299e, Loeb Classical Library (London: Heinemann, 1925), 146–152. For additional examples of craft as an analogy for statecraft see J. R. Bambrough, "Plato's Political

been pointed out by G. R. E. Lloyd, Bruno Snell and others[10] the introduction of order into disorder and the necessary skillful action directed toward a clearly conceived and good end involved in the production of an artifact by the artisan was a powerful analogy for correct and knowledgeable action in Greek thought. Plato finds craft so useful as an example that Callicles must complain to Socrates in the *Gorgias* that he never stops talking about cobblers, fullers, cooks and doctors as if the argument were about them.[11] At the same time Plato describes crafts, at least as practiced by actual craftsmen, as base and degrading.[12] In Plato's metaphysical world the bed made by the carpenter is a "shadowy thing," only one step removed in its level of imitation or unreality from the bed produced by the painter.[13] According to Plato, it is the user of an object, not its maker, who possesses knowledge of it.[14] Used didactically, craft is presented as a paradigm of what knowledge should be, yet in other contexts craft, for Plato, does not appear to constitute knowledge, in its proper sense, at all. A simpler discussion of opposing judgments on craft occurs in Seneca's *Epistolae*. Seneca reports Posidonius as asserting that it was a philosopher and wise man who first invented buildings, tools and weaving and to this Seneca answers that philosophy has nothing to do with tools or anything else which involves a bent body and a mind gazing upon the ground.[15] This double-edged attitude passes into Latin Christianity and, from there, into the medieval tradition. One of the most effective statements of ancient ambivalence toward craft occurs in Book 22.24 of Augustine's *City of God*. Here Augustine, in a deliberately oxymoronic statement, describes crafts as at once exemplifying the "natural genius" of man and, at the same time, as "superfluous, perilous and pernicious."[16]

Analogies," in *Philosophy, Politics and Society*, ed. Peter Laslett (Oxford: Basil Blackwell, 1963), 98–115.

[10] G. R. E. Lloyd, *Polarity and Analogy: Two Types of Argumentation in Early Greek Thought* (Cambridge: Cambridge University Press, 1961), 292–294; Bruno Snell, *The Discovery of the Mind: The Origins of European Thought* (Cambridge, Mass.: Harvard University Press, 1953; rpt. New York: Harper, 1960), 185–186, 222; Bambrough, "Plato's Political Analogies," 100.

[11] Plato, *Gorgias* 491a, ed. E. R. Dodds (Oxford: Clarendon Press, 1959), 132.

[12] Plato, *Republic* 495d, 522b, 590c, Loeb Classical Library, 2:48, 148, 406.

[13] Ibid., 495d, 522b, 590c, 596, Loeb Classical Library, 2:48, 148, 406, 422–426.

[14] Ibid., Loeb Classical Library, 2:446.

[15] Seneca, *Ad Lucilium epistulae morales* 90.13, Loeb Classical Library (London: Heinemann, 1930), 2:403.

[16] Augustine, *De civitate Dei* 22.24, ed. B. Dombart (Leipzig: B. G. Teubner, 1918) 2:612:

> Praeter enim artes bene vivendi et ad inmortalem perveniendi felicitatem, quae virtutes vocantur et sola Dei gratia, quae in Christe est, filiis promissionis regnique donantur, nonne humano ingenio tot tantaeque artes sunt inventae et exercitae, partim necessariae artim voluptariae, ut tam excellens vis mentis atque rationis in his etiam rebus, quas superfluas, immo et periculosas perniciosasque appetit, quantum bonum haveat in natura, unde ista potuit vel invenire vel discere vel exercere, testetur?

For further discussion of Augustine's meaning and intent in this passage, see below, pp. 52–55.

Although not absolutely contradictory, these various conceptions of crafts suggest very different judgments on the legitimacy and worth of technology as a branch of knowledge. Both viewpoints were reflected in the way technical arts appeared in classifications of the arts and sciences. When authors wished to emphasize the physical and inferior character of all or some crafts, they labeled these crafts as banausic (βάναυσος), a pejorative term which served to separate unworthy from worthy arts. Yet it is misleading to conclude, as some historians have done,[17] that ancient thinkers condemned all technical arts and systematically opposed them to the liberal arts. Crafts were also classified in a variety of ways which established them as fully legitimate parts of knowledge: as productive arts, as parts of mathematics, as liberal and "semi-liberal" arts. If we look at these classifications more closely, the complexity of ancient attitudes toward technology can be seen from another perspective and more evidence is gained for the view that antiquity was neither uniformly hostile nor indifferent to technology.

The Banausic Arts

In the *Republic* when Socrates casually remarks that manual crafts debase the human mind and body, the word he uses for crafts is not the neutral τέχνη but τὰς βαναυσίας.[18] Xenophon takes the same position

---

[17] See, for example, E. J. Dijksterhuis, *The Mechanization of the World Picture*, trans. C. Dikshoorn (Oxford: Clarendon Press, 1969), 74: ". . . whatever called for purely mental work (the later *artes liberales*) was regarded by society as greatly superior to handicraft, whether aided by machines or not, to the trades, and to mechanical engineering, which can be covered by the name of *artes mechanicae*, and to which the plastic arts may also be added. The *artes mechanicae* did not befit the free Hellene, any activity bringing man into too close a contact with matter has a degrading effect. The existence of a free citizen ought to be characterized by σχολή *otium* (leisure), compared with this, being tied down to a duty ἀσχολία *negotium*, is inferior." Another instance of an over-sharp distinction occurs in Robert James Forbes, *Studies in Ancient Technology*, 2d rev. ed. (Leiden: E. J. Brill, 1965), 2:100: "This typical Greek contrast between the liberal arts and the 'artes mechanicae' precluded all efficient cooperation between science and technology." See also the discussion in Ernst Robert Curtius, *European Literature and the Latin Middle Ages*, trans. Willard R. Trask, Bollingen Series, 36 (New York: Harper, 1963; rpt. Princeton: Princeton University Press, 1973), 37. The Greek term βαναυσικὰι and its Latin equivalents are often translated into English as "mechanical arts" (as, for example, in Liddell and Scott *Greek-English Lexicon* and in the two examples quoted above). This translation is misleading for several reasons. Although the Romans used the singular form *ars mechanica* to refer to the art of mechanics, i.e. the art of making engines of war, astronomical models or lifting devices, the plural form in Latin does not seem to be used in antiquity. On this point see Peter Sternagel, *Die artes mechanicae im Mittelalter: Begriffs- und Bedeutungsgeschichte bis zum Ende des 13. Jahrhunderts* (Kallmung: Lassleben, 1966), 13–17. The Latin *artes mechanicae* is a medieval term, first known to be used in the ninth century, which referred to all crafts as a group and carried a generally favorable connotation (see Chaps. III and IV below). The terms βαναυσικὰι, *artes illiberales*, on the other hand, referred only to certain crafts which were regarded as unworthy or degrading and not necessarily to all crafts. The translation of mechanical arts for the Greek banausic arts therefore tends to confuse in the mind of the reader the more positive medieval tradition with the limited and pejorative meaning signified by the Greek word. For this reason I have used the transliteration banausic rather than the more common "mechanical arts."

[18] Plato, *Republic* 495e, Loeb Classical Library, 2:48.

when he explains that the banausic arts (βαναυσικὰι), "as they are called, are spoken against, and are, naturally enough, held in utter disdain in our states," because they soften the body and weaken the mind.[19] Both before and after Plato the term banausic for crafts was strongly pejorative and was associated with philosophical and social attitudes which labeled certain occupations or activities, primarily but not exclusively those requiring physical, rather than mental, labor, as inferior and base.[20] In Latin a similar set of ideas and value-judgments was conveyed by the expressions *artes illiberales, artes vulgares* and *artes sordidae*.[21]

The standard by which some arts were labeled inferior was that of the ἐγκύκλιος παιδεία or liberal arts. The liberal arts were those arts pursued for the sake of a liberated mind rather than for the satisfaction of any vocational or physical need. The precise curriculum and focus of the arts was flexible throughout antiquity and into the early Middle Ages; the liberal arts might be construed narrowly, including only the specific subjects prerequisite for the study of philosophy or broadly, including all of general culture.[22] Yet the liberal arts were always regarded as contributing toward intellectual and moral wisdom.[23]

The banausic arts, on the other hand, were considered hostile, or, at least unhelpful, to the pursuit of virtue. Aristotle (384–322 B.C.) provides a succinct definition of the banausic arts in the *Politics* (8.2 1337b):

> A task and also an art or a science must be deemed vulgar [βάναυσον] if it renders the body or soul or mind of free men useless for the employments and actions of virtue. Hence we entitle vulgar all such arts as deteriorate the condition of the body, and also the industries that earn wages; for they make the mind preoccupied and degraded.[24]

---

[19] Xenophon, *Oeconomicus* 4.2, trans. G. Cyril Armstrong, Loeb Classical Library (London: Heinemann, 1936), 390–391:

> Ἀλλὰ καλῶς, ἔφη, λέγεις, ὦ Κριτόβουλε. καὶ γάρ αἵ γε βαναυσικαὶ καλούμεναι καὶ ἐπίρρητοί τέ εἰσι καὶ εἰκότως μέντοι πάνυ ἀδοξοῦνται πρὸς τῶν πόλεων.

See also Xenophon, *Oeconomicus* 6.5, 408: "βαναυσικὰς . . .τέχνας"

[20] For example, Herodotus, *Persian Wars* 2.165, Loeb Classical Library (London: Heinemann, 1921):478; Aristotle, *Politics* 1277b, 1278a, 1289b33, 1328b39, 1329a20, 1338b34, Loeb Classical Library (London: Heinemann, 1932), 190, 196, 286, 574, 576, 646; Plutarch, *Lives.Marcellus* 17.4, Loeb Classical Library (London: Heinemann, 1916), 5:472; Galen, *Protreptikos* 14 in *Scripta minora*, ed. Ioannis Marquardt (Leipzig: B. G. Teubner, 1893; rpt. Amsterdam: Hakkert, 1967), 1:120; Jerome, *Dialogus contra Pelagianus* 1.21, ed. Migne, *PG* 23:537.

[21] For example, Seneca, *Ad Lucilium epistulae morales* 88.21, Loeb Classical Library, 2:362 and Cicero, *De officiis* 1.42.150, Loeb Classical Library (London: Heinemann, 1913), 152.

[22] H. I. Marrou, *A History of Education in Antiquity*, trans. George Lamb (New York: Mentor, 1964), 244; H. Parker, "The Seven Liberal Arts," *English Historical Review* 5 (1890):424, 427.

[23] See Seneca, *Ad Lucilium* 88, especially sections 2, 20, 29–33, Loeb Classical Library, 2:348, 360, 366–368.

[24] Aristotle, *Politics* 1337b, trans. H. Rackham, Loeb Classical Library (London: Heine-

Aristotle expresses clearly the connection often made in antiquity between manual labor, work for money and mental sluggishness. It should be noted that for Aristotle it is not physical activity *per se* which is vulgar but physical activity that leads to the worsening of the condition of the body or which is ungoverned by higher aims. Thus Aristotle includes gymnastics among the parts of a liberal education because it teaches the proper use of the body but also points out that training *only* in gymnastics again renders young men vulgar (*Politics* 8.3.1–4.2).[25]

Comparable ideas appear in the work of Galen, Plutarch, Cicero and Seneca. Galen (c. A.D. 129–199) strongly distinguishes between arts which are rational and noble and those, called the banausic arts, that work through the body or physical exertion.[26] Plutarch's (fl. A.D. 66) famous description of Archimedes cites both Plato's objection to mechanics as involving mean and manual labor (βαναυσουργίας) and Archimedes's repudiation of engineering because its purpose is mere utility and profit.[27] Cicero (106–43 B.C.) in the *De officiis* divides trades which are *liberales* (in which group he includes agriculture, medicine and architecture) from those which are *sordidi;* the latter category includes tax-gatherers and usurers because they incur ill-will, retailers because they lie, manual laborers, all mechanics because they are engaged in vulgar trades (*in sordida arte*) and "no workshop can have anything liberal about it," and as an afterthought fishmongers, butchers, cooks, poulterers and dancers.[28] Seneca (d. A.D. 66) also excludes from the liberal arts painting, wrestling, perfumers, cooks, "other helps toward luxury," and *any* art, even mathematical ones, practised for monetary payment.[29] In the early fifth century, Martianus Capella helped transfer this radical distinction between worthy and unworthy arts to the Middle Ages by excluding medicine and architecture from the celestial company of the liberal arts

---

mann, 1932), 638–639:

> βάναυσον δ' ἔργον εἶναι δεῖ τοῦτο νομίζειν καὶ τέχνην ταύτην καὶ μάθησιν ὅσαι πρὸς τὰς χρήσεις καὶ τὰς πράξεις τὰς τῆς ἀρετῆς ἄχρηστον ἀπεργάζονται τὸ σῶμα τῶν ἐλευθέρων ἢ τὴν ψυχὴν ἢ τὴν διάνοιαν. διὸ τάς τε τοιαύτας τέχνας ὅσαι τὸ σῶμα παρασκευάζουσι χεῖρον διακεῖσθαι βαναύσους καλοῦμεν καὶ τὰς μισθαρνικὰς ἐργασίας· ἄσχολον γὰρ ποιοῦσι τὴν διάνοιαν καὶ ταπεινήν.

[25] Aristotle, *Politics* 8.3.1–8.4.2, Loeb Classical Library, 642–648.
[26] Galen, *Protreptikos* 14 in *Scripta minora*, ed. Marquardt, 1:120.
[27] Plutarch, *Lives.Marcellus* 17.4, Loeb Classical Library, 5:472.
[28] Cicero, *De Officiis* 1.42.150, Loeb Classical Library, 152.
[29] Seneca, *Ad Lucilium* 88.18, Loeb Classical Library, 2:358–359: "Non enim adducor, ut in numerum liberalium artium pictores recipiam, non magis quam statuarios aut marmorarios aut ceteros luxuriae ministros."

because they "are concerned with mortal subjects and their skill lies in mundane matters."[30]

These examples are among the most explicit we possess on the definition of the banausic arts.[31] They show that the appellation banausic and its Latin equivalents were frequently associated with physical activity and the satisfaction of physical needs or pleasures but did not refer to any strictly defined category of arts. These terms were used as general labels for arts or trades which supply merely necessary needs or have degrading effects on their practitioners, whether because they deform the body, involve the transfer of money or encourage immoral behavior. The inferiority of the banausic arts is derived neither from their technological character nor their physicality alone but from the idea that these particular arts do not involve the soul in either its intellectual or its moral capacities but are practiced *merely* to satisfy physical needs or pleasures. If technical arts or crafts comprise the main type of arts labeled banausic, they are not the only type; dancing and tax-gathering are equally illiberal, and, according to Seneca, even geometry is illiberal if one is paid to practice it. Moreover, as we shall see, certain crafts were regarded as elevating the mind and were, therefore, consistently excluded from the category of the banausic arts.

The disjunction between the banausic arts and crafts is important not only because it leaves open the possibility that some crafts might be considered liberal rather than illiberal, but because it helps make more explicit the grounds upon which crafts could be regarded as non-rational activities. One of the clearest statements of the idea underlying the conception of the banausic arts is found in Plato's *Gorgias*. Socrates explains why cookery, his analogue for oratory, is not an art:

> . . . cookery puts on the mask of medicine and pretends to know what foods are best for the body. . . . Now I call this sort of thing pandering and I declare that it is dishonourable—I'm speaking to you now, Polus—because it makes pleasure its aim instead of good, and I maintain that it is merely a knack and not an art because it has no rational account to give of the nature of the various things which it offers.[32]

---

[30] Martianus Capella, *Martianus Capella and the Seven Liberal Arts*, trans. William Harris Stahl, vol. 2: *The Marriage of Philology and Mercury* (New York: Columbia University Press, 1971), 346; *Martianus Capella*, ed. Adolfus Dick and Jean Préaux (Stuttgart: B. G. Teubner, 1978), 471–472: "cui Delius Medicinam suggerit Architectonicamque in prae paratis assistere. 'sed quoniam his mortalium rerum cura terrenorumque sollertia est nec cum aethere quicquam habent superisque confine, non incongrue, si fastidio respuuntur, in senatu caelico reticebunt ab ipsa deinceps uirgine explorandae discussius.'"

[31] As far as I know, no systematic collection of texts has been made. Tatkiewicz, "Classification of Arts," 233 finds the distinction between vulgar and liberal arts the "best known and most generally accepted" classification of the arts in the ancient world but gives only Galen as an example.

[32] Plato, *Gorgias* 464d–465a, trans. W. Hamilton (London: Penguin, 1960), 46 (ed. Dodds,

The twin charges of irrationality and pandering brought by Plato against cookery were often leveled against crafts in general. It is this conception of craft which is behind much of ancient primitivism, or the belief that a simpler life, one less encumbered with the products of crafts and other arts, is more desirable.[33] Arthur O. Lovejoy in his important work on classical primitivism finds that the arts were often described as allowing and encouraging men to act on their evil impulses toward luxury, hubris and excessive pleasure and as leading men astray from the ideals of moderation, self-sufficiency and the contemplative life.[34] According to Lovejoy, "nearly all the crafts . . . could more or less plausibly be, and, as the texts show, in antiquity were, brought under a similar indictment [of promoting greed and violence]."[35]

The issue of negative attitudes toward crafts in antiquity is, of course, complicated by the question of the effects of ancient social and economic conditions, especially slavery, on ideas.[36] Leaving this complex problem aside as beyond the scope of this paper, however, one can point to several elements within the intellectual tradition itself which made it difficult for technical arts to be treated as fully rational and legitimate parts of knowledge. Carl Mitcham explores how the conception of matter as an organic entity already ordered toward form limited the Greek idea of technology.[37] For Ludwig Edelstein, the important point is the prevailing notion that scientific knowledge was important for its own sake rather than for any use which might be made of it.[38] Related to both

---

94–95):

ὑπὸ μὲν οὖν τὴν ἰατρικὴν ἡ ὀψοποιικὴ ὑποδέδυκεν, καὶ προσποιεῖται τὰ βέλτιστα σιτία τῷ σώματι εἰδέναι.

κολακείαν μὲν οὖν αὐτὸ καλῶ, καὶ αἰσχρόν φημι εἶναι τὸ τοιοῦτον, ὦ Πῶλε—τοῦτο γὰρ πρὸς σὲ λέγω—ὅτι τοῦ ἡδέος στοχάζεται ἄνευ τοῦ βελτίστου· τέχνην δὲ αὐτὴν οὔ φημι εἶναι ἀλλ' ἐμπειρίαν, ὅτι οὐκ ἔχει λόγον οὐδένα ᾧ προσφέρει ⟨ἣ⟩ ἃ προσφέρει ὁποῖ' ἄττα τὴν φύσιν ἐστίν, ὥστε τὴν αἰτίαν ἑκάστου μὴ ἔχειν εἰπεῖν·

[33] Arthur O. Lovejoy and George Boas, *Primitivism and Related Ideas in Antiquity* (Baltimore: Johns Hopkins, 1935), 7.

[34] Lovejoy and Boas, *Primitivism*, 7–21, for sources and commentary, passim. Lovejoy and Boas also discuss classical anti-primitivism, or the belief that the invention of the arts improved the conditions of human life, *Primitivism*, 192–221.

[35] Lovejoy and Boas, *Primitivism*, 16.

[36] For an excellent summary of the literature on this topic see Edelstein, "Recent Interpretations," 579–583. See also Finley, "Technical Innovation," for the view that economic dependence on slavery in antiquity inspired contempt for technology and labor but cf. Desmond Lee, "Science, Philosophy and Technology in the Greco-Roman World," *Greece and Rome* 20 (1973): 69–75, 193 for the opposite view that slavery was an effect rather than a cause of the lack of technological development.

[37] Mitcham, "Philosophy," 185–187.

[38] Edelstein, "Recent Interpretations," 583.

attitudes was the tendency to identify rationality with virtue, as in Plato's contrast of cookery and medicine. Linking the questions of rationality and morality was the teleological character of ancient thought. True knowledge could only be knowledge of a final end, transcending the immediate satisfaction of physical needs or pleasures and focusing on higher purposes. Technology, as the ancients were well aware, remains a means to an end rather than an end in itself. For both Plato and Aristotle, the person who uses an object and, therefore, knows its proper purpose possesses *scientia;* the craftsman who makes the object holds at best correct opinion about it.[39] In an almost complete reversal of modern values, utility *per se* and divorced from higher considerations of virtue, remains the least important product of the arts and sciences, ranking even below recreation.[40] True knowledge must ask "for the sake of what." The answer "for the sake of utility" was merely to beg the question, in much the same way (but from the opposite perspective) that today advocates of the humanities in education are often greeted with the question, "Yes, but what are they good for?" The danger of technology, according to one strand of classical thought, is that it provides technique but not purpose and increases human powers without also supplying guidance for the proper use, if any, of inventions.[41] Jacques Ellul's suggestion that the Greeks rejected technology (and magic) because its "potentialities" threatened their sense of balance, harmony and moderation points up this opposition between moral and intellectual restraint and technological possibility.[42] The labeling of crafts as banausic or illiberal reflected and perpetuated this persistent theme of means *versus* final ends, techniques *versus* wisdom.

The Productive Arts

Unlike the designation of arts as liberal and banausic, other ancient classifications of knowledge did not pass a moral judgment on different human activities but instead assumed the rationality of all arts and grouped them according to the kind of process each involved. The basis of all later versions of this type of classification was Aristotle's division

---

[39] Plato, *Republic* 601c–602, Loeb Classical Library (London: Heinemann, 1933), 6.

[40] Aristotle, *Metaphysics* 1.1981b16, Loeb Classical Library (London: Heinemann, 1933, 34).

[41] Jean-Pierre Vernant, "Prométhée et la function technique," in *Myth et pensée chez les grecs: Études de psychologie historique* (Paris: François Maspero, 1965), 185–195; Wolfgang Schadewaldt, "The Concepts of Nature and Technique according to the Greeks," *Research in Philosophy and Technology* 2 (1979):168–169. For the important classical texts on the danger of the arts and crafts, with commentary, see Lovejoy and Boas, *Primitivism*.

[42] Jacques Ellul, *The Technological Society*, trans. John Wilkinson (New York: Vintage-Knopf, 1964), 29. See also Karl F. Morrison, *The Mimetic Tradition of Reform in the West* (Princeton: Princeton University Press, 1982), 15, in which Morrison discusses Aristotle's distinction between the "natural" and liberal acquiring of wealth, which enables one to live well, and the "unnatural" and dishonorable acquiring of excess wealth and unlimited profit.

of human knowledge into the fundamental categories of thinking, doing and making. The last category, that of "making arts" or ποιητικάι was defined as arts which produced a concrete result, and was composed mainly or exclusively of crafts.

Prior to Aristotle, arts had been classified on the basis of production by the Sophists and by Plato, but these classifications were not developed and remained only incidental comments. The Sophists separated arts whose purpose was to produce the necessities of life from those which promoted pleasure and amusement.[43] This distinction was long-lived and was repeated, with variations, by Plato, Aristotle, Cicero, Posidonius and Augustine, yet acquired little further substance.[44]

More elaborate classifications along the same lines appear in Plato's *Sophist* and *Statesman*. These classifications seem to have no direct influence on other classifications of the arts in antiquity or the Middle Ages. Yet they deserve attention because Plato's use of them illuminates the paradoxical role craft plays in his thought. In the *Sophist* (219b–d) Plato compares "productive arts" (ποιητικός) or arts which bring into existence something that did not exist before and "acquisitive arts" (κτητικός) or arts which conquer by word or deed, or prevent others from acquiring things which have already been produced. Among the productive arts he includes agriculture, medicine, construction or molding of vessels and the arts of imitation (painting and sculpture) and among the acquisitive arts all ways of learning and acquiring knowledge, cognition, trade, fighting, hunting and fishing. In the *Statesman* (281d–e) Plato contrasts productive arts, in this case arts which produce objects from raw materials, with "contributory arts" (ξυναιτικός) or arts which produce the tools needed by the productive arts. These Platonic classifications are remarkable for their precision, detail and knowledge of crafts.[45] Under contributory arts, for example, Plato discusses arts which make instruments, containers, carriages, "defenses" (including weaving, clothing, armor, walls, stonework and others), diversions (visual arts, poetry, music), nourishments (farming, hunting, gymnastics, medicine, butchering) as well as those handling raw material such as mining, lumbering, the currier's art, the art of stripping bark and the arts of making cork, papyrus and rope (287b–289c). Under weaving, he sep-

[43] Isocrates, *Panegyrics* 40, Loeb Classical Library (Cambridge: Harvard University Press, 1928), 1:143.

[44] Ps.-Plato, *Epinomis* 975d, in *Platonis Opera*, ed. Ioannes Burnet, Scriptorum classicorum bibliotheca Oxoniensis (Oxford: Clarendon Press, 1907), 5:975d; Aristotle, *Metaphysics* 981b17, Loeb Classical Library, 6; Cicero, *De natura deorum* 2.59.148 and 2.60.150, Loeb Classical Library (London: Heinemann, 1933), 266, 268; Seneca, *Ad Lucilium* 88.21–24, Loeb Classical Library, 2:362; Augustine, *De civitate Dei* 22.24, ed. Dombart, 612.

[45] These classifications are discussed in Pierre-Maxime Schuhl, "Remarques sur Platon et la technologie," *Revue des études grecques* 66 (1953):469–472. To them might be added the classification in the *Epinomis* (attributed to Plato) 975a–976c which divided the arts into arts of recreation (music, drawing), necessity (agriculture, architecture, manufacture of furniture, tools, pottery, weaving, smithing, hunting and prophecy) and defense (medicine, military arts, navigation and law).

arates weaving from felting, garments made from hair from garments made from vegetable products, stitched and unstitched garments and coverings which we spread under us from coverings we wrap around us (279e).

Pierre-Maxime Schuhl has claimed that Plato's classifications of technological arts were not superseded in complexity and detail under Francis Bacon;[46] although this judgment fails to take into account the Middle Ages, it carries some weight with respect to antiquity. The precise knowledge of specific crafts displayed in the passages cited above goes far to dispel the notion that Plato had nothing but contempt for manual crafts.[47] Nevertheless, despite the detail, the limitations of Plato's classifications are soon evident. In none are crafts integrated with other sorts of knowledge; where Plato does discuss his basic division of knowledge into mathematics, physics and dialectics (*Republic* 509d–511e), no mention is made of any but purely speculative knowledge. Crafts do not appear as a subdivision of any broader classification, but are introduced for rhetorical and didactic purposes as part of an extended analogy or example. The acquisitive arts defined in the *Sophist* are found to encompass sophistry, which hunts young men (233b), the deceptive nature of which is the subject of the dialogue. The lengthy discussion of various technological arts in the *Statesman* provided analogies for the more difficult task of defining the art of kingship (278b). Plato's classifications of the arts, elaborate and knowledgeable but lacking in substance, are, in fact, instances of his frequent use of technical illustrations or imagery to explain a point of moral or speculative philosophy. In the *Statesman* (285d–286d), after some two hundred lines discussing the details of weaving, the stranger remarks, "Of course, no man of sense could wish to pursue a discussion of weaving for its own sake. . . . But it is always easier to practice in small matters than in greater ones."[48] Craft, for Plato, is finally, a "small thing" in comparison to ethical questions, but it remains, also, a valuable focus through which Plato defines his ideas.

In all likelihood, Aristotle borrowed the term productive arts from Plato. Unlike Plato, however, Aristotle not only integrated crafts into

---

[46] Schuhl, "Remarques sur Platon," 466.

[47] Plato's knowledgeability about crafts has been often remarked upon. See, for example, discussion in Lloyd, *Polarity and Analogy*, 292, 277, 293–294; Friedrich Solmsen, "Nature as Craftsman in Greek Thought," *Journal of the History of Ideas* 24 (1963):473–496; Alison Burford, *Craftsmen in Greek and Roman Society* (Ithaca: Cornell University Press, 1972), 130–131; Vernant, "Prométhée," 185–193.

[48] Plato, *Statesman* 285d–286b, trans. Harold N. Fowler (London: Heinemann, 1925), 106–107:

Ἦ που τὸν τῆς ὑφαντικῆς γε λόγον αὐτῆς
ταύτης ἕνεκα θηρεύειν οὐδεὶς ἂν ἐθελήσειε νοῦν ἔχων·

ῥᾴων δ' ἐν τοῖς ἐλάττοσιν ἡ μελέτη
παντὸς πέρι μᾶλλον ἢ περὶ τὰ μείζω.

an overall classification but provided a framework within which the nature of craft could be further explored. His rigorous definition of art was the philosophical underpinning for much of ancient and medieval thought on craft. Further, Aristotle supplied a flexible and useful method of organizing all branches of human knowledge, including craft, which lent itself to later elaboration and expansion.

Using some of Plato's terminology but in a far more systematic fashion, Aristotle distinguishes theoretical knowledge (mathematics, physics and metaphysics) which deals with necessary being and ends in truth (*Metaphysics* 21.993b, 6.1025b, 6.1 1026a, 11.7 1064b), practical arts (economics, ethics and politics) or knowledge expressed in action (*Nicomachean Ethics* 6.1140, *Metaphysics* 2.1 993b) and productive arts or knowledge by which some product such as a shoe or a poem is brought into being (*Metaphysics* 11.7 1064a). Aristotle also mentions subalternate or subordinate arts which pursue particular ends included within a larger purpose, as, for example, all arts concerned with equipping horses fall under the general category of the art of riding (*Nicomachean Ethics* 1.1. 1094a).

Aristotle does little to further refine his remarks and, on the whole, crafts play an inconspicuous part in his classification of the arts and sciences. His notion of subalternate sciences, however, contains great potential for relating specific arts, particularly technical arts, to each other and to higher sciences. One step Aristotle takes in this direction is the inclusion of mechanics as a more physical kind of mathematics (*Metaphysics* 1078a). Another context for discussion of crafts in relation to other arts occurs in the first book of the *Politics*, in which Aristotle explains how various occupations, including agriculture, mining, commerce and other manual arts, pertain to wealth-getting and, therefore, to economics.[49] Later commentators on Aristotle's works, especially the Hellenistic and medieval Arabic philosophers, developed his basic scheme into comprehensive and highly precise classifications which frequently gave a substantial place to crafts.

The integration of craft into an overall scheme of knowledge, moreover, opened the door for further thought on the epistemological status of craft. By developing Plato's use of art as a model of skillful work toward an end, Aristotle made explicit the analogical relationship between art and nature and thereby supplied a philosophical understanding of craft which was to last through the Renaissance. Aristotle defines art as "a reasoned state of capacity to make" (*Nicomachean Ethics* 1140a). Art was rational and could be distinguished from simple experience because the artist, unlike, for example, the manual laborer, knows the reason why he does what he does (*Metaphysics* 981a–b.) Art, furthermore, differs from other kinds of knowledge because it makes or produces something, although not necessarily a physical object. All art,

---

[49] Aristotle, *Politics* 8.3.1–8.4.2, Loeb Classical Library, 642–648.

according to Aristotle, is concerned with bringing into existence a thing which may exist or not and is distinct from both action, or doing, and scientific knowledge.[50]

The definition of art as the human activity which causes something to "come-to-be" creates an analogy between art and nature. Both nature and art impose a form upon matter for the sake of a final end; the purposeful and intelligent shaping of matter by human craft is, therefore, analogous to natural causation.[51] Art imitates nature (*Physics* 199a-15–17) by its method of production, not as some later thinkers understood, in the products themselves.[52] Nature, however, possesses a primacy which art does not have; although Aristotle leaves open the possibility that art could in some sense go beyond nature, "imitation" generally retains the Platonic connotation of inferiority. Nature, unlike art, is self-moving and the principle of movement in a natural thing is within itself. For artificial things, however, the principle of movement is extrinsic, that is, in the maker rather than in the thing made.[53] Consequently, man may make use of nature but he cannot direct her; his abilities are sharply circumscribed by art's inferior power only to "imitate." Yet Aristotle himself sometimes speaks of art completing nature (*Physics* 199c15) or adding to nature what nature itself cannot do (*Politics* 1337a2) and he suggests the possibility that art could in some sense correct or go beyond nature. The reworking of Aristotle's complex and fertile discussion of the relationship of art and nature, as art became the rival of nature and, finally, nature's obedient commander, continued to be a major part of the history of the philosophy of technology through the seventeenth century.[54]

Certain Hellenistic writers developed the Aristotelian division of the arts and sciences into more elaborate and systematic classifications which emphasized technological arts. This tendency may reflect advances in the practical sciences of mechanics, optics, medicine and ge-

---

[50] Aristotle, *Nicomachean Ethics* 6.3.4 1140a, *The Ethics of Aristotle*, ed. John Burnet (New York: Arno Press, 1972), 259–262.

[51] On Aristotle's use of craft as an analogy with natural processes, see Lloyd, *Polarity*, 288; Solmsen, "Nature as Craftsman," 488, 491; and, especially, J. M. Le Blond, *Logique et méthode chez Aristote* (Paris: J. Vrin, 1939), 326–346.

[52] Seneca, *Ad Lucilium* 90.24, Loeb Classical Library, 412; Hugh of St. Victor, *Didascalicon* 1.9, ed. Charles Henry Buttimer, The Catholic University of America Studies in Medieval and Renaissance Latin, 10 (Washington, D.C.: The Catholic University Press, 1939), 16–17.

[53] For an excellent and lucid explication of Aristotle on nature and art see M. J. Charlesworth, *Aristotle on Art and Nature*, Auckland University College Bulletin No. 50, Philosophy Series No. 2 (Auckland: Auckland University Press, 1957). For a more interpretative discussion see Le Blond, *Logique et méthode*, 330–331, who suggests that art was not only an exceptionally useful example for Aristotle, but the basic source of his ideas on causation. See also Morrison, *Mimetic Tradition*, 10–13.

[54] See Paolo Rossi, *Philosophy, Technology and the Arts in the Early Modern Era*, trans. Salvator Attanasio (New York: Harper, 1970).

ography, as well as the more organized approach to knowledge characteristic of the Alexandrian school.[55]

One of the most important of these classifications is a scheme, remarkable for the importance which it gives to crafts, put forward in an early scholium to the *Ars Grammatica* of Dionysius Thrax.[56] The arts are divided into four groups: the productive, theoretical, practical and mixed. Of these four categories, three have a technological element. Productive arts are those which fashion "a certain matter which has been wrought" into an artificial thing; metal-working, shoemaking and carpentry are given as examples. Practical arts are arts executed by means of instruments, for example, military art which prevails against the adversary using machines. Theoretical arts are the familiar category: astronomy and philosophy are the examples. Finally, "mixed" arts are those which seem to combine the other categories, for instance, medicine, which is evidently theoretical but is also executed by hand and, therefore, practical.[57]

In the same commentary variations on the main scheme also demonstrate a strong interest in classifying technical arts. Attributed to Lucius Tarrhaeus is a fourfold division into apotelesmatic, practical, instrumental and theoretical. Apotelesmatic arts are described as arts using one or more materials, as carpentry works with wood, metal-working with metal and architecture with lime and stone. The practical arts are arts using actions, subdivided into five types based on the type of action involved: self-movement (for example, dancing), moving against (wrestling), aiming at (javelin throwing and oratory), moving after (hunting and fishing) and assisting in movement (driving horses or steering a ship). Instrumental arts are confined to the playing of musical instruments, by blowing, touch or both. Astronomy and geometry are the examples of theoretical arts. Lucius Tarrhaeus ends his classification by saying that all the arts together are called knowledge (ἡ γνῶσις ἐπιστήμη) and cites Homer to prove his point.[58] A combination classification is given later in the treatise in which arts are divided into theoretical, practical (zitherplaying and dancing), apotelesmatic (statuary and building) and acquiring (hunting and fishing).[59]

The most striking aspect of the scholia is the emphasis on technology. The authors of these classifications have made use of Aristotelian cate-

---

[55] On Hellenistic technology and science see, especially, Bertrand Gille, *Les mécaniciens grecs: La naissance de la technologie* (Paris: Editions du Seuil, 1980). The liberal arts were also more distinctly defined as a category of knowledge in this period. See Marrou, *Saint Augustin*, 211–235 and Marrou, "Les arts libéraux," 23–27.

[56] *Scholia ad Dionysius Thrac*, in Immanuelis Bekker, ed., *Anecdota Graeca* (Berlin: Apud G. Reimerum, 1816), 2:652–670. On Dionysius Thrax see R. H. Robins, "Dionysius Thrax and the Western Grammatical Tradition," in *Diversions of Bloomsbury: Selected Writings on Linguistics* (Amsterdam: North Holland, 1970), 113–154.

[57] *Scholia ad Dionysius Thrac*, ed. Bekker, *Anecdota Graeca*, 2:652; cf. 2:655.

[58] Ibid., 2:652–654.

[59] Ibid., 2:670.

gories but have redefined their content. In the first scholium all but one of the four kinds of knowledge are associated with technical arts and in all the classifications the productive arts, skimmed over by Aristotle, receive as much emphasis as the theoretical arts. The definition of productive arts has been narrowed to include only arts producing material objects, thus excluding poetry, and focusing attention on crafts. The practical arts, on the other hand, have partially or completely lost the ethical and social element of Aristotle's conception and have been reduced to physical actions, particularly actions using instruments or machines. The dignity conferred on crafts in these classifications is reinforced by Lucius Tarrhaeus's quotation from the *Iliad*: "The apotelesmatic arts are 'the overseer of many cunningly made things.'"[60]

Classifications of technical arts based on Aristotle's flourished in the last centuries of antiquity. These usually modified Aristotle's original classification in characteristic ways. The more narrow definition of productive arts as arts producing a physical object, found in the scholia but not in Aristotle (who had included poetry among the productive arts), appears to have become standard, strengthening the focus on crafts. A possible echo of the scholia can even be seen in Plotinus. Although the overall structure of Plotinus's classification of the arts derives from Platonic, rather than Aristotelian, sources, he includes the category of the productive arts and names building and carpentry as examples.[61] Diogenes Laertius repeats the basic Aristotelian division of the arts into practical, productive and theoretical, although he attributes this classification to Plato. Practical arts are those which do or perform something but produce nothing visible, as, for example, politics, fluteplaying and harpplaying; productive arts, such as architecture and shipbuilding, produce a work which can be seen.[62] These definitions, with different examples, also appeared in the classical Latin tradition in Quintilian[63] and, in a very abbreviated form, in Cicero.[64]

Although it was only rarely alluded to in the context of classifications of knowledge, the conception of craft as the intelligent and purposeful shaping of matter by which a mental form was imposed upon a physical substance continued to be associated with the productive arts. Thus Plotinus describes carpentry as drawing upon intellectual patterns in order to give form to matter.[65] The Church Fathers used the idea of the

---

[60] Ibid., 2:654: "*ὡς μαρτυρεῖ καὶ ὁ ποιητής, ἐπὶ μὲν ἀποτελεσματικῆς . . . ὅς χερσὶν ἐπίστατο δαίδαλα πολλὰ τεύχειν.*"

[61] Plotinus, *Enneads* 5.9.11, in *Opera*, ed. Paul Henry and Hans-Rudolf Schwyzer, Museum Lessianum Series philosophica, 34 (Paris: Desclée de Brouwer et Cie, 1959), 2:424.

[62] Diogenes Laertius, *Lives of Eminent Philosophers. Plato* 3.84, Loeb Classical Library (London: Heinemann, 1925), 1:350.

[63] Quintilian, *Institutio oratoria* 2.18.1, Loeb Classical Library (London: Heinemann, 1921), 346. Quintilian names dancing and painting as examples of practical and productive arts, respectively.

[64] Cicero, *Academica* 2.7, Loeb Classical Library (London: Heinemann, 1933), 496.

[65] Plotinus, *Enneads* 5.9.11, in *Opera*, ed. Henry and Schwyzer, 2:424.

productive arts not only as a method of classification but also to point out the produced, or created, nature of the world. In Basil's *Hexameron* the world is presented as a work of art, and an analogy is drawn between God's production of the universe and the production of the craftsman:

> The aim of the theoretical skills is action of the mind; but that of the practical, the motion itself of the body, and, if that should cease, nothing would subsist or remain for those beholding it. In fact, there is no aim in dancing and flute playing; on the contrary, the very action ends with itself. However, in the case of the productive arts, the work remains, as that of architecture, carpentry, metalwork, weaving and of as many such arts as, even if the craftsman is not present, ably manifest in themselves the artistic processes of thoughts, and make it possible for you to admire the architect from his work, as well as the metal-worker and the weaver. That it might be shown, then, that the world is a work of art, set before all for contemplation, so that through it the wisdom of Him who created it should be known. . . .[66]

Ambrose paraphrases this passage in his own *Hexaemeron*.[67] Augustine uses the same contrast between a category of arts which produce a physical object and those consisting only in action in the *De doctrina christiana* as part of a general classification of knowledge.[68] He more rigorously distinguishes between the productive powers of man and God, consistently stressing the inferiority of human art and the inadequacy of the analogy. Nevertheless, he seems to have found the comparison a compelling one and he framed the problem several times from different perspectives.[69]

The productive arts served as a useful and convenient rubric for crafts throughout the fifth century. Yet the term seems to have died out in the Latin West sometime after this date. Although Boethius translated Aristotle's *Topics*, which mentions the productive arts, and although his own classification of the arts and sciences generally follows Aristotelian lines, Boethius does not include the productive arts among the parts of knowledge.[70] Early medieval classifications of knowledge, while some-

---

[66] Basil, *Exegetic Homilies*, trans. Sister Agnes Clare Way (Washington D.C.: The Catholic University of America Press, 1963), 12; In *Hexaemeron. Homily* 1.7 in *Opera omnia*, ed. Julian Garnier (Paris: Apud Gaume Fratres Bibliopolis, 1839), 1:9.

[67] Ambrose, *Hexaemeron* 1.5, in *Opera, Corpus Scriptorum Ecclesiasticorum latinorum* (Leipzig: G. Freytag, 1896), 32:14. For the relationship of *hexaemera* of Basil and Ambrose, see F. E. Robbins, *The Hexaemeral Literature: A Study of the Greek and Latin Commentaries on Genesis* (Chicago: University of Chicago, 1912), 57–59.

[68] Augustine, *De doctrina christiana* 2.30 (47), in *Opera, Corpus christianorum*, series latina (Turnholt: Brepols Editores Pontificii, 1962), 32:65.

[69] For example, Augustine compares human and divine art in the *Confessions* 11.5, *De diversis quaestionibus* 83 and *De genesi ad litteram* 8.10 and 8.12. For a more detailed discussion of God as craftsman in the hexaemeral literature, see George Ovitt, Jr., *The Restoration of Paradise: Labor and Technology in Medieval Culture* (New Brunswick, N.J.: Rutgers University Press, 1987), 57–70.

[70] James A. Weisheipl, "Classification of the Sciences in Medieval Thought," *Medieval Studies* 27 (1965):58–62.

times including a group of "making" arts, do so under the rubric *mechanica* and associate these arts with physics or the mathematical arts.[71]

The disappearance of the threefold division of knowledge into productive, practical and theoretical knowledge perhaps reflected the increasing unavailability of the Aristotelian corpus as a whole in the Latin West. A symptom of the resulting confusion is the lack of any standard Latin translation for ποιητικάι: whereas Quintilian left the Greek term untranslated, Ambrose and Augustine defined the idea but provided no name, Boethius translated it as *effective* and the sixth-century translator of Basil's *Hexaemeron* gave the Latin translation as *factrices*.[72]

The Greek East, on the other hand, retained contact with all of the Aristotelian corpus, and there the classification of the productive arts had a continuous tradition into the medieval period. Greek mathematicians of late antiquity, as we shall see below, began to identify mechanics with both the productive arts and a physically-oriented branch of mathematics. Through the intermediary of John Philoponus, the Aristotelian classification passed into Arabic and Hebrew classifications and appeared in modified form in the works of Alfarabi, Algazali, Averroes, Al-Mukammas, Ihwan al-Safa, Maimonides and others.[73] These treatises, which were highly elaborate and systematic, often interchanged the terms productive arts and practical arts, mixed magical arts with technical arts and also classified crafts as the practical parts of theoretical sciences.[74] The Aristotelian classification in its Arabic variations was reintroduced into the West in the twelfth century through Domingo Gundisalvo's translation of Alfarabi's *De ortu scientiarum* and thereafter again influenced Latin classifications of the arts.[75]

Crafts and Mathematics

The liberal arts in antiquity included the traditional branches of mathematics, geometry, arithmetic, astronomy and music, which later became the medieval *quadrivium*. Despite the sharp distinction made by some authors between the liberal and banausic arts, certain technical arts were often recognized as possessing a mathematical character and, hence, as being in some sense theoretical. Plato, for instance, distinguishes in the *Philebus* between crafts on the basis of a greater or lesser use of mathematics (55e–56b). The more exact and scientific arts, which

---

[71] See below, Chapter III.

[72] Boethius, *De topicis differentiis* 6.4, *Boethius's De topicis differentiis*, ed. Eleanore Stump (New York: Cornell University Press, 1978), 25. For the translation of Basil's *Hexaemeron*, see Migne, *PL* 53:874.

[73] Harry A. Wolfson, "The Classification of the Sciences in Medieval Jewish Philosophy," *Hebrew Union College Jubilee Volume (1875–1925)* vol. 2 (Philadelphia: Jewish Publication Society Press, 1925), 264–265, vol. 3 (Philadelphia: Jewish Publication Society Press, 1926), 371.

[74] Wolfson, "Classification," 2:264, 266, 280–281, 298.

[75] See below, Chapter V.

use measurements and instruments, include building. The less exact, which attain only unreliable and uncertain results, include lyreplaying, medicine, agriculture, navigation and military science.[76] Although Plato is quick to suggest that the calculation used in commerce and building is of a different sort than that used in philosophy (57a), his discussion is an interesting instance in which Plato appears willing to apply his interest in mathematics to practical pursuits. Aristotle classifies mechanics as a branch of mathematics, but one which, like optics and harmonics, had a physical orientation (*Physics* 194a7–13).[77] The pseudo-Aristotelian *Mechanical Problems* treats mechanics as a mathematical discipline which, nevertheless, overcomes nature.[78] Contrary to Plutarch's claim that Plato's disapproval caused mechanics to become entirely distinct from geometry and ignored by philosophers,[79] Hero and later Greek mathematicians continued to regard mechanics as a branch of mathematics, without denying its association with manual arts. Hero (first century A.D.) implies a parallelism between philosophers, who deduce properties theoretically, and mechanics, who deduce them from sensible bodies.[80] The fifth-century Neoplatonist, Proclus, tells us that Geminus (fl. first century B.C.?) and other mathematicians divided mathematics into arithmetic and geometry, which dealt with theoretical forms only, and mechanics, optics, astronomy and other arts (sometimes including military tactics) which dealt with sensible objects.[81] Pappus in the fourth century explicitly named metal-working, architecture, carpentry, painting and the manual activities connected with these arts as the practical part of mechanics, whose theoretical part includes geometry, arithmetic, astronomy and physics.[82] He defends a close association between purely theoretical mathematics and manual skills as beneficial to both.[83] For Proclus himself, mechanics, which he characterizes as a "making" or productive art or science, is an important part of mathematics; it includes not only the making of instruments of war and de-

[76] Plato, *Philebus* 55e–56b, Loeb Classical Library (London: Heinemann, 1925), 358. Aristotle also describes medicine, navigation, gymnastics and business as less certain and requiring more deliberation than other arts (*Nicomachean Ethics* [3.3.8]; cf. Nemesius of Emessa (fl. late 4th c.), *On the Nature of Man* chap. 34 which lists medicine, gymnastics and navigation as arts depending on conjecture.

[77] Aristotle, *Physics* 194a7–13, Loeb Classical Library (London: 1929)1:120.

[78] Ps.-Aristotelian *Mechanical Problems*, edited under the name of Aristotle in *Minor Works*, Loeb Classical Library (London: Heinemann, 1936), 331.

[79] Plutarch, *Lives.Marcellus* 14.5–6, Loeb Classical Library, 5:470, 472.

[80] Hero, *Treatise on Pneumatics* 1.1 in *The Pneumatics of Hero of Alexandria: A facsimile of the 1851 Woodcroft Edition* (London: Macdonald, 1971), 1.

[81] Proclus, *Commentary on the First Book of Euclid's Elements* 1.13.38–39, trans. Glenn R. Morrow (Princeton: Princeton University Press, 1970), 31–32; ed. Gottfried Friedlein, *Procli Diadochi in primum Euclidis Elementorum librum Commentarii, ex recognitione Godofred Friedlein* (Leipzig: Teubner, 1873), 38.

[82] Pappus Alexandrinus, *Collectio* 8.1 in *Selections illustrating the History of Greek Mathematics*, Loeb Classical Library (London: Heinemann, 1941), 2:614.

[83] Pappus, *Mechanics* 8.3, Loeb Classical Library, 2:618, 620.

fense, astronomical models and marvelous devices with moving figures, but every art concerned with the moving of material things.[84]

These Greek mathematicians of late antiquity exerted little, if any, direct influence, as far as is known, on the early development of classifications of the sciences in the Latin West, although Pappus's and Proclus's arrangements of the manual and mathematical arts suggest a possible connection with Isidore of Seville's list of the arts in the *Liber numerorum* and the *Differentiae*.[85] Among medieval Arabic philosophers, however, parallelism between theoretical sciences and physically oriented arts became a major element in the organization of knowledge and, as we shall see below (Chapter V), these classifications in turn profoundly affected Western approaches toward the integration of technology with other branches of knowledge in the work of Domingo Gundisalvo (Dominicus Gundissalinus), Robert Kilwardby, Roger Bacon and others.

Crafts and the Liberal Arts

The distinction between the liberal and illiberal or banausic arts was, as we have seen, not a clear-cut opposition between theoretical arts and crafts. The banausic arts included not only manual arts but any activity which was pursued for physical need or pleasure, entertainment or monetary gain. Trade, dancing and wrestling were as much banausic arts as metal-working; on the other hand, geometry or astronomy, if performed for payment or pursued in the wrong spirit, could be considered illiberal.[86] Conversely, in antiquity the liberal arts were not a fixed canon of disciplines but a loosely defined group of arts characterized in terms of their function and value in society; although the center of the liberal arts remained the seven literary and mathematical arts which later became the medieval *trivium* and *quadrivium*, the classical conception of the liberal arts focused on the general development of intellectual and moral abilities rather than on specific subject matter.[87] Even though handicrafts in general were commonly called banausic arts, some arts with a physical aspect were consistently associated with the liberal arts or placed in an intermediate category, neither fully "liberal" nor entirely "banausic."

These arts, most often medicine, gymnastics, agriculture, mechanics, navigation and, sometimes, painting, could be regarded as in some sense liberal, despite the fact that they dealt with the physical world,

[84] Proclus, *Commentary* 1.13.41, trans. Morrow, 34; ed. Friedlein, 41.

[85] Isidore of Seville, *Liber numerorum* 7.44 (*PL* 83:188) and *Differentiae* 2.39 (*PL* 83:94); on these classifications and the possible connection with Pappus or Proclus, see Chapter III, 61–65.

[86] See, for example, Seneca, *Ad Lucilium* 88.1, Loeb Classical Library, 348 and Aristotle *Politics* 1337b, Loeb Classical Library, 638.

[87] Marrou, *A History of Education in Antiquity*, 244, 288, 299, 302–304.

because they, like the fully-fledged liberal arts, had virtue or intellectual wisdom as their end. More specifically, if an art could be linked to theoretical knowledge or could be seen as possessing a special moral value, it acquired a different and higher status than other physically oriented arts. A mathematical, and, therefore, theoretical character could easily be attributed to mechanics, which, although it included manual arts, was, as we have seen, often included as a subdivision of geometry.[88] Similarly, medicine, while often regarded as a manual craft, could also be considered a science.[89] Doctors and others since the Hippocratic school had asserted that medicine was part of philosophy.[90] The authors of the scholia to Dionysius Thrax placed medicine in a special category because it mixed theoretical science and practical art.[91] Even agriculture, if, as Cassiodorus says, "it studies the seasons," and navigation could be associated with astronomy and, hence, with theoretical knowledge.[92]

A closeness to nature and natural processes also served to give some physically oriented arts, especially agriculture and medicine, a moral value. Agriculture was strongly associated with the simple and, therefore, virtuous, life. A telling example is the remainder of the passage in Xenophon's *Oeconomicus* quoted above.[93] This passage had been cited in the truncated form previously quoted as an example of contempt for the banausic arts.[94] However, the work in which this passage occurs is a treatise on household management and the passage in question is immediately followed by advice to pursue "husbandry and the art of war . . . two of the noblest and most necessary pursuits."[95] Xenophon goes on to praise agriculture, clearly not a "banausic" art, because it increases one's estate without depriving other men, teaches righteousness, trains the body in all that a free man should be able to do, yields

---

[88] Above, p. 41.

[89] Owsei Temkin, "Greek Medicine as Science and Craft," *Isis* 44 (1953):213–225.

[90] Hippocrates, *Decorum* 2.5–6, Loeb Classical Library, 2:286, 288. See also below, p. 44 and Temkin, "Medicine," 224–225.

[91] *Scholia ad Dionysius Thrac*, ed. Bekker, *Anecdota Graeca*, 2:652.

[92] Cassiodorus, *An Introduction to Divine and Human Readings*, trans. Leslie Webber Jones (New York: Columbia University Press, 1946; rpt. New York: Octagon Books, 1966), 202–203; *Institutiones divinarum et saecularium lectionum*, ed. R. A. B. Mynors (Oxford: Clarendon Press, 1961), 71–72, 78. Philostratus also associates agriculture with astronomy; see below p. 45.

[93] Above, 27–28.

[94] Benjamin Farrington, *Greek Science* (London: Penguin, 1944), 28–29.

[95] Xenophon, *Oeconomicus* 4.4, Loeb Classical Library, 390, 391:

Ἡμῖν δὲ δὴ ποίαις συμβουλεύεις, ὦ Σώκρατες, χρῆσθαι;

Ἆρα, ἔφη ὁ Σωκράτης, μὴ αἰσχυνθῶμεν τὸν Περσῶν βασιλέα μιμήσασθαι; ἐκεῖνον γάρ φασιν ἐν τοῖς καλλίστοις τε καὶ ἀναγκαιοτάτοις ἡγούμενον εἶναι ἐπιμελήμασι γεωργίαν τε καὶ τὴν πολεμικὴν τέχνην τούτων ἀμφοτέρων ἰσχυρῶς ἐπιμελεῖσθαι.

food and luxuries, gives strength and exercise and prepares the *mind* and body for other activities.[96] Jean-Pierre Vernant in his study of classical attitudes toward work and nature concludes that agriculture, unlike other forms of labor, had a moral and religious value for the Greeks; whereas mining, for example, was sometimes represented as an arrogant attack on nature, agriculture conformed man to nature and, therefore, to virtue.[97] Hesiod, Virgil, Lucretius, Varro and Cicero praise the farmer and farming as exemplifying the simple, moral life.[98] For Augustine, agriculture is specially blessed: Adam and Eve farmed the garden of Paradise before the Fall, not as painful labor but with spontaneous joy.[99] Where, according to Augustine, is "human reason better able to speak, as it were, to nature than when man sows the seed, plants a tree, transplants a bush. . . ?"[100]

Medicine, like agriculture, had a special place because it clearly sought a human good within the context of natural processes. Plato's example in the *Gorgias* of true and proper knowledge is medicine, because it knows the welfare of its subject and does not pander to unworthy desires.[101] In the Platonic and Neoplatonic tradition of Plotinus and Augustine, both agriculture and medicine are elevated beyond ordinary crafts because they help bring nature or natural products to fruition.[102] For Cassiodorus the practice of medicine and agriculture is an act of charity and comes under the heading of divine reading.[103]

Ancient classifications of the arts often reflected these ideas. Classical authors not infrequently lifted some technical or physically oriented arts out of the general category of craft and directly associated them with philosophy or liberal arts.[104] Cicero singles out agriculture, medicine, architecture, and, with some hesitation, wholesale trade as liberal.[105] The encyclopedia planned by Celsus (first century A.D.?) was to cover agriculture, medicine and military arts as well as rhetoric, philosophy and law.[106] Varro (116–27 B.C.) includes medicine and architecture as

---

[96] Xenophon, *Oeconomicus* 5.12–18, 6.4–12, Loeb Classical Library, 404, 408–410.

[97] Jean-Pierre Vernant, "Travail et nature dans le Grèce ancienne," in *Mythe et pensée chez les grecs*, 206, 217.

[98] Clarence J. Glacken, *Traces on the Rhodian Shore: Nature and Culture in Western Thought from Ancient Times to the End of the Eighteenth Century* (Berkeley: University of California Press, 1967), 130–134, 163–167; Lovejoy and Boas, *Primitivism*, 279, 285, 353.

[99] Augustine, *De genesi ad litteram* 8.8 and 8.10, in *Oeuvres de Saint Augustin* (Paris: Desclée de Brouwer, 1972), 49:34, 42.

[100] Augustine, *De genesi ad litteram* 8.8, *The Literal Meaning of Genesis*, trans. John Hammond Taylor, *Ancient Christian Writers*, 42 (New York: Newman Press, 1982), 2:45; *Oeuvres de Saint Augustin*, 49:36: "Quod enim malus mirabiliusque spectaculum est aut ubi magis cum rerum humana ratio quodammodo loqui potest, quam cum positis seminibus, plantatis surculis, translatis arbusculis, insitis malleolis. . . ."

[101] Plato, *Gorgia* 465a, ed. Dodds, 94–95.

[102] See below, 45–48.

[103] Cassiodorus, *Institutiones*, ed. Mynors, 71–72, 78.

[104] Galen, *Protreptikos* 14 in *Scripta minora*, ed. Marquardt, 1:120.

[105] Cicero, *De officiis* 1.42, Loeb Classical Library, 154.

[106] See Marrou, "Les arts libéraux," 23.

the eighth and ninth liberal arts.[107] Vitruvius (first century B.C.), although not explicit, seems to regard architecture as liberal and part of philosophy.[108] Jerome (c. 340–420) and Fulgentius (fifth century) also consider medicine to be among the liberal arts.[109]

The crossover between crafts and liberal arts developed further in late antiquity. Authors from the second through the fifth centuries classified some arts as neither liberal nor banausic but as belonging to some intermediate category, which mixed mental and physical elements. H. L. Marrou has cited Galen, the fifth-century grammarian Maximus Victorinus and the popular Greek philosopher, Philostratus, as having grouped the arts in this way.[110] One may add to these Plotinus, and Augustine's *De doctrina christiana*. Although for Marrou these classifications are of interest primarily as stages in the development of the concept of the *artes liberales*, they also demonstrate the range of ancient attitudes toward technical arts. Taken together with those lists of the liberal arts which included arts such as agriculture, medicine, architecture, elsewhere regarded as crafts, these classifications indicate a considerable degree of flexibility toward defining technological arts as knowledge.

Philostratus (c. A.D. 165 or 170–240) separates the banausic arts from those which were learned or wise (σοφαί) and from those which were somewhat or less learned (ὑπόσοφοι).[111] The latter group includes painting, sculpture, navigation and agriculture "if it waits upon the seasons"; these, he remarks, are "not very inferior to the liberal professions."[112]

---

[107] Ibid., 23.

[108] Vitruvius, *Ten Books on Architecture* 1.1, Loeb Classical Library (London: Heinemann, 1931), 1:6–32.

[109] Jerome, *Letter* 53.6 in *Opera*, ed. Isidorus Hilberg, *Corpus Scriptorum Ecclesiasticorum Latinorum* (Leipzig: G. Freytag, 1910) 54:452; Fulgentius, *Mitologiae* 3.8, ed. R. Helm (Leipzig: Teubner, 1898). Gregory of Nyssa lumped together geometry, logic, physics, mechanical inventions, agriculture, navigation and "other pursuits of our life" as proceeding from the same mental processes; see *Contra Eunomium* 2.181, ed. Werner Jaeger (Leiden: E. J. Brill, 1960), 1:277. This passage is discussed and translated in Alcuin A. Weiswurm, *The Nature of Human Knowledge According to Saint Gregory of Nyssa*, The Catholic University of America Philosophical Studies, 136 (Washington, D.C.: The Catholic University of America Press, 1952), 141–144.

[110] Marrou, "Les arts libéraux," 9–11.

[111] Philostratus, *The Life of Apollonius of Tyana* 8.7, trans. F.C. Conybeare, Loeb Classical Library (London: Heinemann, 1912), 2:298.

[112] Ibid., 2:299:

> Προσήκει δέ, ὦ βασιλεῦ, κἀκεῖνα ἐπεσκέφθαι· τέχναι ὁπόσαι κατ᾽ ἀνθρώπους εἰσί, πράττουσι μὲν ἄλλο ἄλλη, πᾶσαι δ᾽ ὑπὲρ χρημάτων, αἱ μὲν σμικρῶν, αἱ δ᾽ αὖ μεγάλων, αἱ δ᾽ ἀφ᾽ ὧν θρέψονται· καὶ οὐχ αἱ βάναυσοι μόνον, ἀλλὰ καὶ τῶν ἄλλων τεχνῶν σοφαί τε ὁμοίως καὶ ὑπόσοφοι, πλὴν ἀληθοῦς φιλοσοφίας. καλῶ δὲ

Philostratus elsewhere also exempts military command and gymnastics from the banausic arts.[113] Galen, in addition to the simple distinction between banausic and liberal arts, arranges the arts and their practitioners in a three-part hierarchy according to their closeness to the divine; geometers, arithmeticians, philosophers, doctors, astronomers and grammarians are in the first, or highest, rank; painters, modelers, schoolmasters, carpenters, architects, and sculptors are in the second; and all the remaining arts are in the third, or last, rank.[114]

A comparable classification was outlined by Maximus Victorinus, who divided the arts into those which are entirely physical, those entirely intellectual and those requiring both human faculties:

What is art? How many are the kinds of art? Three. What are they? Certain ones are of the body, certain ones are of the soul and body. Which ones are only of the soul? These are poetry, music, astrology, grammar, rhetoric, law, philosophy. Which are of the body? Shouting, leaping, fleetness, carrying burdens. Which are of the soul and body? Cultivation of a farm, gymnastics, medicine, mechanics [μηχανικά], carpentry [τεκτονική][115]

Plotinus (c. 203–262) also classifies knowledge in a hierarchical fashion. In the *Enneads,* he distinguishes between the arts on the basis of the quality of the substance or material with which they deal and their consequent distance or closeness to the Intelligible World:

As for the arts: such as look to housebuilding and the like are exhausted when the object is achieved; there are again those—medicine, farming, and other serviceable pursuits—which deal helpfully with natural products, seeking to bring them to natural efficiency; and there is a class—rhetoric, music, and every other method of swaying mind or soul, with their power of modifying for better or

---

σοφὰς μὲν ποιητικὴν μουσικὴν ἀστρονομίαν, σοφιστὰς καὶ τῶν ῥητόρων τοὺς μὴ ἀγοραίους, ὑποσόφους δὲ ζωγραφίαν πλαστικὴν ἀγαλματοποιοὺς κυβερνήτας γεωργούς, ἣν ταῖς ὥραις ἕπωνται, καὶ γὰρ αἵδε αἱ τέχναι σοφίας οὐ πολὺ λείπονται.

[113] Philostratus, *Über Gymnastik* 261, ed. Julius Jünther (Leipzig and Berlin: B. G. Teubner, 1909; rpt. Chicago: Argonaut Publishers Inc., 1969). On gymnastics as an art comparable to medicine rather than a sport in the modern sense, see Marrou, "Les arts libéraux," 10–11.

[114] Galen, *Protreptikos* 5 in *Scripta minora,* ed. Marquardt, 1:107.

[115] Maximus Victorinus, *Ars Victorini Grammatici* in *Grammatici Latini,* ed. Henrici Keil (Leipzig: Teubner, 1870; rpt. Hildesheim: Georg Olms, 1961), 6:187: "Ars quid est? Vnius cuiusque rei scientia. Artium genera quot sunt? Tria. Quae? Sunt quaedam animi tantum, quaedam corporis, quaedam animi et corporis. Quae sunt animi tantum? Hac sunt, poetice, musice, astrologice, grammatice, rhetorice, iuris scientia, philosophia. Quae sunt corporis? Iaculatio, saltus, velocitas, oneris gestamen. Quae sunt animi et corporis? Ruris cultus, palaestra, medicina, μηχανικά, τεκτονική."

for worse—and we have to ascertain what those arts come to and what kind of power lies in them.[116]

Now as to the arts and crafts and their productions: The imitative arts—painting, sculpture, dancing, pantomimic gesturing—are, largely, earth-based; they follow models found in sense, since they copy forms and movements and reproduce seen symmetries; they cannot therefore be referred to that higher sphere except indirectly, through the Reason-Principle in humanity. On the other hand any skill which, beginning with the observation of the symmetry of living things, grows to the symmetry of all life, will be a portion of the Power There which observes and mediates the symmetry reigning among all beings in the Intellectual Cosmos. Thus all music—since its thought is upon melody and rhythm—must be the earthly representation of the music there is in the rhythm of the Ideal Realm. The crafts such as building and carpentry which give us Matter in wrought forms, may be said, in that they draw on pattern, to take their principles from that realm and from the thinking There: but in that they bring these down into contact with the sense-order, they are not wholly in the Intellectual, except as contained in the Idea of man. So agriculture, dealing with material growths; so medicine watching over physical health; so the art which aims at corporeal strength and well-being; power and well-being mean something else There, the fearlessness and self-sufficing quality of all that lives.

Oratory and generalship, administration and sovereignty—under any forms in which their activities are associated with Good and when they look to that—possess something derived thence and building up their knowledge from the knowledge There.

Geometry, as a science of the Intellectual entities, holds place There: so, too, philosophy, whose high concern is Being.

For the arts and products of art, these observations may suffice.[117]

---

[116] Plotinus, *Enneads* 4.4.31, trans. Stephen MacKenna (London: Faber and Faber, 1962), 314 (in *Opera*, ed. Henry and Schwyzer, 2:120):

> Τέχναι δὲ αἱ μὲν οἰκίαν ποιοῦσαι καὶ τὰ ἄλλα τεχνητὰ εἰς τοιοῦτον ἔληξαν· ἰατρικὴ δὲ καὶ γεωργία καὶ αἱ τοιαῦται ὑπηρετικαὶ καὶ βοήθειαν εἰς τὰ φύσει εἰσφερόμεναι. ὡς κατὰ φύσιν ἔχειν ῥητορείαν δὲ καὶ μουσικὴν καὶ πᾶσαν ψυχαγωγίαν ἢ πρὸς τὸ βέλτιον ἢ πρὸς τὸ χεῖρον ἄγειν ἀλλοιούσας. ἐν αἷς ζητητέον, ὅσαι αἱ τέχναι καὶ τίνα τὴν δύναμιν ἔχουσι

[117] Ibid., 5.9.11, trans. MacKenna, 440–441 (in *Opera*, 2:423–424):

> Τὰ οὖν κατὰ τέχνην καὶ αἱ τέχναι; τῶν δὴ τεχνῶν ὅσαι μιμητικαί, γραφικὴ μὲν καὶ ἀνδριαντοποιία, ὄρχησίς τε καὶ χειρονομία, ἐνταῦθά που τὴν σύστασιν λαβοῦσαι καὶ αἰσθητῷ προσχρώμεναι παραδείγματι καὶ μιμούμεναι εἴδη τε καὶ κινήσεις τάς τε συμμετρίας ἃς ὁρῶσι μετατιθεῖσαι οὐκ ἂν εἰκότως ἐκεῖ ἀνάγοιντο, εἰ μὴ τῷ ἀνθρώπου λόγῳ.

The overall graduated arrangement in these classifications reflects Plotinus's conception of the universe as a series of levels of reality or being. For the purposes of this paper, the important point is that Plotinus distinguishes between crafts which impress a mental form on non-living matter, such as architecture, (i.e., the Aristotelian productive arts), and those which help bring nature to its "natural efficiency." All crafts participate to some extent in both the sensible and the intelligible realms; they, in Plotinus's words, "draw upon pattern." But some crafts exist on a level closer to the Intellectual because they deal with sensible things which themselves exist on a higher plane: architecture and carpentry produce products of "wrought Matter," but agriculture, medicine and gymnastics deal with living beings, whose life derives from a higher sphere, that is, Life itself.

A passage in Plato's *Laws* may have been one of Plotinus's sources. In this dialogue, the Athenian, first dismissing the products of the arts of painting, music and other crafts as "toys" or "simulacre," remarks that "if there are arts which really produce anything of genuine worth, they are those which lend their aid to nature, like medicine, husbandry, gymnastics."[118] He goes on to list statesmanship and legislation, thus closely paralleling the order of the arts given in the *Enneads*.

Plotinus's ideas on the arts may, in turn, have influenced Augus-

---

εἰ δέ τις ἕξις ἐκ τῆς περὶ τὰ ζῷα συμμετρίας ὅλως ζῴων πούσης καὶ θεωρούσης τὴν ἐν τῷ νοητῷ περὶ πάντα συμμετρίαν. καὶ μὴν καὶ μουσικὴ πᾶσα [περὶ ἁρμονίαν ἔχουσα καὶ ῥυθμὸν ἡ μὲν] περὶ ῥυθμὸν καὶ ἁρμονίαν ἔχουσα τὰ νοήματα τὸν αὐτὸν τρόπον ἂν εἴη, ὥσπερ καὶ ἡ περὶ τὸν νοητὸν ἀριθμὸν ἔχουσα. ὅσαι δὲ ποιητικαὶ αἰσθητῶν τῶν κατὰ τέχνην, οἷον οἰκοδομικὴ καὶ τεκτονική, καθόσον συμμετρίαις προσχρῶνται, ἀρχὰς ἂν ἐκεῖθεν ἔχοιεν καὶ τῶν ἐκεῖ φρονήσεων· τῷ δὲ αἰσθητῷ ταῦτα συγκερασάμεναι τὸ ὅλον οὐκ ἂν εἶεν ἐκεῖ ἢ ἐν τῷ ἀνθρώπῳ. οὐ μὴν οὐδὲ γεωργία συλλαμβάνουσα αἰσθητῷ φυτῷ, ἰατρική τε τὴν ἐνταῦθα ὑγίειαν θεωροῦσα ἥ τε περὶ ἰσχὺν τήνδε καὶ εὐεξίαν· ἄλλη γὰρ ἐκεῖ δύναμις καὶ ὑγίεια, καθ' ἣν ἀτρεμῆ πάντα καὶ ἱκανά, ὅσα ζῷα. ῥητορεία δὲ καὶ στρατηγία, οἰκονομία τε καὶ βασιλική, εἴ τινες αὐτῶν τὸ καλὸν κοινωνοῦσι ταῖς πράξεσιν, εἰ ἐκεῖνο θεωροῖεν, μοῖραν ἐκεῖθεν εἰς ἐπιστήμην ἔχουσιν ἐκ τῆς ἐπιστήμης τῆς ἐκεῖ. γεωμετρία δὲ νοητῶν οὖσα τακτέα ἐκεῖ, σοφία τε ἀνωτάτω περὶ τὸ ὂν οὖσα. καὶ περὶ μὲν τεχνῶν καὶ τῶν κατὰ τέχνας ταῦτα.

118 Plato, *Laws* 889c, in *Opera*, ed. Ioannes Burnet (Oxford: Clarendon Press, 1907), 5:889c:

tine.[119] In the *De doctrina christiana,* Augustine echoes Plotinus when he divides corporeal arts into those which manufacture a product, those which result in an action and those, namely medicine, agriculture and navigation, which "display a kind of service to the work of God."[120] This classification, like that of Plotinus, includes a distinctive category of arts which aid the processes of life in nature.[121] It seems probable in the light of Augustine's intellectual history that Plotinus is an indirect or direct source for this additional group of arts. If so, Augustine has

---

> τέχνην δὲ ὕστερον ἐκ τούτων ὑστέραν γενομένην, αὐτὴν θνητὴν ἐκ θνητῶν ὕστερα γεγεννηκέναι παιδιάς τινας, ἀληθείας οὐ σφόδρα μετεχούσας, ἀλλὰ εἴδωλ' ἄττα συγγενῆ ἑαυτῶν, οἷ' ἡ γραφικὴ γεννᾷ καὶ μουσικὴ καὶ ὅσαι ταύταις εἰσὶν συνέριθοι τέχναι· αἳ δέ τι καὶ σπουδαῖον ἄρα γεννῶσι τῶν τεχνῶν, εἶναι ταύτας ὁπόσαι τῇ φύσει ἐκοίνωσαν τὴν αὑτῶν δύναμιν, οἷον αὖ ἰατρικὴ καὶ γεωργικὴ καὶ γυμναστική. καὶ δὴ καὶ τὴν πολιτικὴν σμικρόν τι μέρος εἶναί φασιν κοινωνοῦν φύσει, τέχνῃ δὲ τὸ πολύ, οὕτω δὲ καὶ τὴν νομοθεσίαν πᾶσαν οὐ φύσει, τέχνῃ δέ, ἧς οὐκ ἀληθεῖς εἶναι τὰς θέσεις.

[119] On Plotinus's influence in general on Augustine's thought see Pierre Courcelle, *Late Latin Writers and their Greek Sources,* trans. Harry E. Wedeck (Cambridge, Mass.: Harvard University Press, 1969), 169–180. Augustine lists the arts in a hierarchy from the physical to the intellectual, possibly influenced by Plotinus, in his *De quantitate animae* 32.72 and the *City of God* 22.24.

[120] Augustine, *De doctrina christiana* 2.30.47, *On Christian Doctrine,* trans. D. W. Robertson, jr. (Indianapolis: Bobbs-Merrill, The Liberal Arts Press, Inc., 1958), 66; text in *Opera, Corpus Christianorum, series latina* 32:65:

> Artium etiam ceterarum, quibus aliquid fabricatur uel quod remaneat post operationem artificis ab illo effectum, sicut domus et scaninum et uas aliquod atque alia huiuscemodi, uel quae ministerium quoddam exhibent operanti deo sicut medicina et agricultura et gubernatio, uel quarum omnis effectus est actio sicut saltationum et cursionum et luctaminum: harum ergo cunctarum artium de praeteritis experimenta faciunt etiam futura conici; nam nullus earum artifex membra mouet in operando, nisi praeteritorum memoriam cum futurorum exspectatione contexat.

Gubernatio can be translated as both navigation and government.

[121] Earlier (*De doctrina christiana,* 2.29.45) Augustine distinguishes between superstitions which are valid only because of a special sign and sciences such as medicine and agriculture which are valid because of the force of nature; *Corpus Christianorum* 32:64:

> Aliud est enim dicere 'tritam istam herbam si biberis, uenter non dolebit' et aliud est dicere 'istam herbam collo si suspenderis, uenter non dolebit'. Ibi enim probatur contemperatio salubris, hic significatio superstitiosa damnatur. Quamquam ubi praecantationes et inuocationes et characteres non sunt, plerumque dubium est, utrum res, quae alligatur aut quoquo modo adiungitur sanando corpori, ui naturae ualeat, quod libere adhibendum est, an significatiua quadam obligatione proueniat, quod tanto prudentius oportet cauere christianum, quanto efficacius prodesse uidebitur. Sed ubi latet, qua causa quid ualeat, quo animo quisque utatur interest, dumtaxat in sanandis uel temperandis corporibus siue in medicina siue in agricultura.

In *De genesi ad litteram* 8.9.18 Augustine describes agriculture and medicine as external helps for internal natural forces. Cf. Plotinus, *Enneads* 4.4.31, trans. MacKenna, 314: "the artificial either remains, as it began, within the limit of the art-attaining finality in the artificial product alone—or is the expression of an art which calls to its aid natural forces and agencies, and so sets up act and experience within the sphere of the natural."

modified details, perhaps to bring the scheme into a more specifically Christian ambiance. First, he replaces the possibly morally suspect gymnastics with navigation. Second, although Plotinus described agriculture and medicine as aiding nature, according to Augustine these arts are in the service of God. Both Augustine and Plotinus, as well as Plato, however, place a higher value on agriculture and medicine than on crafts in general because they connect human activity to nature and through nature to the divine.

The classifications of Philostratus, Galen, Maximus Victorinus, Plotinus and Augustine fall into no precisely repeated pattern. Each, however, uses a hierarchy or graduated scale from the physical to the intellectual as a principle around which to organize the various arts and sciences. Those same technical arts which were sometimes included among the liberal arts—agriculture, medicine and with less consistency, gymnastics, mechanics, architecture, navigation, sculpture and painting—appear along this scale not with the purely physical or banausic arts, but in a center position as arts of both the body and soul. The softening of the radical distinction between banausic and liberal arts suggests that technical arts might occupy a middle ground, retaining a corporeal nature but also participating in the intellectual realm. This blurring of categories may, in turn, have influenced early medieval classifications of philosophy.[122] To an extent, these classifications overcame the dichotomy of mental and physical labor which made it difficult for classical thinkers to accept crafts as possessing intellectual and moral worth. By perceiving crafts such as agriculture, medicine, mechanics, navigation and others as linking men to a higher level of reality than the purely material, some philosophers suggested that these arts had ends or purposes beyond pleasure, convenience or the satisfaction of physical necessity and that they directed men to some extent toward the spiritual or intellectual, as well as the physical, world.

Conclusion

Despite the emphasis of classical thought on purely theoretical philosophy and science, technological arts were often described as a basic part of knowledge in antiquity. Under the rubric of the productive arts, or by association with the liberal arts, crafts were included within the realm of approved arts and sciences, and, to a great degree, these definitions of crafts countered the negative label of "banausic" arts given to many arts with a physical component.

Although classification of the arts and sciences became increasingly detailed and elaborate over the course of time, basic attitudes toward craft had already been formulated in the time of Plato and Aristotle. A view of knowledge as hierarchically ordered from the lowest arts to those

[122] See below, Chapter III.

closest to the divine and an emphasis on the moral value of knowledge was primarily associated with Plato and thinkers influenced by him, who often defined crafts as banausic or liberal arts. These two categories were, in fact, opposite points on an ascending scale of arts and sciences from the least to the most valued; individual crafts were assigned to one or the other group as they were perceived to lead men away from virtue or toward it. Although a blend of Platonic and Aristotelian influences is evident in many of these classifications, the strongest and clearest definitions of crafts as liberal or semi-liberal arts were made by thinkers deeply influenced by Platonic or Neoplatonic thought, such as Plotinus, Augustine, and Maximus Victorinus.

The more neutral, simpler and far less value-laden concept of the productive arts, defined by Aristotle as arts which made a product according to rational rules, was used alongside the banausic and liberal arts as a rubric for crafts throughout antiquity and was sometimes incorporated into hierarchical schemes of the Platonic type. Aristotle also described crafts as related to other sciences through the principle of subalternation, or subordination, or in special cases as applying mathematics to physical problems, as, for example, in mechanics. Although Aristotle himself made only scattered comments on these subjects, his ideas suggested systematic methods of defining technology as a part of knowledge which were developed by Hellenistic and late ancient thinkers into comprehensive schemes giving a major place to crafts.

At the same time, classical thinkers did not develop a rigorous framework within which to consider crafts or technical arts as parts of knowledge. No single ancient classification of the arts subsumed all the arts or activities now called technology under one heading. The productive arts most clearly and comprehensively defined crafts as a group; it is not clear, however, whether such arts as medicine, agriculture and navigation, which did not obviously "make" or produce something, were considered productive arts. They were rarely mentioned as examples of productive arts and were almost always placed in a distinct category under a variety of rubrics. The idea of the productive arts, moreover, was limited in that it did not incorporate implications about final ends or purposes, an issue which we have seen was virtually inseparable in classical thought from the problem of knowledge. Significantly, it was precisely the arts which were most commonly accorded a higher intellectual status because they were more easily associated with higher human values, such as medicine and agriculture, which were excluded from the productive arts. The banausic, "semi-liberal" and liberal arts, on the other hand, were defined largely in terms of perceived value and only loosely in terms of subject matter; depending upon the individual perspectives of particular authors, these categories included some, many or no crafts. This discontinuity accurately reflects the difficulties in defining technology faced by a system of thought which emphasized the dichotomy of mind and matter and identified moral virtue with intellectual knowledge.

The complexity of the classical philosophical tradition on the place of technology as a part of knowledge is aptly illustrated by the views of St. Augustine, who was in many ways both an heir to classical thought and a parent of a new and distinctive culture. In his formal classifications of knowledge Augustine combined the Aristotelian classification of the productive arts and the Platonic-Neoplatonic hierarchical arrangement of arts from the most physical to the most spiritual. The same hierarchy underlies a famous passage in the *City of God,* which places human knowledge, including technology, in the context of man's natural and supernatural ends. This passage, which remained a touchstone for attitudes about crafts through the thirteenth century, is both a culmination of classical ideas on technology and a link to the medieval *artes mechanicae.*

And, quite apart from those supernatural arts of living in virtue and of reaching immortal beatitude which nothing but the grace of God which is in Christ can communicate to the sons of promise and heirs of the kingdom, there have been discovered and perfected, by the natural genius of man, innumerable arts and skills which minister not only to the necessities of life but also to human enjoyment. And even in those arts where the purposes may seem superfluous, perilous and pernicious, there is exercised an acuteness of intelligence of so high an order that it reveals how richly endowed our human nature is. For, it has the power of inventing, learning and applying all such arts.

Just think of the progress and perfection which human skill has reached in the astonishing achievements of cloth-making, architecture, agriculture and navigation. Or think of the originality and range of what has been done by experts in ceramics, by sculptors and by painters; of the dramas and theatrical spectacles so stupendous that those who have not seen them simply refuse to believe the accounts of those who have. Think even of the contrivances and traps which have been devised for the capturing, killing, or training of wild animals; or, again, of the number of drugs and appliances that medical science has discovered in its zeal for the preservation and restoration of men's health; or, again, of the poisons, weapons, and equipment used in wars, devised by military art for defense against enemy attack; or even of the endless variety of condiments and sauces which culinary art has discovered to minister to the pleasures of the palate.

It was human ingenuity, too, that devised the multitude of signs we use to express and communicate our thoughts and, especially, speech and writing. The arts of rhetoric and poetry have brought delight to men's spirits by their ornaments of style and varieties of verse; musicians have solaced human ears by their instruments and songs; both theoretical and applied mathematics have made great progress; astronomy has been most ingenious in tracing the movements, and in distinguishing the magnitudes, of the stars. In general, the completeness of scientific knowledge is beyond all words and becomes all the more astonishing when one pursues any single aspect of this immense corpus of information. Last, but not least, is the brilliance of talent displayed by both pagan philosophers and Christian heretics in the defense of error and falsehood. (In saying this, of course, I am thinking only of the nature of the human mind as a glory of this mortal life, not of faith and the way of truth that leads to eternal life.)[123]

The mood of this account of the arts is one of ambivalence and paradox. Augustine, of course, is drawing upon an explicitly Christian view of knowledge and the human condition and his exclusion of the arts and sciences from the sphere of "immortal beatitude" clearly reflects Christian rather than classical values. Augustine, however, wrote this passage specifically as an answer to Cicero's praise of crafts in the *De natura deorum*[124] and in doing so he made use of the classical, as well as a Christian, critique of technology. Cicero's discussion in the *De natura deorum* ties human dignity and power closely to man's ability to change his environment through technology and to create a "second nature" for himself.[125] It is one of the most positive statements on technology in classical literature and although elsewhere Cicero criticizes and even attacks certain crafts, here he unequivocally espouses the view placed in the mouth of the Stoic, Balbus, that technological arts are a product of human reason well and properly used.[126] Augustine's reply, however, finds technology to be an expression of the "natural genius" of

---

[123] Augustine, *De civitate Dei* 22.24, trans. Gerald G. Walsh and Daniel J. Honan in *The Fathers of the Church: A New Translation* (Washington, D.C.: The Catholic University of America Press, 1954), 24:484 (ed. B. Dombart, revised by A. Kalb [Leipzig: Teubner, 1928], 2:612–613);

> Praeter enim artes bene vivendi et ad immortalem perveniendi felicitatem, quae virtutes vocantur et sola Dei gratia, quae in Christo est, filiis promissionis regnique donantur, nonne humano ingenio tot tantaeque artes sunt inventae et exercitae, partim necessariae partim voluptariae, ut tam excellens vis mentis atque rationis in his etiam rebus, quas superfluas, immo et periculosas perniciosasque appetit, quantum bonum habeat in natura, unde ista potuit vel invenire vel discere vel exercere, testetur? Vestimentorum et aedificiorum ad opera quam mirabilia, quam stupenda industria humana pervenerit; quo in agricultura, quo in navigatione profecerit; quae in fabricatione quorumque vasorum vel etiam statuarum, et picturarum varietate excogitaverit et impleverit; quae in theatris mirabilia spectantibus, audientibus incredibilia facienda et exhibenda molita sit; in capiendis occidendis domandis inrationalibus animantibus quae et quanta repperit; adversus ipsos homines tot genera venenorum, tot armorum, tot machinamentorum, et pro sainte moriali tuenda atque reparanda quot medicamenta atque adiumenta conprehenderit; pro voluptate faucium quot condimenta et gulae inritamenta repperit; ad indicandas et suadendas cogitationes quam multitudinem varietatemque signorum, ubi praecipuum locum verba et litterae tenent; ad delectandos animos quos elocutionis ornatus, quam diversorum carminum copiam; ad mulcendas aures quot organa musica, quos cantilenae modos excogitaverit; quantam peritiam dimensionum atque numerorum, meatu que et ordines siderum quanta sagacitate conprehenderit; quam multa rerum mundanarum cognitione se impleverit, quis possit eloqui, maxime si velimus non acervatim cuncta congerere, sed in singulis inmorari? In ipsis postremo erroribus et falsitatibus defendendis quam magna claruerint ingenia philosophorum atque haereticorum, quis aestimare sufficiat? Loquimur enim nunc de natura mentis humanae, qua ista vita mortalis ornatur, non de fide atque itinere veritatis, qua illa inmortalis adquiritur.

[124] Maurice Testard, *Saint Augustin et Cicéron* (Paris: Études Augustiniennes, 1958), 1:76–77.

[125] Cicero, *De natura deorum* 2.50, Loeb Classical Library (London: Heinemann, 1933), 270–271.

[126] Ibid., 2.50–2.51, Loeb Classical Library, 266–271.

man but, *at the same time*, to be "superfluous, perilous and pernicious." The oxymoron is intentional, and an analysis of Augustine's catalogue of the arts and sciences reveals his purpose in speaking in an apparent contradiction.

Augustine begins with the distinction between arts which are necessary and those which are for pleasure, a comparison which goes back to the Sophists and was transmitted through Augustine to the Middle Ages.[127] Yet he does not tell us which arts are "necessary" and which "for pleasure," and he arranges the arts not into two distinct groups but hierarchically in the Platonic or Neoplatonic pattern. Beginning with arts producing material objects (cloth-making, architecture) he follows with the arts he describes in the *De doctrina christiana* as "aiding God" (agriculture, navigation), the arts we would now call "fine arts" (sculpture, painting), a group of arts perhaps characterized by the importance of process rather than product (hunting, medicine, warfare and cookery) and ends with the liberal arts and, finally, philosophy.

Although some commentators have taken both the introduction and catalogue of arts at face value as straightforward praise of the ingenuity and power of the human intellect, in fact Augustine's tone is heavily ironic.[128] His subject is the condition of our mortal life, which, he carefully points out, is divorced from faith, truth and eternal life, and which he describes elsewhere in the same chapter as depraved and condemned to sin.[129] His list of the arts, it should be noted, includes heresy, theatrical spectacles, traps, poisons, weapons and war machines. (The pairing of heresy with philosophy, as well as medicine with poisons and cookery suggests a delicate sense of irony.) The arts, despite their status as expressions of human genius, are not only irrelevant to man's final beatitude but are potentially dangerous and immoral even in the miserable mortal life for which they were intended to console us. The argument is essentially the same as that implied by the labeling of crafts as banausic, i.e., that the ability to invent or use inventions does not imply the ability to know how to use inventions for proper and moral ends, and that the latter requirement should condition the former. Yet Augustine clearly does not deny that technology is a product of intelligence. Like the classical philosophical tradition as a whole, Augustine leaves us with a paradoxical view of technology as part of human knowledge and achievement and yet as antithetical to mankind's highest and truest ends.

Augustine, perhaps inadvertently, however, also provides a way out of the dilemma posed by the ambivalence of his statement. If all the arts together suffered the limitations of reason *vis-à-vis* faith, as implied by

---

[127] See above, p. 33, for the Sophists and below, Chapter IV, for this distinction in Bonaventure and Vincent of Beauvais.

[128] See below, Chapter IV, n. 98, for modern scholarly interpretations of this passage.

[129] Augustine, *De civitate Dei* 22.24, ed. Dombart, 2:609.

his inclusion of philosophy as well as heresy, then, conversely all the arts together, including crafts, could be put in the service of God as long as they were properly subordinated to religious purposes. This interpretation of the Augustinian view of knowledge as dependent upon religion was one of the sources for the striking re-evaluation of technology in the twelfth century. This re-evaluation would have been impossible, however, without the groundwork laid down by classical thought which frequently, if not consistently, related technology to other parts of knowledge. Although the persistent ambivalence of general comments on the arts and crafts in antiquity, which tied crafts as much to the misery of man as to his dignity, had a parallel in the fragmentation of categories under which crafts were included within, or excluded from, knowledge, ancient classifications of the arts and sciences also suggested mechanisms by which this fragmentation could be resolved. Medieval classifiers of the arts developed these suggestions into comprehensive schema which for the first time included all crafts in a group as an essential part of knowledge.

TRANS. AMER. PHIL. SOC.
VOL. 80 PT. 1, 1990

III. Crafts, Philosophy, and the Liberal Arts in the Early Middle Ages

The transition from the ancient to the medieval world, if not as sudden and decisive as once thought, was nevertheless profound.[1] Between the fifth and the ninth centuries, Roman, Germanic, and Christian influences combined to form a new Western European society. Isolated economically, politically, and culturally from the Eastern empire, the increasingly rural and localized Germanic kingdoms oriented themselves toward Northern Europe rather than the Mediterranean, and developed new forms of political, social, and military organization. As awareness of classical philosophy and science declined, so did the ancient system of education, and the Church became the sole focus and agent of culture and schooling.

One of the characteristics which marked the early medieval world as a new culture was its technological dynamism. Richard Lefebvre des Noëttes, Marc Bloch, and especially Lynn White have pictured a society remarkably innovative in the invention of new technical devices and methods, such as the rigid horsecollar, three-field system and heavy wheeled plow, and aggressive in its use of older inventions, such as the stirrup and watermill.[2] These new and adapted technologies helped shape early medieval society and set the stage for the technological development of the twelfth and thirteenth centuries.[3]

---

[1] For an overall examination of this complex issue and extensive bibliography, see William Carroll Bark, *Origins of the Medieval World* (Stanford, Calif.: Stanford University Press, 1958).

[2] The most thorough explication of this thesis is found in Lynn White, jr., *Medieval Technology and Social Change* (Oxford: Clarendon Press, 1962); White provides excellent bibliographical material and a provocative discussion. Lynn White's views on the importance of the early Middle Ages for the history of technology and the reasons for the technological vitality of this period are summarized in "What Accelerated Technological Progress in the Western Middle Ages?" *Creation: The Impact of an Idea*, ed. Daniel O'Conner and Francis Oakley (New York: Scribner, 1969), 84–104. The pioneering studies on early medieval technology are Richard Lefebvre des Noëttes, *La force motrice animale à travers les âges* (Paris: Berger-Levrault, 1924); *L'attelage; le cheval de selle à travers les âges* (Paris: A. Picard, 1939); "La 'nuit' du Moyen Âge et son inventaire," *Mercure de France* 235 (1932):572–599. A useful and balanced view is presented in Marc Bloch, "The Advent and Triumph of the Watermill," in *Land and Work in Mediaeval Europe: Selected Papers by Marc Bloch*, trans. J. E. Anderson (Berkeley and Los Angeles: University of California Press, 1967), 136–168; "Mediaeval 'Inventions,'" in *Land and Work*, 169–185; and Maurice Daumas, *Historie générale des techniques* (Paris: Presses Universitaires de France, 1962), 1:431–438.

[3] Lynn White's arguments connecting technological change and social change are somewhat overstated; see reviews of White's book by R. H. Hilton and P. H. Sawyer, "Technical Determinism: The Stirrup and the Plough," *Past and Present* 24 (1963):90–100, and Bernard S. Bachrach, "Charles Martel, Mounted Shock Combat, the Stirrup and Feudalism," *Studies in Medieval and Renaissance History* 7 (1970):49–75.

The intellectual environment surrounding early medieval technology has come under scrutiny from several different directions. Jacques Le Goff, for example, has emphasized the ambivalence of attitudes toward craft and manual labor in all three cultures—classical, Judeo-Christian, and Germanic—which influenced early medieval society. He further suggests, however, that the Carolingian period experienced a "Renaissance of Labor" in which this ambivalence was at least partially resolved and manual work and laborers given a new legal and social status.[4]

Lynn White, on the other hand, has argued that the voluntaristic and active piety of early medieval Latin Christianity, together with the displacement of animism by the cult of the saints, encouraged and supported an exploitative attitude toward nature.[5] White's position, in turn, has been modified by George Ovitt. Ovitt concurs that the early medieval period saw a more positive evaluation of labor and craftsmanship but suggests that labor was always placed within the context of personal spiritual (rather than secular) ends. Thus, both biblical commentaries and early medieval monastic rules defined labor as normative for the Christian but at the same time subordinated "labors of the hands" to "labors of the soul."[6]

Classifications of the parts of knowledge provide another useful perspective from which to evaluate early medieval attitudes toward craft and manual labor. Not only do classifications of knowledge give us insight into how craftsmanship might have been considered from a philosophical (rather than from a more broadly theological) point of view but the schematic literature touches on one of the central questions inherited from antiquity: in what way could craftsmanship, which deals physically with the material world, be considered rational?

This question of the intellectual status of craft was raised most explicitly by Martianus Capella, a fifth-century grammarian and rhetorician, whose *Marriage of Philology and Mercury* was an important influence on later medieval iconography of the arts. In his allegory Capella dismisses medicine and architecture from the celestial company of the liberal arts because their "mundane" and "mortal" nature made it appro-

---

[4] Jacques Le Goff, "Labor, Techniques, and Craftsmen in Value Systems of the Early Middle Ages (Fifth to Tenth Centuries)," trans. Arthur Goldhammer in *Time, Work and Culture in the Middle Ages* (Chicago and London: University of Chicago Press, 1980), 71–86. Le Goff mentions *techne versus* labor, the prestige of the warrior *versus* the prestige of the craftsman, a creator God *versus* work as punishment for original sin, "Labor, Techniques, and Craftsmen," 74–77; "Early medieval man inherited a variety of mental traditions, in which the attitude toward labor ranged from contempt to respect," 73. See Chapter I, pp. 11–15, for discussion of these issues.

[5] Lynn White, "Technological Progress," 95–104. See also Lynn White, "Cultural Climates and Technological Advance in the Middle Ages," *Viator* 2 (1979):171–201. See Chapter I, pp. 13–17 for discussion of White's ideas.

[6] George Ovitt, Jr., *The Restoration of Paradise: Labor and Technology in Medieval Culture* (New Brunswick, N.J.: Rutgers University Press, 1987), 105–106. See also Ovitt, "The Cultural Context of Western Technology: Early Christian Attitudes toward Manual Labor," *Technology and Culture* 27 (1986):477–500.

priate to disdain and reject them.[7] Here Capella appears to be not only accepting a prejudice for theoretical over practical knowledge but also reinforcing the authority of this attitude for later medieval thinkers.

The continuing influence of classical suspicion of crafts, however, was only one element in early medieval thought. Several scholars since the 1950s have noted an alternative pattern of relating craft and the liberal arts. Bernard Bischoff, Peter Sternagel and Manuel Díaz y Díaz identified a secondary classification first appearing in the work of Isidore of Seville in which medicine, mechanics (*mechanica*), and astrology are given equal weight with the four mathematical liberal arts, arithmetic, geometry, astronomy, and music, as parts of philosophy.[8] These and other historians have, however, attached little significance to Isidore's classification. Assuming that Capella's contempt for craft represented the standard or "normal" philosophical attitude, they have dismissed the mixing of crafts and liberal arts as eccentric and confused, a symptom of the general breakdown of intellectual life in the early Middle Ages. Díaz y Díaz, for example, finds Isidore's classification "confused," "curious," "very strange," and its transmission to later authors an "erudite detail."[9] Peter Sternagel, on the other hand, simply sees the classification as the product of Isidore's "faulty understanding."[10] In his classic article on medieval classifications of the sciences, James A. Weisheipl refers to this classification as it appears in the work of Rhabanus Maurus as "confused."[11]

The impression of confusion, however, is largely illusory, a result of treating Isidore's classification as an isolated comment rather than placing it within a broad historical context. As we shall see, many aspects of contemporary intellectual life had an impact on how thinkers viewed the relationship between crafts and philosophy. Martianus Capella's treatise on the arts rejecting medicine and architecture, for instance, was

---

[7] *Martianus Capella and the Seven Liberal Arts*, trans. William Harris Stahl, vol. 2: *The Marriage of Philology and Mercury* (New York: Columbia University Press, 1971), 346; *Martianus Capella*, ed. Adolfus Dick and Jean Préaux (Stuttgart: Teubner, 1978), 471–472. For the Latin text, see Chapter II, n. 29.

[8] Peter Sternagel, *Die Artes Mechanicae im Mittelalter. Begriffs- und Bedeutungsgeschichte bis zum Ende des 13. Jahrhunderts* (Kallmung über Regensburg: Lassleben, 1966); Bernard Bischoff, "Eine verschollene Einteilung der Wissenschaften," *Archives d'Histoire Doctrinale et Littéraire au Moyen Âge* 33 (1958):5–20; Manuel Díaz y Díaz, "Les arts libéraux d' après les écrivains espagnols et insulaires aux VIIe et VIIIe siècles," in *Arts libéraux et philosophie au Moyen Âge: Actes du Quatrième Congrès International de Philosophie Médiévale* (Montreal: Institut d'études médiévales, 1969; Paris: Libraire philosophique J. Vrin, 1969), 37–46. These studies are invaluable for textual and bibliographical information. The classifications appear in Isidore of Seville's (c. 560–636) *Differentiae* 2.39 (*PL* 83:94) and *Liber numerorum* 8.44 (*PL* 83:188). Bischoff, "Eine erschollene Einteilung der Wissenschaften," discusses the complex transmission of Isidore's classification. On Isidore's definition of *mechanica* see below, p. 68 and for Isidore and astrology see Jacques Fontaine, "Isidore de Séville et l'astrologie," *Revue des études latines* 31 (1953):276–277.

[9] Díaz y Díaz, "Arts libéraux," 40, 41, 46.

[10] Sternagel, *Artes Mechanicae*, 17.

[11] James Weisheipl, "Classification of the Sciences in Medieval Thought," *Medieval Studies* 27 (1965):65.

rarely read in the period before the ninth century.[12] On the other hand, a number of late ancient authors had defined crafts as liberal or "semi-liberal" arts. These classifications survived in texts known to the early Middle Ages and may have had an impact on Isidore and others. The persistence of a classificatory tradition including crafts as a part of legitimate knowledge was supported by the very practical conception of the function of philosophy and the arts characteristic of early medieval thought. Especially prior to the revival of intellectual life in the ninth century, secular knowledge was considered important more for its usefulness in scriptural exegesis, intellectual training and the practical needs of daily life than for any inherent abstract value. In this pragmatic atmosphere, the line between applied and theoretical science blurred and many early medieval authors blended philosophy with an enthusiastic interest in the mundane aspects of crafts. Ultimately, the attention paid to crafts by early medieval thinkers generated a new concept of technology as a category of knowledge in which crafts became a standard division of the arts and sciences under the rubric *artes mechanicae*. Far from being mere details of terminology or arbitrary variations, these changes were important steps in the formation of European ideas about technology as a legitimate and worthy area of human thought and endeavor. Although the full elaboration of the concept of the mechanical arts did not appear until the twelfth and thirteenth centuries when Hugh of St. Victor and his followers described seven crafts—fabric-making, armament and building, commerce, agriculture, hunting and food preparation, medicine and theatrics—as corporeal arts parallel in form and function to the seven liberal arts, the roots of later medieval intellectual assimilation of technology lie in the early Middle Ages.

Crafts and the Liberal Arts

The naming of certain crafts as parts of philosophy or in other ways associating crafts with the liberal arts was not a rare or occasional occurrence but a consistent pattern in the early Middle Ages. Even though compendia of the more traditional liberal arts restricted to the *quadrivium* and *trivium* and excluding crafts from legitimate knowledge were common in this period, many of the authors of these works elsewhere associate technical arts with the liberal arts or philosophy. Cassiodorus, for example, in his formal treatise on the arts, the *Institutiones*, names only the seven usual liberal arts, yet the section on divine readings includes a discussion of medicine and agriculture.[13] In his letters, moreover, Cassiodorus groups mechanics, architecture and medicine with

[12] For the influence of Capella's treatise in this period, see below note 66.

[13] Cassiodorus, *An Introduction to Divine and Human Readings*, trans. Leslie Webber Jones (New York: Columbia University Press, 1946; reprint New York: Octagon Books, 1966), 130, 135–136, 143–145; *Institutiones divinarum et saecularium lectionum*, ed. R. A. B. Mynors (Oxford: Clarendon Press, 1961), 71–72, 78.

the *quadrivium* as the mathematical sciences dealing with general principles.[14] Similarly, although Isidore of Seville's *Etymologiae* does not name technical arts as specific parts of knowledge, an echo of his alternative classification appears in his definition of medicine as a "second philosophy" which makes use of all the liberal arts.[15] A ninth-century manuscript attributed to Boethius associates geometry not only with philosophers, but also with mechanicians, architects, and physicians.[16] A comparable mixing of liberal arts and crafts reappears as late as the twelfth century in Honorius Augustodunensis's *De animae exsilio et patria* which names physics (defined as medicine), mechanics and *oeconomica*, or economics, as the eighth, ninth, and tenth liberal arts.[17]

It was Isidore of Seville's classification of mechanics, astrology and medicine as parts of physics or philosophy and variations stemming from it, however, which became the most important and widely diffused alternative or addition to the standard divisions of philosophy. In the *Liber numerorum*, a work on the scriptural significance of numbers, Isidore divides philosophy into seven parts: arithmetic, geometry, music and astronomy plus astrology, mechanics, and medicine.[18] The *Differentiae* repeats the list of disciplines but this time as divisions of physics, which, together with logic and ethics, made up philosophy.[19]

---

[14] Cassiodorus, *Variae* 3.52, ed. Å. J. Fridh, *Corpus Christianorum, series latina* (Turnholt: Brepols Editores Pontifici, 1973), 96, 136: "Geometriam quippe, ut est hominum genus nimis acutissimum atque sollicititum, Chaldaei primum invenisse memorantur, qui rationem ipsius disciplinae generaliter colligentes et in astronomicis rebus et in musicis et in mechanicis et in architectis et in medicinam et in musicis logisticam, uel quicquid potest formis generalibus contineri"; see also ibid. 1.45 (ed. Å. J. Fridh, 49): "Translationibus enim tuis [Boethius] Pythagoras musicus, Ptolemaeus astronomus leguntur Itali: Nicomachus arithmeticus, geometricus Euclides audiuntur Ausonii; Plato theologus, Aristoteles logicus Quirinali uoce disceptant: mechanicum etiam Archimedem Latialem Siculis reddidisti." These letters were written c. 510.

[15] Isidore of Seville, *Etymologiae*, ed. W. M. Lindsay (Oxford: Clarendon Press, 1911), 4:xiii: "Quaeritur a quibusdam quare inter ceteras liberales disciplinas Medicinae ars non contineatur. Proptera, quia singulares continent causas ista vero omnium . . . Hinc est quod Medicina secunda Philosophia dicitur." Medicine had a special place among the arts in the early Middle Ages; see Bruce Stansfield Eastwood, "The Place of Medicine in a Hierarchy of Knowledge: The Illustration in Lyon Palais des Arts, ms. 22, f. 1r, from the Eleventh Century," *Sudhoffs Archiv* 66 (1982):20–37. Cf. Rhabanus Maurus (c. 776–856) who names only the *quadrivium* and *trivium* in his *De institutione clericorum* (*PL* 107: 395ff.) but in his *De universo* (*PL* 111:413) gives mechanics, medicine and astrology as parts of physics.

[16] Ps.-Boethius, in Sternagel, *Artes Mechanicae*, 24: "Utilitas geometriae triplex est, ad facultatem, ad sanitatem, ad animam. Ad facultatem ut mechanici et architecti. Ad sanitatem ut medici. Ad animam ut philosophi."

[17] Honorius Augustodunensis, *PL* 72:1241–1246; *Concerning the Exile of the Soul and its Fatherland, also called, About the Arts*, trans. Joseph M. Miller in *Readings in Medieval Rhetoric*, ed. Joseph M. Miller, Michael H. Prosser, Thomas W. Benson (Bloomington and London: Indiana University Press, 1973), 198–206.

[18] Isidore of Seville, *Liber numeroruum* 8.44 (*PL* 83):188: "Septum apud veteres annumerantur genera philosophiae, prima arithmetica, seconda geometria, tertia musica, quarta astronomia, quinta astrologia, sexta mechanica, septem medicina."

[19] Isidore of Seville, *Differentiae* 2.39 (*PL* 83:94):"Ad physicam pertinere aiunt disciplinas septem, quarum prima est arithmetica, secunda geometria, tertia musica, quarta astro-

The classification linking medicine, astrology and mechanics with the *quadrivium* and hence to the liberal arts and philosophy became widespread, first among the Irish and Anglo-Saxon scholars of the late seventh through the ninth centuries and later among the masters of the Carolingian Renaissance. It appears, but without the mention of mechanics, in an anonymous work sometimes attributed to Isidore, the *Institutionum disciplinae.*[20] The anonymous *Letter to Cuimnanus,* which closely follows Isidore's wording, dated by Bischoff to the mid-seventh century, is a possible early link between Spain, Ireland, and the Continent.[21] Later in the seventh century the poet Aldhelm of Malmesbury repeated this ordering of the arts twice in his *De virginitate* and once in *De metris et enigmatibus ac pedum regulis.*[22] It also appears, but again without mechanics, in a ninth-century work attributed to Bede.[23] During the eighth and ninth centuries variations on Isidore's classification appear in many works of Carolingian provenience, including an anonymous appendix to Alcuin's *Rhetoric,* works by Ermenrich of Ellwagen (a pupil of Rhabanus Maurus) and Clemens the Grammarian, as well as several anonymous and unedited manuscripts cited by Sternagel.[24]

---

nomia, quinta astrologia, sexta mechanica, septima medicina"; *PL* 83:93: "Hujus philosophiae partes tres esse dixerunt, id est, physicam, logicam, ethicam."

20 Edited in Paul Pascal, "The 'Institutionum disciplinae' of Isidore of Seville," *Traditio* 13 (1957):425–432; "Iuris quoque scientiae artem retineat, philosophiam etiam, medicinam, musicam, geometricam, astrologiam comprehendat atque ita his disciplinis omnibus perornetur ut nequaquam expers nobilissimarum artium esse videatur," 427. For a summary and bibliography of the arguments on the authenticity of this text, see Pascal, "'Institutionum disciplinae,'" 425–426, 428–431 (who accepts the text as Isidore's) and Díaz y Díaz, "Les arts libéraux d'après les écrivains," 41–42 (who does not). Pascal is unaware of the classification of the arts in Isidore's *Differentiae* and *Liber numerorum,* but suggests a connection with Jerome, *Adversus Pelagianos* 1.21 which includes law, astrology and medicine among the liberal arts, 429.

21 "John Scottus, Martin Hiberniensis, The Liberal Arts, and Teaching," in *Studies: Papers on Latin Texts and Manuscripts of the British: 550–1066,* ed. (Toronto: Pontifical Institute of Mediaeval Studies, 1981), 23.

21 Bischoff, "Eine verschollene Einteilung der Wissenschaften," 19. See also Vivien Law, *The Insular Latin Grammarians* (Woodbridge, Suffolk: The Boydell Press, 1982), 87–90.

22 Aldhelm, *De virginitate* 35: "Igitur consummatis grammaticorum studiis et philosophorum disciplinis, quae. VII. speciebus astrologia, mechanica, medicina" (ed. R. Ehwald, *MGH, Auctores antiquissimi,* 15:277). Ibid. 59 (ed. Ehwald, 320): ". . . omnes propemodem philosphorum disciplinas, hoc est arithmeticam, geometricam, musicam, astronomiam, astrologiam, et mechanicam. . . .," and Aldhelm, *De metris* 3. "Saeculares quoque et forasticae philosophorum disciplinae totidem supputationum partibus calculari cernuntur arithmetica, scilicet, geometrica, musica, astronomia, astrologia, mechanica, medicina" (ed. R. Ehwald, *MGH, Auct. antiqu.,* 15:71).

23 Ps.-Bede, *PL* 90:908: "Naturalis vero dividitur in sex, scilicet, arithmeticam, geometriam, musicam, astronomiam, astrologiam, medicinam."

24 *Schemata* 10 (*PL* 101:947–948): "De physica—Arithmetica, astronomia, astrologia, mechanicia, medicina, geometria, musica." See also Sternagel, *Artes Mechanicae,* 19, for additional references. Ermenrich, *Epistola ad Grimaldum Abbatem* 7 *MGH, Epistolae,* 5:541: "Item physica dividitur in arithmeticam, astronomiam, astrologiam, mechanitiam, medicinam, geometricam, musicam." See also Law, *Insular Latin Grammarians,* 105. Clemens, *Ars grammatica* 7, ed. Johannes Tolkiehn, *Philologus. Supplementband* 20, fasc. 3 (1928), 6: "Physica in quot partes dividitur? M. Plato, ut praediximus, eam in quattuor principales divisit partes id est: arithmeticam, geometricam, musicam, astronomiam, et est hos illud quad-

By the ninth century Isidore's classification had been absorbed into the mainstream of early medieval thought. It appears in the work of two of the most influential masters of the ninth century, Rhabanus Maurus and Martin of Laon. Rhabanus Maurus, a pupil of Alcuin, enjoyed a high reputation and his encyclopedia, the *De universo*, was widely read.[25] In general the *De universo* closely follows Isidore's *Etymologiae*, upon which it is modeled. Yet while the *Etymologiae* names only the seven conventional liberal arts, Rhabanus Maurus prefers Isidore's alternative classification including medicine, mechanics, and astrology as parts of philosophy.[26] Martin of Laon's version of the Isidorean classification appears in what John Contreni has described as "an excellent representative of ninth-century teaching manuals."[27] The presence of Isidore's classification in educational handbooks both reflected and ensured its continuing influence. The strength of this tradition is demonstrated by its survival in a twelfth-century work by Thierry of Chartres.[28]

Such a widespread and persistent pattern of classification deserves serious attention and a higher status than that of "detail." Moreover, if compared to earlier classifications of the arts it becomes clear that the Isidorian classification represents the continuation of late classical practice. Henri Marrou has shown that late ancient classifications of the sciences often placed certain arts with a physical or practical aspect among the liberal arts or in an intermediate category between the liberal and illiberal, or corporeal, arts. Medicine had been associated with philosophy or the liberal arts by Galen, Cicero, Celsus, Varro, Jerome and Augustine and had a special status for Plotinus and Maximus Victori-

---

ruvium philosophiae, quo, ut Boethius dicit, his viandum quibus excellentior est animus; quibus adhaerent astrologia et medicina"; ibid. 7 (ed. Tolkiehn, 9): "In physica quoque etiam artes minores sunt, quas aratores et fullones et caementarii excercent et disponunt." On this variation see below, 68. On the attribution of this work, see Law, *Insular Latin Grammarians*, 102. Sternagel, *Artes Mechanicae*, 22; Díaz y Díaz, "Arts libéraux," cites several tenth-century English manuscripts, 45.

[25] M. L. W. Laistner, *Thought and Letters in Western Europe A.D. 500 to 900* (Ithaca, New York: Cornell University Press, Cornell Paperback, 1966), 201, 221.

[26] Rhabanus Maurus, *De universo* 15.1 (*PL* 111:413): "Dividitur autem Physica in septem partes, hoc est, Arithmeticam, Astrologiam, Mechaniam, Medicinam, Geometriam et Musicam."

[27] Martin of Laon, text in John J. Contreni, "John Scottus, Martin Hiberniensis, the Liberal Arts and Teaching," in *Insular Latin Studies: Papers on Latin Texts and Manuscripts of the British: 550–1066*, ed. Michael W. Herren (Toronto: Pontifical Institute of Mediaeval Studies, 1981), 32: "Physica autem in quattuor divisiones partitur, id est arithmeticam, geometricam, musicam, astronomiam quibus adhaerent astrologia, medicina, et etiam minores artes quas aratores, et fullones, et cimentarii exercent." For Martin of Laon, also called Martin Hiberniensis (819–875), see John J. Contreni, *The Cathedral School of Laon from 850 to 930: Its Manuscripts and Masters*, Münchener Beiträge zur Mediävistik und Renaissance-Forschung, 29 (Munich: Bei der Arbeo-Gesellschaft, 1978). For the importance of the differences from Isidore's version, see below, pp. 68–69.

[28] *Heptateuchon*. This text has not been edited but the scheme of the sciences is discussed in Martin Grabmann, *Die Geschichte der scholastischen Methode* (Graz: Akademische Druck- u. Verlagsanstalt, 1957), 2:44. See Bischoff, "Einteilung," 6.

nus.[29] In the fifth century Fulgentius's list of the liberal arts included medicine, astrology and divination.[30] Xenophon, Cicero, Celsus, Plotinus, Marius Victorinus, Augustine, and others regarded agriculture as in some sense liberal.[31] Architecture was a liberal art for Cicero and Varro; Vitruvius, although not explicit, seems to have considered architecture as "liberal" and as part of philosophy.[32] Mechanics had retained an uneasy position between geometry and craft ever since Aristotle and several of the Greek mathematicians and Latin authors in late antiquity regarded mechanics as including both theoretical mathematics and manual crafts.[33]

A late classical source precisely anticipating Isidore's classification has not yet been identified. Jacques Fontaine in his thorough study of the intellectual context of Isidore's thought suggests a possible connection to Proclus.[34] An even closer correspondence occurs between the *Collectio* of Pappus Alexandrinus, which describes mechanics as composed of a theoretical part including geometry, arithmetic, astronomy and physics, and a manual part, including metal-working, architecture, carpentry, painting and all skills involving the use of the hands.[35] Díaz y Díaz argues for a hypothetical Hellenistic source and Sternagel points to Varro, on the one hand, because he includes medicine and architecture among his list of nine liberal arts and to Vitruvius who associated architecture with mechanics, on the other.[36] Another possible source is Audax, a grammarian of the fifth or sixth century whom Isidore is known to have read. Audax repeats Maximus Victorinus's classification of the arts:

How many are the kinds of art? What are they? Certain ones are only of the

[29] Henri Irénée Marrou, "Les arts libéraux dans l'antiquité classique," in *Arts libéraux et philosophie au Moyen Âge*, 5–19. For Plotinus, see the *Enneads* 4.4.31 and 5.9.11 in *Opera* ed. Paul Henry and Hans-Rudolf Schwyzer (Paris: Desclée de Brouwer et Cie., 1959), 2:120, 423–24.

[30] Fulgentius, *Mitologiae* 3.8., ed. R. Helm (Leipzig, 1898).

[31] Marrou, "Arts libéraux," 6–12.

[32] Cicero, *De officiis* 1.42; Vitruvius, *Ten Books on Architecture* 1.1; for Varro, see Marrou, "Arts libéraux," 19.

[33] Hero, *Treatise on Pneumatics* 1.1; Proclus, *Commentary on the First Book of Euclid's Elements* 1.13.38–39, ed. Gottfried Friedlein (Leipzig, 1873); Pappus Alexandrinus, *Collectio* 8.1.

[34] Jacques Fontaine, *Isidore de Séville et la culture classique dans l'Espagne wisigothique* (Paris: Études Augustiniennes, 1959), 1:345–348.

[35] Pappus Alexandrinus, *Mathematical Collection*, in *Selections illustrating the History of Greek Mathematics*, Loeb Classical Library (London: Heinemann, 1941), 2:614. How Isidore might have directly or indirectly known the Greek treatises of Proclus or Pappus is, of course, something of a puzzle. For the absence of any extant Latin translations of Pappus prior to the twelfth century see Marjorie Nice Boyer, "Pappus Alexandrinus," in *Catalogus translationum et commentariorum: Medieval and Renaissance Latin translations and commentaries*, ed. Paul O. Kristeller and F. Cranz (Washington: Catholic University of America Press, 1971), 2:206.

[36] For the view of Díaz y Díaz, see "Questiones et discussions," *Arts libéraux et philosophie au Moyen Âge*, 67; Sternagel, *Artes Mechanicae*, 20–21; Paul Pascal also suggests Varro as the ultimate source of the classification in the *Institutionum disciplinae*; see "'Institutionum disciplinae,'" 430–431.

soul, certain ones are of the body, certain ones are of the soul and body. Which ones are only of the soul? These are poetry, music, astrology, grammar, rhetoric, law, philosophy. Which are of the body? Shouting, leaping, fleetness, carrying burdens. Which are of the soul and body? Cultivation of a farm, gymnastics, medicine, mechanics, carpentry.[37]

Audax's classification is particularly interesting for the explicitness with which it asserts that technological arts involve both the mind or "soul" and the body and thus both mental and physical labor. Although its structure clearly differs from Isidore's designation of mechanics, astrology and medicine as liberal arts, certain similarities suggest a possible influence. Both Audax and Isidore refer to astrology rather than to astronomy and there is some evidence that Isidore may have considered naming law as a liberal art in the *Etymologiae*.[38] Isidore may well have conflated gymnastics, which was regarded as a method of hygiene, with medicine. Isidore's definition of mechanics, further, as we shall see, was so broad as to be virtually coextensive with craft and therefore agriculture and carpentry might have been included under *mechanica*.

Although a direct link between Isidore and classical texts remains elusive, these texts provide a background to Isidore's classification which lends it seriousness and weight. They demonstrate that the dichotomy of body and soul, or mind and matter, so thoroughly developed in ancient thought, did not necessarily mean that all physically oriented arts or crafts were considered completely corporeal activities, substantially different from the liberal arts. Specific crafts were not infrequently considered "liberal." Viewed against the framework of this varied and complicated tradition, Isidore's classification of the arts appears more as the product of complexity than of confusion.

The significance of early medieval classifications of the arts, however, lies not only in the continuation of ancient ideas but also in the way

---

[37] Texts of Maximus Victorinus and Audax published in Henrici Keil, *Grammatici Latini* (Leipzig: Teubner, 1870; rpt. Hildesheim: Georg Olms, 1969), 6:187 and 7:320–321. Audax in Keil, *Grammatici Latini*, 7:320; "Artium genera. Quot sunt? Tria. Quae? Sunt quaedam animi tantum, quaedam corporis, quaedam animi et corporis: animi tantum, ut poetica, musica, astrologia, grammatica, rhetorica, iuris scientia, philosophia; corporis, iaculatio, saltus, velocitas, oneris gestamem; animi autem et corporis, ruris cultus, palaestra, medicina, mechanica, tectonica." For discussion of Maximus Victorinus, see Chapter II, p. 46, above. For the medieval manuscripts repeating Audax's classification, see Keil, 7: xxxii–xxxv and xliv–xlviii. On Audax himself, see Martin Schanz, *Geschichte der Romischen Litteratur* (Munich: C. H. Becktsche, 1920) 4:2:214–221. For Isidore's knowledge of Audax see Fontaine, *Isidore de Séville*, 1:107–108, 197–199. Audax was known to English authors after Isidore, including Bede and Aldhelm; see J. D. A. Ogilvy, *Books Known to Anglo-Latin Writers from Aldhelm to Alcuin (670–804)*, Studies and Documents, 2 (Cambridge, Mass.: The Mediaeval Academy of America, 1936), 13, and Law, *Insular Latin Grammarians*, 24. According to Jocelyn N. Hillgarth, "A Critical Review of the Literature since 1935," in *Isidoriana: Estudios sobre San Isidore de Sevilla en el XIV centenario de su nacimiento* (Leon: Centro de Estudios "San Isidoro," 1961), 1: 34–35: "The sources he [Isidore] actually employed were almost always late, of the Fourth or Fifth centuries A.D. or even later. . . ."

[38] Díaz y Díaz, "Arts libéraux," 40. Cf. the *Institutionum disciplinae*, probably by Isidore, which includes law, astrology and medicine among the liberal arts.

these ideas were changed. Isidore and his successors shaped their classical heritage according to their interests, which were pragmatic rather than philosophical. One can discern in the history of these classifications hints of a characteristic enthusiasm for the products of technical skill. Early medieval culture transformed ancient traditions even as it perpetuated them. If the ways in which knowledge was organized remained intact, the content of knowledge and the uses to which it was put were modified.[39] Much of classical science and philosophy became either unavailable or unintelligible; what remained of secular knowledge was increasingly subordinated to practical needs.

These tendencies contributed, on the one hand, to a very practical conception of the purposes of the liberal arts and, on the other hand, to a lively interest in the everyday aspects of technology. As Pierre Riché has pointed out, Western thinkers from the sixth through the eighth centuries reduced philosophy to physics and medicine, and mathematics to surveying, building and calendar computation.[40] The writers we have been dealing with often seemed to have had a fondness for concrete details about everyday tools and artifacts. Of the twenty books of the *Etymologiae*, Isidore, for example, devotes six to technical subjects, compared to only three on the liberal arts. The six books are largely given to naming the types and parts of ships, buildings, clothing, weapons, and household and farm utensils.[41] These sections are often detailed; for example, the section on horsemanship mentions the trappings of the harness, bridle, curbs, reins, halter, saddle, saddlecloths, lasso and branding-irons.[42]

Aldhelm of Malmesbury and the Anglo-Saxon grammarian, Tatwine, wrote riddles not only about plants and animals but also on household tools and furniture, such as cups, sewing needles and tables, and tech-

---

[39] Weisheipl, "Classification of the Sciences," 64–65: "As the early Middle Ages were unaware of the numerous Greek works on natural science, metaphysics and ethics, repetition of the Boethian and Stoic classification of the sciences had little significance and no practical value for teachers of the arts. Misunderstandings of the original divisions and confusions of the issues involved were the inevitable result of not having the Aristotelian corpus."

[40] Pierre Riché, *Education and Culture in the Barbarian West from the Sixth Through the Eighth Century*, trans. John J. Contreni (Columbia, South Carolina: University of South Carolina Press, 1978), 46–47, 68–71; "Only the applied sciences . . . still attracted attention" (47).

[41] Isidore of Seville, *Etymologiae*, ed. W. M. Lindsay, 1, Index Librorum:

> IV. De Medicina; XV. De Civitatibus, de Aedificiis Vrbanis et Rusticis, de Agris, de Finibus et Mensuris Agrorum de Itineribus; XVI. De Glebis ex Terra vel Aquis, de omni genere Gemmarum et Lapidum pretiosorum et vilium, de Ebore quoque inter Marmora notato, de Vitro, de Metallis omnibus, de Ponderibus et Mensuris; XVII. De Culturis Agrorum, de Frugibus universi generis, de Bitibus et Arboribus omnis generis, de Herbis et Holeribus universis; XVIII. De Bellis et Triumphis ac Instrumentis Bellicis, de Foro, de Spectaculis, Alea et Pila; XIX. De Navibus, Funibus et Retibus, de Fabris Ferrariis et Fabricis Parietum et cunctis Instrumentis Aedificiorum, de Lanificiis quoque, Ornamentis et Vestibus universis; XX. De Mensis et Escis et Potibus et Vasculis eorum, de Vasis Vinariis, Aquariis et Oleariis, Cocorum, Pistorum, et Luminariorum, de Lectis, Sellis et Vehiculis, Rusticis et Hortorum, sive de Instrumentis Equorum.

[42] Isidore of Seville, *Etymologiae*, ed. Lindsay, 20:xvi.

nical devices, such as mill, spindle, whetstone, sieve, lighthouse and bellows.[43]

Cassiodorus, especially, displays an interest in the mundane and practical in his descriptions of the projected technological comforts of Vivarium: its fishponds, gardens, sundial, and waterclock and self-regulating lamp for the copy-room,[44] and in his comments in his letters in praise of aqueducts, bridges, roads, iron tools and weapons, mills, sewers, clothing dyes and surveying.[45] Typical, if unusually appealing, is his account of the virtues of writing on papryus:

> An excellent work in truth ingenious Memphis conceived, so that it adorned all the bookcases of the world. . . . Before [papyrus was discovered] the sayings of the wise, the thoughts of the ancients were in danger. For how could the writer have been able to write quickly, when, the hardness of the bark resisting him he would scarcely have been able to be ready? The excitement of the mind submits to the unfitting hindrances; when the words are harassed, the mental powers are compelled to grow lukewarm. . . . This was fit only for the beginnings of the world. Then papyrus was discovered, and therewith was eloquence made possible. . . . So smooth and so continuous, the snowy entrails of a green herb, which keeps the sweet harvest of the mind, and restores it to the reader whenever he chooses to consult it; which is the faithful witness to all human action.[46]

This strong concern for the everyday utility of technology is reflected in the changing uses of the term *mechanica*.[47] The original Greek meaning was a mathematical discipline which dealt with problems of the moving

---

[43] Aldhelm, *De metris et enigmatibus*, ed. Ehwald, 15:127, 129, 124 and Tatwine, *Aenigmata*, in Thomas Wright, *The Anglo-Latin Satirical Poets and Epigrammatists* (London: Her Majesty's Stationery Office, 1872), 2:528, 531, 532, 533. On Tatwine, see Law, *Insular Latin Grammarians*, 23, 64–67.

[44] Cassiodorus, *Divinarum et saecularium lectionum* 1.29, 30; *Divine and Human Readings*, 131, 134–135. Cassiodorus also recommends the study of medicine (1.31; *Divine and Human Readings*, 135–136) and, in special cases, agriculture (1.28; *Readings*, 129–131).

[45] Cassiodorus, *Variae* 1.2, 2, 45, 52, 53; 5.38; 7.6, 17; 3.25. (ed. Fridh, 11, 17, 52, 115–116, 276–277).

[46] Translation adapted from *The Letters of Cassiodorus*, trans. Thomas Hodgkin (London: Henry Frowde, 1886), 483; *Variae* 11.38 (ed. Fridh, 455–456):

> Pulchrum plane opus Memphis ingeniosa concepit, ut universa scrinia vestiret . . . . Periclitabantur ante hic dicta sapientium, cogitata maiorum. Nam quemadmodum velociter potuisset scribi, quod repugnante duritia corticis vix poterat expediri? Ineptas nimirum moras calor animi sustinebat et cum differebantur verba, tepescere cogebantur ingenia . . . . Sed hoc primordiis consentaneum fuit. . . . Haec enim tergo niveo aperit eloquentibus campum, copiosa semper assistit et quo fiat habilis. . . .Inunctura sine rimis, continuitas de minutiis, viscera nivea virentium herbarum. . .ubi apicibus elevatis fecundissima verborum plantata seges fructum mentibus totiens suauissiumum reddit, quotiens disiderium lectoris invenerit. . . .

[47] In addition to the tendency toward defining *mechanica* as craft, traced below, many early medieval authors continued to associate *mechanica ars* with magical-mathematical arts (mostly in contexts other than the classificiation of the arts); see Sternagel, *Artes Mechanicae*, 37–47. For the close association of technological information and magic in the early Middle Ages, see Lynn Thorndike, *A History of Magic and Experimental Science* (New York: Columbia University Press, 1947), 1:551ff.

of objects and hence "overcame nature," or at least gave the illusion of doing so.[48] This meaning is still evident in Cassiodorus, who describes mechanics as a wonderful art which is "almost Nature's comrade, opening her secrets, changing her manifestations, sporting with miracles, feigning so beautifully, that what we know to be an illusion is accepted by us as truth."[49]

For Isidore, mechanics, even if still associated with the mathematical sciences, is simply any kind of handicrafts. He defines *mechanica* in the *Differentiae* as a certain skill or *doctrina* to which belongs the production (or making) of all things.[50] After Isidore, the definition of *mechanica* becomes even more concrete. In the late eighth century mechanics is defined in the appendix to Alcuin's *Rhetoric* as skill in the art of making things out of metal, wood and stone and this definition reappears in Rhabanus Maurus's *De universo* in the early ninth century.[51] At some later point the definition of *mechanica* became conflated with a portion of a letter by Jerome defining what he calls the "minor arts."[52] By the

---

[48] For example, the ps.-Aristotelian *Mechanical Problems* which describes mechanics as an art producing an effect contrary to nature, in Aristotle, *Minor Works*, Loeb Classical Library (Harvard: Harvard University Press, 1936), 331. The close association of the marvelous and the technological was also an important element in the ancient attitude toward craft and was transmitted to medieval culture; see Sternagel, *Artes Mechanicae*, 37–47.

[49] Cassiodorus, *Variae* 1.45, translation adapted from Hodgkin, *Cassiodorus*, 170 (ed. Fridh, 51): "Mechanicus, si fas est dicere, paene socius est naturae, occulta reserans, manifesta conuertens, miraculis ludens, ita pulchre simulans, ut quod compositum non ambigitur, ueritas aestimetur."

[50] Isidore of Seville, *Differentiae* 2.52. (*PL* 83:94): "Mechica est quaedam peritia, vel doctrina, ad quam subtiliter fabricas omnium rerum concurrere dicunt." Cf. *Differentiae* 1.8 (*PL* 83:11): "Ars est natura liberalis, artificium vero gestum manibus constat." This practical interpretation may also be operative in Isidore's understanding of astrology. According to Jacques Fontaine, "Isidore de Séville et l'astrologie," 276–277, Isidore "understood natural astrology, as opposed to superstitious astrology, to mean calendar computation, observations of weather and the heavens used in farming and navigation by the stars." Cf. Cassiodorus on astronomy: "There is another advantage arising from studies of this sort, which is not to be despised, if we learn from them the proper season for sailing, the time for ploughing, the date of the summer's heat and of the autumn's suspected rains"; *Divine and Human Readings*, 202–203. On the relationship between astronomy and astrology in the early Middle Ages, see M. L. W. Laistner, "The Western Church and Astrology during the Early Middle Ages," in *The Intellectual Heritage of the Early Middle Ages*, ed. Chester G. Starr (New York: Octagon Books, 1966), 57–82. The *Anonymous ad Cuimnanum* repeats Isidore's definition of *mechanica* virtually word for word; Bischoff, "Einteilung," 19. This definition is not dissimilar from the definition of the productive arts—arts which produce objects—but how this idea became attached to the word *mechanica* is not clear.

[51] *Schemata* 10 (*PL* 101:947–948): "Mechanica est peritia fabricae artis in metallis et in lignis et in lapidibus"; *De universo*, 15.1 (*PL* 111:413): "Mechnia (sic) est peritia fabricae artis in metallis et in lignis et lapidibus." This definition also appears in Ermenrich's letter to Grimaldum in *MGH, Ep.*, 5.541.

[52] Letter 53.6 in which Jerome compares the knowledge of grammarians, rhetoricians, philosophers, geometers, musicians, astronomers, astrologers, physicians and logicians with the knowledge of the minor crafts requiring manual dexterity more than reason used by farmers, masons, carpenters, workers in wool and metal, fullers and artisans who make furniture and utensils (*PL* 22:544): "Taceo de Grammaticis, Rhetoribus, Philosophis, Geometris, Dialecticis, Musicis, Astronomis, Astrologis, Medicis, quorum scientia mortalibus vel utilissima est, et in tres partes scinditur, τό δόγμα, τὴν μέθοδον, τὴν ἐμπειρίαν.

late ninth century even the word *mechanica* has dropped out and for Clemens the Grammarian and Martin of Laon physics consists of arithmetic, geometry, music, and astronomy, to which are attached astrology, medicine and the minor arts which farmers, clothing-fullers and stone-workers employ.[53]

Thus between the fifth and ninth centuries the notion of what might constitute philosophy or the liberal arts broadens considerably. Whereas Cassiodorus added three specific technical arts, each with an obviously mathematical character, to the *quadrivium*, by the ninth century at least some authors include the whole range of handicrafts, naming farming, cloth-making and stone-working, as parts of physics and hence of philosophy. This change continued to be influential as late as the twelfth century when it appears in Honorius Augustodunensis's treatise on the arts. Honorius describes and defines ten liberal arts, the usual *quadrivium* and *trivium* plus *physica*, economics and *mechanica*.[54] *Physica* is described as medicine.[55] The definition of *mechanica*[56] shows how completely the early Middle Ages had transformed its original classical meaning:

Concerning mechanics, the ninth city through which our native land ought to be approached is mechanics. It teaches travelers every work in metals, wood or stones, in addition to painting, sculpture and all arts which are done with the hands. By this art Nimrod erected his tower, Solomon constructed his temple. By it Noah fashioned his ark as well as all protections in the entire world, and it taught the manifold weavings of garments.[57]

The beginning of this description of *mechanica* mentioning work with metals, wood and stone demonstrates its origins in the later versions of

Ad minores artes veniam, et quae non tam λογῳ, quam manus administrantur. Agricolae, caementarii, fabri, metallorum, lignormve caesores, lanarii quoque et fullones, et caeteri qui variam supellectilem et vilia opuscula fabricatur, absque doctore non possunt esse quod cupiunt."

[53] This portion of Martin of Laon's treatise in John J. Contreni, "John Scottus," 32: "Phisica autem in quattuor divisiones partitur, id est arithmeticam geometricam, musicam, astronomian quibus adhaerent astrologia, et medicina, et etiam minores artes quas aratores, et fullones, et cimentarii exercent." For Clemens the Grammarian see note 24.

[54] *De animae exsilio, PL* 172:1241–1246.

[55] Honorius Augustodunensis, *De animae exsilio*, 9 (*PL* 172:1245): "Octava civitas est physica per quam petitur patria. In hac docet Hippocrates viatores vires et naturas herbarum, arborum, lapidum, animalium; et per medelam corporum deducit ad medelam animarum,"

[56] The translation of *De animae exsilio*, 10 in Miller et al., *Readings in Medieval Rhetoric*, suffers from several problems including the translation of "De mechanica" (*PL* 172:1245) as "Concerning the mechanical arts," obscuring the connection with Isidore.

[57] Honorius Augustodunensis, *De animae exsilio, PL* 172:1245: "Nona civitas est mechanica, per quam subeunda est patria, haec doces viantes omne opus metallorum, lignorum, marmorum, insuper picturas, sculpturas, et omnes artes, quae manibus fiunt. Haec turrim Nemrod erexit, haec templum Salomonis construxit. Haec arcam Noe et omnia moenia totius orbis instituit, et varias texturas vestium docuit." Robert Darwin Crouse, "Honorius Augustodunensis: The Arts as *via ad patriam*," *Arts libéraux et philosophie*, 531–539 provides a useful summary of Honorius's ideas on the arts but misses the connection with the Isidorian classification.

the Isidorean classification of the technical arts. But its expansion to include painting, statuary, building, shipbuilding and weaving, and thus to include virtually all the crafts, as well as the addition of illustrations from biblical history, shows how much more developed the concept of craft as a part of knowledge had become. Classification of the arts in the centuries after the end of the ancient world, therefore, both continued old patterns and introduced new ones. The gradual expansion of the term *mechanica* into a generic term for crafts was an important innovation which reached its full development only in later centuries. Taken seriously on their own terms and looked at in the context of broad developments in intellectual history, these early medieval classifications are part of a coherent set of ideas about the relationship of craft and philosophy and suggest a greater intellectual appreciation of technology in this period than is usually recognized. Moreover, these classifications, by reinforcing the importance of crafts as a division of knowledge, contributed to the genesis of a new, characteristically medieval, classification of technical arts, the *artes mechanicae*.

The "artes mechanicae"

The earliest known use of the term *artes mechanicae* in the plural and referring to a category or group of arts occurs in John the Scot's commentary on Martianus Capella's *Marriage of Philology and Mercury*.[58] Although John's remarks are brief, they are extremely significant. Not only does he outline a way of classifying technical arts which is different in important ways from ancient and earlier medieval classifications, but later thinkers, in particular the twelfth-century theologian Hugh of St. Victor, drew upon John's ideas to develop a comprehensive philosophy of technology.

In his commentary on Capella's allegory, John the Scot remarks that after Mercury gave the seven liberal arts to his bride, Philology, she gave him the seven mechanical arts.[59] The seven mechanical arts are not named here, but later in the work the phrase "architecture and certain other arts" replaces the term *artes mechanicae*.[60] This second passage contains the other element in John's conception of the mechanical arts:

---

58 Sternagel, *Artes Mechanicae*, 30.

59 John the Scot, 79,12: "DOS A VIRGINE ac si dixisset: Postquam Mercurius dederit septem liberales artes, tunc virgo dabit septem mechanicas," *Annotationes in Marcianum*, ed. Cora E. Lutz (Cambridge, Mass.: The Mediaeval Academy of America, 1939), 74; 47,13: "MANCIPIAQUE id est que dotales erant, id est septem artes mechanicas quas Philologia Mercurio donaret," *Annotationes*, 59. The mechanical arts are also mentioned in 475, 1: "ALIAS id est mechanicis," *Annotationes*, 189 and 475,4: "Consequentibus ed est VII mechanicis," *Annotationes*, 189.

60 170, 14: "Percepte artes dicuntur que communi animi perceptione iudicantur ut septem liberales artes . . . sed naturaliter in anima intelliguntur. Non sic ceterae artes quae imitatione quadam vel excogitatione humana fiunt, ut architectoria et caetere," *Annotationes*, 96, 97: "[the liberal arts] naturaliter in ipsa anima intelliguntur. Mechanicae enim artes non naturaliter insunt sed quadam excogitatione humana," *Annotationes*, 86.

the liberal arts "understood naturally in the soul" are compared with the mechanical arts which come by "some imitation or human devising."[61]

Although John's remarks are little more than a sketch, they nevertheless imply a coherent concept of craft as a kind of knowledge which differs substantially from previous classifications. Unlike the classical idea of the banausic arts, which *opposed* unworthy physical and worthy mental arts, John's mechanical arts are *parallel* in form and function to the liberal arts. The Aristotelian notion of the productive arts, which died out in the Latin West by the fifth century and had no discernible influence on John the Scot, defined the arts in terms of results produced (thought, action, objects) rather than in terms of a hierarchy of innate and transcendent (liberal) arts and invented (mechanical) arts. Although John contrasts the two sets of arts, suggesting that the liberal arts are in some sense like the soul, "divine,"[62] while the mechanical arts are "human," they remain linked to each other and there is no trace of the pejorative tone associated with the banausic, or illiberal, arts. In this respect, John's classification most closely resembles the late ancient idea of "semi-liberal" arts. But, unlike these and the later classifications of Martin of Laon and other Carolingian masters, John names technical arts or crafts as a completely separate category of arts, clearly distinguished from the liberal arts and, thereby, focuses attention on the distinctive nature of craft.

An intellectual appreciation of technical arts was fed by cultural changes in the Carolingian period. Indeed, the establishment of a new classification of crafts at this time can best be explained by placing the problem within a broad cultural context.[70] From the eighth century, the study of philosophy and, especially, the arts had been generally revived and emphasized.[63] For John the Scot, in particular, the arts are an essential element in the effort to attain Wisdom. The arts, according to John, are "man's link with the Divine, their cultivation a means to salvation."[64] Innate in man, the arts belong naturally to him, and knowledge of them, obscured because of original sin, must be stimulated through teaching.[65] The continued popularity of Isidore's classification of crafts, combined with John's concern to define and establish the arts

---

[61] John the Scot, *Annotationes, 170, 14* (ed. Lutz, 86, 96–97).

[62] See note 60 and note 65.

[63] Laistner, *Thought and Letters* and *Intellectual Heritage;* for a useful overview of the issues surrounding the Carolingian Renaissance, see John J. Contreni, "Inharmonious Harmony: Education in the Carolingian World," *Annals of Scholarship* 1 (1980):81–96.

[64] Contreni, "John Scottus," 25.

[65] Contreni, "John Scottus," 25. This passage is translated on p. 41: "Every natural art (therefore) is found materially in human nature. It follows that all men by nature possess natural arts, but because, on account of the punishment for the sin of the first man, they (are obscured) in the souls of men and are sunk in a profound ignorance, in teaching we do nothing but recall to our present understanding the same arts which are stored deep in our memory." On the "Christianization of the arts" in Martin of Laon, see Contreni, "John Scottus," and *Cathedral School of Laon,* 113–117.

as a necessary part of education, most probably led to the establishment of the *artes mechanicae*.

Martianus Capella's *Marriage of Philology and Mercury*, in which architecture and medicine, and by implication all crafts, are excluded from the liberal arts, was only rarely read in the period prior to the ninth century.[66] In its absence, as we have seen, classifications of the arts including technical arts flourished. John the Scot, as part of the Carolingian revival of philosophy and the arts, was largely responsible for bringing Martianus Capella into a prominence which lasted until the end of the Middle Ages.[67] Yet in writing his commentary on the *Marriage*, John had to reconcile two contradictory traditions on crafts: Capella's rejection of them and the Irish-Carolingian practice of including crafts under the rubrics of *mechanica*, astrology and medicine among the liberal arts. He seems to have resolved the problem by inventing a new category of arts, thereby neither eliminating technical arts from the divisions of knowledge nor incorporating them among the liberal arts. Taking his cue from his contemporaries, he called them the mechanical arts.

The notion of the mechanical arts was sustained by a new interest in craftsmanship and manual labor from the ninth century on.[68] For the first time, calendars, encyclopedias and biblical commentaries were illustrated with realistic depictions of agricultural and artisan labor.[69] The mechanical arts reappeared in Remigius of Auxerre's commentary on Martianus Capella, although Remigius does not further develop the idea.[70] Its full potential was reached only in the twelfth century when Hugh of St. Victor fleshed out the meaning of the mechanical arts by enumerating and describing in detail seven crafts—fabric-making, armament and building, commerce, agriculture, hunting and food prepa-

---

[66] Stahl, *Martianus Capella*, Vol. 1: *The Quadrivium of Martianus Capella*, 56; Cora E. Lutz, "Martianus Capella," in *Catalogus translationum et commentariorum: Mediaeval and Renaissance Latin translations and commentaries*, ed. Paul O. Kristeller and F. Cranz (Washington: Catholic University of America Press, 1971), 2:36.

[67] Stahl, *Martianus Capella*, 1:61, Lutz, "Martianus Capella," 368.

[68] Le Goff, "Labor," argues for a "Carolingian Renaissance of Labor," 83–86.

[69] Le Goff, "Labor," 84–86, points to changes in calendar illustration around 800 and 1023 A.D. in manuscripts of Rhabanus Maurus's *De universo*; Lynn White, "Cultural Climates," 198 emphasizes an illumination of the Utrecht Psalter, c. 830, which shows King David's troops using a crank-driven grindstone to sharpen their swords, while the enemy uses a whetstone. The calendar illustrations are published and discussed in J. C. Webster, *The Labors of the Months in Antique and Mediaeval Art to the End of the XIIth Century* (Evanston and Chicago: Northwestern Press, 1938). For the calendars, see also, H. Stern, "Poésis et représentations carolingiennes et byzantines des mois," *Revue archéologique*, 6e series (1955):45–46 and for the psalter see Ernest DeWald, *The Illustrations of the Utrecht Psalter* (Princeton: Princeton University Press, 1932).

[70] *Remigii Autissiodorensis Commentum in Martianum Capellam, Libri I–II*, ed. Cora E. Lutz (Leyden: E. J. Brill, 1962); *Libri III–IX* (Leyden: E. J. Brill, 1965), 208, 200, 302, 304, 305. Remigius does refer to "architecture, medicine and certain other arts which consist more in experience than in reason," Lutz, *Commentum*, 17–18 (my translation). Remigius's commentary was extremely influential; Lutz, *Commentum*, 2, 38–40. For Remigius on the liberal arts, see Cora E. Lutz, "Remigius' Ideas on the Classification of the Liberal Arts," *Traditio* 12 (1956):65–86.

ration, medicine and theatrics—and, drawing upon John's ideas about the arts in general, linked the mechanical as well as the liberal arts directly to salvation and restoration of fallen man. This remarkable vision of technology as a part of philosophy derives ultimately from early medieval classifications which joined philosophy, the liberal arts and crafts.

Trans. Amer. Phil. Soc.
Vol. 80 Pt. 1, 1990

IV. Paradise Restored: Hugh of St. Victor and the Mechanical Arts in the Twelfth and Thirteenth Centuries

The revival of the European world, which began in the late eleventh century and extended into the twelfth, cut across all areas of life. An increasing population, in part the result of improved agricultural techniques, contributed to the rapid growth of cities, the settlement of new areas in Eastern Europe and the Levant, and a greatly expanded network of industry and trade.[1] This economic growth, which soon acquired its own self-sustaining momentum, in turn, produced profound social changes. As a new fluidity in social relationships appeared, the artisan and merchant, already increasingly important in the functioning of a more industrialized and commercial society, began to achieve new recognition from secular governments and the Church.[2]

This economic and social expansion had its counterpart in the intellectual sphere. The revival of thought and letters still generally referred to as the Renaissance of the Twelfth Century, despite increasing evidence that it was rooted in the eleventh century, involved both a more thorough application of reason and dialectic to philosophical and theological problems and an increased awareness of secular concerns and the natural world.[3] Late eleventh-, twelfth- and thirteenth-century

---

[1] On these topics see Georges Duby, *Rural Economy and Country Life in the Medieval West*, trans. Cynthia Postan (Columbia, S.C.: University of South Carolina Press, 1968); *The Cambridge Economic History of Europe* (Cambridge: Cambridge University Press, 1952–71), vols. 1 and 2; P. Boissonnade, *Land and Work in Medieval Europe: The Evolution of the Medieval Economy from the Fifth to the Fifteenth Century*, trans. Eileen Power (New York: Harper and Row, 1964); Marc Bloch, *Land and Work in Medieval Europe: Selected Papers by Marc Bloch*, trans. J. E. Anderson (London: Routledge and Kegan Paul, 1967, rpt. New York: Harper and Row, 1969); Charles Singer, E. J. Holmyard, and A. R. Hall, eds., *A History of Technology* (Oxford: Clarendon Press, 1965), vol. 2; Lynn White, jr., *Medieval Technology and Social Change* (London: Oxford University Press, 1964); Maurice Daumas, ed., *Histoire générale des techniques* (Paris: 1962), 1:429–598; A. C. Crombie, *Medieval and Early Modern Science* (Garden City, N.Y.: Doubleday, Anchor Books, 1959), vol. 1; Brian Stock, "Science, Technology and Economic Progress in the Middle Ages," in *Science in the Middle Ages*, ed. David C. Lindberg (Chicago: University of Chicago Press, 1978), 1–51 (which covers the twelfth century); and Jacques Le Goff, *Time, Work and Culture in the Middle Ages*, trans. Arthur Goldhammer (Chicago and London: University of Chicago Press, 1980).

[2] Le Goff, *Time, Work and Culture*, 29–42, 58–70, 107–21; Peter Sternagel, *Die Artes Mechanicae im Mittelalter. Begriffs- und Bedeutungsgeschichte bis zum Ende des 13. Jahrhunderts* (Kallmung über Regensburg: Lassleben, 1966), 54–61. For a useful discussion of changes in twelfth-century society from the standpoint of labor and technology, see George Ovitt, Jr., *The Restoration of Perfection: Labor and Technology in Medieval Culture* (New Brunswick, N.J.: Rutgers University Press, 1987), 137–143.

[3] The best short survey of the Twelfth-Century Renaissance remains Charles Homer

scholars not only gave new readings to the writings of the Church Fathers and those classical texts, such as the *Timaeus* in its partial translation by Chalcidius, with which they were already well acquainted, but also sought out a whole range of previously unknown Greek and Arabic philosophical and scientific works. In particular, a greatly expanded knowledge of Aristotle, in both his original and Arabic guises, helped change the direction of medieval thought, forcing thinkers of all intellectual persuasions to take account of a comprehensive natural and ethical philosophy which stood independently of Christian revelation, theology and history. This new philosophical breadth and complexity were served by new institutions, such as the universities, and the further development of older methods and disciplines, such as scholasticism and logic.

Social and economic changes provided both opportunity and stimulus for technological development. Even a partial list of twelfth- and thirteenth-century discoveries reveals the fertile inventiveness of the period: the wheelbarrow, spinning wheel, flying buttress, pole-lathe, rudder and keel, compass, mechanical clock, eyeglasses, chimney, stained glass, and, in the early fourteenth century, the crossbow.[4] Equally indicative of interest in techniques was the rapid adaptation of borrowed or older devices, such as the watermill or windmill, to new industrial uses. By the end of the thirteenth century, mills were employed in fulling, tanning and wood-cutting, for forging metals and powering bel-

---

Haskins, *The Renaissance of the Twelfth Century* (Cambridge, Mass.: Harvard University Press, 1927), but for the results of more recent scholarship, see Robert L. Benson, Giles Constable and Carol D. Lanham, eds., *Renaissance and Renewal in the Twelfth Century* (Cambridge, Mass.: Harvard University Press, 1982). For more specialized treatment of ideas about nature and their connection with philosophical and theological concerns, see especially M.-D. Chenu, *Nature, Man and Society in the Twelfth Century: Essays in New Theological Perspectives in the Latin West*, ed. and trans. Jerome Taylor and Lester K. Little (Chicago: University of Chicago Press, 1968); Brian Stock, *Myth and Science in the Twelfth Century: A Study of Bernard Silvester* (Princeton: Princeton University Press, 1972); J. M. Parent, *La doctrine de la création dans l'école de Chartres* (Paris: J. Vrin, 1938); Tullio Gregory, "L'idea di natura nella filosofia medievale prima del' ingresso della fisca di Aristotele: il secolo xii," in *La filosofia della natura nel Medioevo: Atti del Terzo Congresso Internazionale di Filosofia Medievale, 1964* (Milan: Società editrice Vita e pensiero, 1966), 29–65 and *Anima mundi: La filosofia di Guglielmo di Conches et la Scuola di Chartres* (Florence: G. C. Sansoni, 1955); Franco Alessio, "La filosofia e le 'artes mechanicae' nel secolo XII," *Studi Medievali*, 3rd series, 6 (1965): 71–155 and Richard Lemay, *Abu Ma'shar and Latin Aristotelianism in the Twelfth Century: The Recovery of Aristotle's Natural Philosophy through Arabic Astrology*, American University of Beirut Publication of the Faculty of Arts and Sciences, Oriental Series no. 38 (Beirut: American University of Beirut, 1962). For the bibliography of recent works on twelfth- and thirteenth-century attitudes toward technology in particular, see above Chapter I and for general intellectual trends in the thirteenth century see Frederick Copleston, *Mediaeval Philosophy*, vol. 2, part 2 in *A History of Philosophy* (Garden City, N.Y.: Doubleday, Image Books, 1962) and Maurice De Wulf, *Histoire de la philosophie médiévale* (Louvain: Institute Supérieure de Philosophie, 1924), both of which contain extensive bibliographies, and Fernand van Steenberghen, *Aristotle in the West: The Origins of Latin Aristotelianism*, trans. Leonard Johnston, 2nd ed. (Louvain: Nauwelaerts Pub. House, 1970).

[4] Crombie, *Medieval Science*, 1;191–222; White, *Medieval Technology*, 78–128.

lows, and in the crushing of ore and other materials; they had also been adapted for use in slow-moving rivers and tidal basins.[5]

In this newly "mechanism-minded" world,[6] men developed an increasing awareness of their ability to shape, as well as to understand, the natural world. Twelfth- and thirteenth-century thinkers, who had begun more and more to see nature as a separate macrocosm, open to human understanding, now also began to view their relationship with nature as a dynamic one. In the words of M.-D. Chenu, they "thought of themselves as confronting an external present, intelligible, and active reality as they might confront a partner."[7] This sense of the possibility of mastery, or, at least, confrontation with nature is reflected in contemporary comments on the importance of technological achievement in human life.

Diverse references to crafts in the literature of the period indicate a widespread sensitivity to the value of technology. Several scholars have tied a new emphasis on crafts to trends in religious thought. Chenu, for example, sees an insistence among twelfth-century theologians on man's material nature and a consequent attempt to relate man's efforts to direct nature with religious concerns.[8] Brian Stock finds in the sermons of Bernard of Clairvaux a recognition of the importance for salvation of physical labor.[9] Similarly, early twelfth-century Benedictine thought, in particular, that of Rupert of Deutz and Theophilus, has been linked with a theological justification of craftsmanship.[10]

Favorable comments on crafts occur in many other contexts as well. The technological imagination of Roger Bacon, for example, who envisaged not only new incendiary weapons but also cars which moved by themselves, underwater ships, and flying machines is well known.[11] Alexander Neckham, writing a century earlier in his encyclopedia, the *De naturis rerum*, frequently singled out inventions, tools or machines

---

[5] Crombie, *Medieval Science*, 1:196–199; White, *Medieval Technology*, 79–89; Singer, *History of Technology*, 1:608–614, 619–620.

[6] The phrase is Chenu's from *Nature, Man and Society*, 43.

[7] Chenu, *Nature, Man and Society*, 5.

[8] Chenu, *Nature, Man and Society*, 38–46. For a full discussion of the issues and historiography surrounding the connection between medieval religion and technology, see the Introduction, Chapter I.

[9] Brian Stock, "Experience, Praxis, Work and Planning in Bernard of Clairvaux: Observations on the *Sermones in Cantica*," in *The Cultural Context of Medieval Learning*, Boston Studies in The Philosophy of Science, 26 (Dordrecht and Boston: D. Reidel, 1974), 228.

[10] John Van Engen, "Theophilus Presbyter and Rupert of Deutz: The Manual Arts and Benedictine Theology in the Early Twelfth Century," *Viator* 11 (1980):147–163.

See Ovitt, *Restoration of Perfection*, 143–163 for a valuable account of monastic thought on labor in the twelfth century. Ovitt argues that by the end of the twelfth century, the church had rejected its earlier commitment to labor as an important part of the religious life.

[11] Roger Bacon, *Opus maius* 6. Exemplum 3, *The 'Opus maius' of Roger Bacon*, ed. John Henry Bridges (Oxford: Clarendon Press, 1897; rpt. Frankfurt: Minerva, 1964), 2;217; *Epistola Fratris Rogerii Baconis de Secretis operibus artis et naturae et de nullitate magicae*, 4 in *Fr. Rogerii Bacon Opera quaedam hactenus inedita*, ed. J. S. Brewer, Rerum Britannicarum Medii Aevi Scriptores, 11 (London: Longman, Green, Longman and Roberts, 1859), 532–533.

for praise. Neckham describes the mariner's compass, the construction of a fishing net, the uses of coal and metals, the ways in which plants and animals serve mankind, the operations of the baker and weaver and the parts of the plow and other equipment.[12] Neckham, who also wrote a separate treatise on the names and parts of household and farming utensils, especially praises the plow as a gift from heaven.[13] Machines and crafts were also depicted in manuscript illuminations. The manuscript of Herrad of Landsberg's *Hortus deliciarum*, for example, included representations of a heavy plow, spindle, mason's tools, cart and harness, grain mill and wine press in illustrations of various biblical passages.[14] Drawings of a swing-plow, kitchen and farming utensils, a treadle loom and waterclocks also appear in the Luttrell Psalter (c. 1338) and other illustrated Bibles.[15] By the end of the twelfth century cycles of crafts begin to appear in church sculpture, including Chartres, the Campanile in Florence, Rheims Cathedral and Amiens.[16]

Less systematic but still significant references to crafts are scattered throughout the literature of the period. The discovery of crafts, for example, was incorporated into Christian history. Peter Comestor and Honorius Augustodunensis recount not only that Tubal invented metalworking, as recorded in Genesis, but add the extra-biblical information that his sister Noema invented textile-working.[17] Arnold, Benedictine abbot of Bonneval from 1149 to 1159, prefaced his *Hexaemeron* with a detailed description of the invention and use, "with God's pleasure," of agriculture, metallurgy, textile-working, cookery and medicine at the time of Moses.[18] Arnold was perhaps influenced by a passage in Exodus 35:30–35 cited by his fellow Benedictine, Rupert of Deutz, as proof that all knowledge, including crafts, is a gift from God:

---

[12] Alexander Neckham, *De naturis rerum libri duo* 1.24, 54, 76, 98, 156, ed. Thomas Wright, Rerum Britannicarum Medii Aevi Scriptores, 34 (London: Longman, Green, Longman, Roberts and Green, 1863), 158, 162–163, 173–174, 183, 248–249, 279–283.

[13] Ibid. 1.169:280; see also "The Treatise *De utensilibus* of Alexander Neckham," in *A Volume of Vocabularies*, ed. Thomas Wright (London: private printing, 1857–73), 96–119.

[14] Herrade de Landsberg, *Hortus deliciarum*, ed. Joseph Walter (Strasbourg and Paris: F. X. de Roux, 1952), pl. 7, 9, 10, 30, 61.

[15] E. G. Millar, ed. *'The Luttrell Psalter'. Facsimile Edition* (London: British Museum, 1932) depicts, for example, a watermill, windmill, wheelbarrow, crossbow, bellows, plow, and harrow (pls. 114, 68, 125, 10, 21c, 92, 94); and *La Bible moralisée* (Paris: Société Française de Reproduction des Manuscrits et Peintures, 1911–1927) has illustrations of a polelathe, waterclock and other instruments, 1:183, 2:pl. 213, 5:pl. 181. See R. van Marle, *Iconographie de l'art profane au Moyen-Âge et à la Renaissance* (The Hague: Martines Nijhoff, 1931–1932), vol. 1; and White, *Medieval Technology and Social Change*, 110–117 for additional examples. See also Emile Mâle, *The Gothic Image: Religious Art in France of the Thirteenth Century*, trans. Dora Nussey (New York: Harper and Row, Icon Editions, 1972), 64–75.

[16] Van Marle, *Iconographie de l'art profane*, 2:252–260; Mâle, *The Gothic Image*, 64–75; M. W. Evans, *Medieval Drawings* (Feltham, N.Y.: Hamlyn, 1969), pl. 89, which shows a model-book, early twelfth century, containing a cycle of crafts bound with a copy of Hugh of St. Victor's *Didascalicon*.

[17] Peter Comestor, *Historia scholastica. Liber Genesis* 28 (*PL* 198:1079); Honorius Augustodunensis, *De imagine mundi* 3. *Exhortio* (*PL* 172:165).

[18] This section of Arnold's preface to his *Hexaemeron* has been edited by Jean LeClercq, "Écrits monastiques sur la Bible aux XIe–XIIIe siècles," *Medieval Studies* 15 (1953):96–98.

That, however, all . . . [kinds of knowledge] . . . are gifts of God and on that account the holy spirit is rightly before named the Spirit of knowledge, is established from abundant examples. We, nevertheless, cite briefly only single examples of each. We are informed that illiterate knowledge is a gift of God when we read in Exodus: Behold the Lord called by name Bezaleel, the son of Uri, the son of Hur, of the tribe of Judah; and filled him with the Spirit of God, in wisdom and in understanding and in knowledge of all learning for the contrivance and making of works in gold, silver and brass, and in carving stones and in carpentry work. Whatever can be devised skilfully, he yielded up to his heart. Oliab also the son of Achisamech, of the tribe of Dan. He instructed both, so that they should make works in wood, weaving and embroidery, of blue and purple, and twice-dyed scarlet and in flax.[19]

Theologians also considered the question whether artificial things made by man can be counted among the works of God.[20] For Thomas Aquinas an essential part of human excellence is not man's rational nature alone but also his ability, using both his reason and his hands, to equip himself with an endless catalogue of tools.[21] Monastic writings and records often included expressions of enthusiasm for crafts and machinery. Monks took an active interest in the use of waterpower to accomplish a variety of industrial tasks associated with the management of the monastery, as well as promoting forest clearance, new farming

---

[19] Rupert of Deutz, *De Sancta Trinitate et operibus eius* 40. *De operibus Spiritus Sancti* 7.5, ed. Hrabanus Haacke, Corpus christianorum continuatio mediaevalis, 24 (Turnholt: Brepols Editores Pontificii, 1972), 2042–2043:

> Quod autem omnia quae sub isto genere, id est scientia diuidendo distinximus, dona Dei sint, et idcirco Spiritus sanctus recte Spiritus scientiae praedicetur, examplis comprobare ex abundanti est. Verumtamen singula singulorum breuiter exempla ponamus. Illiteralem scientiam donum Dei esse docemur, cum in Exodo legimus. Ecce vacauit Dominus ex nomine Beselchel filium Huri, filii Hur, de tribu Iuda, impleuitque eum Spiritu Dei, sapientia et intelligentia et scientiae omni doctrina ad excogitandum et faciendum opus in auro, argento et aero sculpendisque lapidibus et opere carpentario. Quidquid fabre adinueniri potest, dedit in corde eius. Oliab quoque filium Achisamech, de tribu Dan. Ambos erudiuit sapientia, ut faciant opera abietarii polymitarii ac plumarii, de hyacintho ac purpura, coccoque bis tincto et lino.

Van Engen, "Theophilus Presbyter and Rupert of Deutz," 153–154, sees this passage as a deliberate retort to Augustine. Cf. Eusebius, *Praeparatione Evangelicae* 9.27 (*PG* 21, 729) who quotes Artapanus (c. 50 B.C.) as saying that Moses invented ships and war machines as well as philosophy; Godfrey of St. Victor, *Microcosmus* 1.52–55, ed. Philippe Delhaye, Mémoires et travaux publiés par les professeurs des Facultés Catholiques de Lille, 56 (Lille: Facultés Catholiques, 1951; Gembloux: J. Duculot, 1951) 72–73 who says that the mechanical arts originated in the law of Moses; Roger Bacon, *Opus maius* 2.9, ed. Bridges, Supplementary volume, 1900, 53–59 who says that philosophy, including experimental science, was revealed by God to the biblical prophets.

[20] See Chenu, *Nature, Man and Society*, 39–40, in which he quotes a twelfth-century manuscript which discusses the question, "Can one consider things manufactured by man—footgear, cheese, and like products—as works of God?" and Robert de Melun, *Oeuvres de Robert de Melun*, ed. Raymond M. Martin, Spicilegium Sacrum Lovaniense, Études et Documents, fascicle 21 (Louvain: Spicilegium Sacrum Lovaniense, 1947), 3, *Sententiae*, 1:73.

[21] Thomas Aquinas, *Summa theologiae*, 1a.91,3.2, ed. and trans. Edmund Hill, in *Summa theologiae*, ed. Blackfriars (New York: McGraw-Hill; London: Eyre and Spottiswoode), 13:28.

techniques and stockbreeding.[22] Indeed, the whole question of the proper relationship of manual labor to the religious life was a major issue in twelfth- and thirteenth-century monastic writings.[23]

The most explicit and developed thought on craftsmanship and the nature of technology itself, apart from the broader and more diffuse issue of the moral and social value of work, however, can be found in works on the divisions of knowledge. In response to the flood of newly available classical and Arabic texts and the further development of scholasticism, the classification of the arts and sciences grew into an independent genre of full-scale works specifically on the parts and organization of the arts and sciences.[24] In part, this reflected the greater complexity of the intellectual and cultural environment. Yet in these works medieval thinkers also displayed a greater interest in technology *per se*. Far more consistently than in antiquity or the early Middle Ages, these treatises included crafts or technical arts as a part of knowledge. Many of these works, moreover, elaborated a philosophical basis which underlay and supported a conception of craftsmanship as an expression of human reason, tied to religious or scientific values. Implicitly or explicitly, the authors of these classifications addressed the critique of technology developed in classical thought and passed on to the medieval world.

The strength of the impulse toward the legitimization of crafts can be seen in the serious attention paid to the problem of including craft as a part of knowledge in authors from quite different intellectual traditions. Honorius Augustodunensis, as we have seen, developed the Isidorian association of medicine and *mechanica* with the *quadrivium* into a far

---

[22] Lynn White, jr., "Cultural Climates and Technological Advance in the Middle Ages," *Viator* 10 (1979):194–195.

Clarence J. Glacken, *Traces on the Rhodian Shore: Nature and Culture in Western Thought from Ancient Times to the End of the Eighteenth Century* (Berkeley: University of California Press, 1967), 304–313, 331–333; Christopher J. Holdsworth, "The Blessings of Work: The Cistercian View," in *Sanctity and Secularity: The Church and The World*, ed. Derek Baker, Studies in Church History, 10 (New York: Harper and Row Publishers, Inc., 1973), 59–76.

[23] Ovitt, *Restoration of Perfection*, 143–163.

[24] The essential works on the classification of the sciences in the twelfth and thirteenth centuries are James A. Weisheipl, "Classification of the Sciences in Medieval Thought," *Medieval Studies* 27 (1965):54–90 and Joseph Mariétan, *Problème de la classification des sciences d'Aristote à s. Thomas* (Paris: F. Alcan, 1901). These, however, treat technological arts only peripherally. The major studies of how crafts or technological arts appeared in classifications of knowledge in this period are Alessio, "Filosofia e le 'artes mechanicae,'" Sternagel, *Artes Mechanicae* and George Ovitt, "The Status of the Mechanical Arts in Medieval Classifications of Learning," *Viator* 14 (1983):89–105 and *Restoration of Perfection*, 107–136. For discussion of the issues raised by these and other works, see Chapter I. Also useful for the liberal and mechanical arts are Richard William Hunt, "The Introductions to the 'Artes' in the Twelfth Century," *Studia mediaevalia in honorem R. J. Martin* (Bruges: De Tempel, 1949), 85–112; G. Pare, A. Brunet and P. Trembley, *La Renaissance du XIIe siècle: Les écoles et l'enseignement* (Paris: Libraire Philosophique J. Vrin, 1933); Ludwig Gompf, "Der Leipziger *Ordo artium*," *Mittel-lateinisches Jahrbuch* 3 (1966):94–128; and *Arts libéraux et philosophie au Moyen Âge: Actes du Quatrième Congrès International de Philosophie Médiévale* (Montreal: Institut d'Études Médiévales, 1969; Paris: J. Vrin, 1969).

broader conception of crafts as part of the liberal arts.[25] In the early twelfth century Rupert of Deutz suggested his own division of knowledge:

> Some knowledge is literate, some illiterate. For there is literate knowledge, which is learned through written records, as are all arts which are contained in books. Illiterate knowledge indeed which is not learned through books, as is sculpture or the artificer's art and any such art, because indeed it is rightly called knowledge, but it is not learned through reading. Again, literate knowledge is both liberal and illiberal. The art of medicine which philosophers do not profess, is both literate and illiberal, although *medici* attribute very much liberality to their art, saying, that it is not numbered among the seven liberal arts because it is formed from all or through all the liberal arts, thus, of course no one can truly be learned in medicine unless he is skilled in all the liberal arts. Again, literate and liberal knowledge is called philosophy.[26]

Although neither Honorius's nor Rupert's division of knowledge spawned any further development, two of their contemporaries introduced new patterns of integrating crafts into a system of knowledge, which were to prove extremely fruitful.[27] Domingo Gundisalvo (fl. 1140), on the one hand, introduced into the Latin West Arabic notions of craftsmanship as the operative or practical aspect of theoretical knowledge. His scheme, for example, associated agriculture, medicine and navigation with physics and carpentry, and stone-working with geometry. Hugh of St. Victor (d. 1140 or 1141), on the other hand, apparently unaware of the new Aristotelian and Arabic scientific learning, developed the notion of the *artes mechanicae* as a discrete and independent group of arts, analogous in form and function to the liberal arts, from patristic and early medieval sources, particularly Augustine and John of Scot. According to Hugh, the mechanical arts supply all the remedies

---

[25] See Chapter III above, p. 69.

[26] Rupert of Deutz, *De Sancta Trinitate et operibus eius 40. De operibus Spiritus Sancti* 7.3, ed. Haacke, 2040:

> Scientia alia litteralis, alia illitteralis. Nam litteralis est, quae litteris addiscitur, ut sunt omnes artes quae libris continentur. Illitteralis uero quae litteris non addiscitur, ut est sculptoria siue fabrilis ars et talium quidlibet, quod recte quidem scientia dicitur, sed non legendo percipitur. Rursus litteralis scientia, alia liberalis, alia illiberalis. Litteralis et illiberalis est medicinae ars, quam philosophi non profitentur, quamuis et medici arti suae liberalitatem plurimum attribuant, dicentes, quod idcirco inter septem liberales artes non numeretur, quia de omnibus uel per omnes ipsa consistat, ita scilicet ut medicus nemo ueraciter esse possit, nisi omnium artium liberalium peritus sit. Porro litteralis et liberalis scientia philosophia dicitur.

Cf. Isidore of Seville, *Etymologiae*, 4.13, ed. W. M. Lindsay (Oxford: Clarendon Press, 1911):4.13 where Isidore says that medicine contains all the liberal arts.

[27] Domingo Gundisalvo, *De divisione philosophiae*, ed. Ludwig Baur in *Beiträge zur Geschichte der Philosophie des Mittelalters, Texte und Untersuchungen*, Band 4, Heft 2–3 (Munster Westfalen: Aschendorffsche Verlagsbuchhandlung, 1903). For discussion of the content and sources of Gundisalvo's treatise, see Chapter V below. For John the Scot as a source for Hugh of St. Victor's *Didascalicon*, see Chapter III above.

for our physical weakness, a result of the Fall and, like the other branches of knowledge, are ultimately subsumed under the religious task of restoring our true, prelapsarian nature.

The twelfth-century push toward the intellectual assimilation of technology continued into the thirteenth century. Both Hugh of St. Victor and Gundisalvo inspired others to integrate technology into discussions of knowledge in a variety of ways. In the twelfth century, Hugh of St. Victor and his followers placed the mechanical arts, defined as an independent category of knowledge, within the religious context of man's effort to restore himself to his prelapsarian condition. In the thirteenth century, although the Victorine understanding of craftsmanship as an aspect of salvation continued to be influential in the thought of Bonaventure, Vincent of Beauvais and others, a concept of the mechanical arts as applied science serving the community predominated.[28] Albertus Magnus, Robert Kilwardby and Roger Bacon, especially, following the lead of Gundisalvo, modified elements taken from the Aristotelian, Arabic and Victorine traditions to define the mechanical arts as the operative or instrumental side of the theoretical sciences.

Medieval thinkers during the twelfth and thirteenth centuries, therefore, attempted in various ways to fashion a coherent and positive view of technology from the diverse body of thought developed by their contemporaries and predecessors. We will follow the somewhat earlier Victorine understanding of the mechanical arts in the present chapter. The Arabic-Aristotelian tradition on the mechanical arts, initiated in the Latin West by Gundisalvo and further developed in the thirteenth century, will be taken up in the fifth chapter.

Hugh of St. Victor

Hugh of St. Victor, first monk and then master at the abbey of St. Victor near Paris from the 1100s until his death in 1141 is, unquestionably, one of the most important figures in the development of medieval ideas about technology.[29] Nicknamed by his contemporaries "a new

[28] See below, Chapter V.

[29] The bibliography on Hugh of St. Victor is extensive. Especially valuable for the intellectual context of the *Didascalicon* are the introduction, notes and bibliography in Jerome Taylor, *The "Didascalicon" of Hugh of St. Victor: A Medieval Guide to the Arts*, trans. Jerome Taylor, Records of Civilization, Sources and Studies, 64 (New York and London: Columbia University Press, 1961). In addition, for Hugh of St. Victor's life, see Jerome Taylor, *The Origin and Early Life of Hugh of St. Victor: An Evaluation of the Tradition*. Texts and Studies in the History of Medieval Education, 5 (Notre Dame, Indiana: The Mediaeval Institute, 1957); for his thought in general, see Roger Baron, *Science et sagesse chez Hugues de Saint-Victor* (Paris: P. Lethielleux, 1957) and *Études sur Hugues de Saint-Victor* (Bruges: Desclée de Brouwer, 1963) and John Phillip Kleinz, *The Theory of Knowledge of Hugh of St. Victor*, Catholic University of America Philosophical Studies, 87 (Washington D.C.: Catholic University of America Press, 1944); and for Hugh's mystical thought, Beryl Smalley, *The Study of the Bible in the Middle Ages* (New York: Philosophical Library, 1952; rpt. Notre Dame, Indiana: University of Notre Dame Press, 1970), 83–105. Hugh of St. Victor figures prominently in recent treatments of medieval technology. For bibliography on this aspect of his thought, see above, Chapter I, pp. 17, 18, 20, and below, n. 32.

Augustine," Hugh was a mystic, as well as a theologian and educator.[30] Besides producing the *Didascalicon* he wrote major works on theology, including the *De sacramentis christianae fidei*, and several short educational texts on practical geometry and grammar.[31]

Hugh is best known among modern scholars, however, for his vision of the mechanical arts as part of man's religious and philosophical quest. As scholarly interest in medieval technology has grown, so, also, have estimations of Hugh's originality and importance. Whereas in 1904 Robert Flint, in his then standard work on the classification of the sciences, described Hugh as a "sickly and feeble" recluse, since the 1950s scholars of medieval science and technology have consistently singled out Hugh for praise, describing him as "remarkable," "revolutionary," "of particular interest," and "one of the most adventurous spirits of his age."[32]

The focus of this praise and attention is Hugh of St. Victor's conception of the mechanical arts, which describes and defines crafts as a distinct category of human knowledge explicitly and comprehensively. In the *Didascalicon* and also, in a condensed version, in the *Epitome Dindimi in philosophiam* Hugh describes seven mechanical arts—fabric-making, armament, commerce, agriculture, hunting, medicine and theatrics—loosely comparing the first three to the *trivium* and the latter four to the *quadrivium*; together, the mechanical arts concern the works of human labor which minister to the necessities of life.[33] The *artes mechanicae* comprise the third major division of philosophy, following theoretical knowledge, made up of mathematics, physics, and theology, and prac-

---

[30] David Knowles, *The Evolution of Medieval Thought* (Baltimore: Helicon Press, 1962), 142.

[31] Hugh of St. Victor, *Hugonis de Sancto Victore Didascalicon de studio legendi: A Critical Text*, ed. Charles Henry Buttimer, Catholic University of America Studies in Medieval and Renaissance Latin, 10 (Washington: Catholic University of America Press, 1939). The *Didascalicon* has been translated by Taylor, *Didascalicon*. Hugh's theological works include *De sacramentis christianae fidei* (*PL* 176: 173–618), *De arca Noe morali* (*PL* 176: 617–680) and *De arca Noe mystica* (*PL* 176: 681–712). Extracts from the latter two works have been translated in *Hugh of Saint Victor: Selected Spiritual Writings*, trans. by a Religious of C.S.M.V. (New York: Harper and Row, 1968). Hugh's minor educational works, *Practica geometriae, De grammatica* and *Epitome Dindimi in philosophiam* are edited in *Hugonis de Sancto Victore opera porpaedevtica*, ed. Roger Baron, Publications in Mediaeval Studies, The University of Notre Dame, 20 (Notre Dame, Indiana: University of Notre Dame Press, 1966). Henceforth references to the *Didascalicon* will include page numbers to both Taylor's translation and Buttimer's edition (for example, Hugh of St. Victor, *Didascalicon* 1.11, Taylor, 60 [Buttimer, 22]). References to the notes or introduction to the translation by Taylor will be given simply as Taylor, ed., *Didascalicon*, 4.

[32] Robert Flint, *Philosophy as Scientia Scientiarum, and A History of Classification of the Sciences* (Edinburgh: W. Blackwood, 1904), 94; Weisheipl, "Classification of the Sciences," 65; Crombie, *Robert Grossteste*, 21; White, "Medieval Engineering," 10; White, "Cultural Climates," 196. See also the comments by Guy Beaujouan, "Réflexions sur les rapports entre théorie et pratique au moyen âge," in *Cultural Context of Medieval Learning*, 438; Alessio, "Filosofia e le 'artes mechanicae,'" 111–116; Sternagel, *Artes Mechanicae*, 67. For further discussion of recent evaluations of Hugh of St. Victor's importance for the history of medieval technology, see above, Chapter I.

[33] Hugh of St. Victor, *Didascalicon* 2.20–27, Taylor, 74–79 (Buttimer, 38–44); cf. *Epitome* 2. 147–153, Baron, *Opera propaedevtica*, 192–193.

tical knowledge, composed of politics, ethics and economics.[34] The functions of the different parts of knowledge parallel each other, for just as the theoretical arts serve as the remedy for ignorance, and the practical arts serve as the remedy for vice, the mechanical arts are the remedy for physical weakness.[35] Hugh adds logic, which includes grammar and the theory of argument, as the fourth part of knowledge.[36]

Hugh's arrangement of theoretical knowledge, practical knowledge and logic is already somewhat unusual, for it combines the Aristotelian and Boethian division of philosophy into theoretical and practical arts with the Platonic and Augustinian division of knowledge into physics, ethics and logic.[37] The addition of the mechanical arts breaks with tradition even more decisively. Prior to the *Didascalicon*, "human" philosophy had generally referred to the pursuit of virtue.[38] Hugh, however, locates philosophy firmly in the totality of life. Because man is both an immortal and a mortal being, knowledge must include the care which man takes to safeguard and make more pleasant his material existence.[39] Since divine wisdom is "a kind of moderator over *all* human actions," the "theoretical consideration of *all* human acts and pursuits *belongs* with equal fitness to philosophy."[40] Moreover, he says, "the same action is able to belong to philosophy as concerns its ideas and to be excluded from it as concerns its actual performance," and therefore, the theory of agriculture belongs to the philosopher, even as the execution belongs to the farmer.[41]

Hugh does not completely overturn the tradition inherited from antiquity that crafts could not properly be considered knowledge. The most obvious holdover is Hugh's designation of the mechanical arts as "adulterate," because they concern human labor and are imitative of nature.[42] This curious association derives from a mistaken ninth-century ety-

---

[34] Hugh of St. Victor, *Didascalicon* 2.1, Taylor, 64 (Buttimer, 24); *Epitome* 2.132–146, Baron, *Opera propaedevtica*, 192.

[35] Hugh of St. Victor, *Didascalicon* 6.14, Taylor, 152 (Buttimer, 130); *Epitome* 2.164–195, Baron, *Opera propaedevtica*, 193–194. This passage is translated by Taylor, *Didascalicon*, 12.

[36] Hugh of St. Victor, *Didascalicon* 1.11, Taylor, 60 (Buttimer, 22).

[37] Taylor, ed., *Didascalicon*, 8.

[38] Taylor, ed., *Didascalicon*, 183, n. 27.

[39] Hugh of St. Victor, *Didascalicon* 1.5, 1.7–8, Taylor, 51–52, 54–55 (Buttimer, 12, 14–16).

[40] Hugh of St. Victor, *Didascalicon* 1.4, Taylor, 51 (Buttimer, 11):

> Quia enim de studio sapientiae loqui suscepimus, idque solis hominibus quodam naturae privilegio competere attestati sumus, consequenter nunc omnium humanorum actuum moderatricem quandam sapientiam posuisse videmur. . . . iam non solum ea studia in quibus vel de rerum natura vel disciplina agitur morum, verum etiam omnium humanorum actuum seu studiorum rationes, non incongrue ad philosophiam pertinere dicemus.

[41] Hugh of St. Victor, *Didascalicon* 1.4, Taylor, 51 (Buttimer, 11): "Potest namque idem actus et ad philosophiam pertinere secundum rationem suam, et ab ea excludi secundum administrationem, verbi gratia, ut de praesenti loquamur: agriculturae ratio philosophi est, administratio rustici."

[42] Hugh of St. Victor, *Didascalicon* 1.8, 1.9, 2.20, Taylor, 55, 56, 75 (Buttimer, 16, 39).

mology which identified the Greek μηχανή (machine) with μοιχός (adulterer).[43] It is symptomatic of Hugh's overall very positive attitude toward the mechanical arts that he does not dwell upon or explain their "adulterate" nature and the designation has proved a puzzle both to his medieval and his modern readers.[44]

Hugh's insistence on the validity of including crafts among the legitimate parts of knowledge comes through not only in his theoretical arguments in support of this view, but also in his descriptions of the arts themselves. Hugh covers each of the mechanical arts in detail, giving them equal space with theology, physics and the mathematical arts. His account displays a pragmatic, lively concern for different aspects of craftmanship. Under "armament," for example, Hugh names various types of weapons and armor, as well as the tools and activities of the carpenter and other builders, who "work with mattocks and hatchets, the file and beam, the saw and auger, planes, vises, the trowel and the level, smoothing, hewing, cutting, filing, carving, joining, daubing in every sort of material."[45] Hugh's description of fabric-making similarly suggests a knowledgeable layman's interest in craft and its products:

> Fabric making includes all the kinds of weaving, sewing, and twisting which are accomplished by hand, needle, spindle, awl, skein winder, comb, loom, crisper, iron, or any other instruments whatever; out of any material made of flax or fleece, or any sort of hide, whether scraped or hairy, out of cane as well, or cork, or rushes, or hair, or tufts, or any material of this sort which can be used for the making of clothes, coverings, drapery, blankets, saddles, carpets, curtains, napkins, felts, strings, nets, ropes; out of straw too, from which men usually make their hats and baskets. All these pursuits belong to fabric making.[46]

---

[43] Taylor, *Didascalicon*, 191, n. 64; M. L. W. Laistner, ed., "Notes on Greek from the Lectures of a Ninth Century Monastery Teacher," *Bulletin of the John Rylands Library* 7 (1922–23):439.

[44] Baron, *Science et sagesse*, 78, dismisses the label "adulterine" as etymological word play and Sternagel, *"Artes Mechanicae,"* sees Hugh's use of the term as an attempt to make an oft-repeated tag more positive (73). Chenu, *Nature, Man and Society*, 44, interprets the phrase as meaning that the mechanical arts adulterate the spiritual dignity of man by associating it with matter but Paolo Rossi, *Philosophy, Technology and the Arts in the Early Modern Era*, trans. Salvator Attanasio (New York: Harper and Row, 1970), 138, stresses the implication of the inferiority of human art to nature. Ovitt, *Restoration of Perfection*, 118, ascribes to Hugh the view that the mechanical arts are "tainted" on the basis of the label as adulterate.

[45] Hugh of St. Victor, *Didascalicon* 2.22, Taylor, 76 (Buttimer, 40): ". . . in dolabris et securibus, lima et assiculo, serra et terebro, runcinis, artavis, examussi, polientes, dolantes, sculpentes, limantes, scalpentes, compingentes, linienties in quadlibet materia."

[46] Hugh of St. Victor, *Didascalicon* 2.21, Taylor, 75 (Buttimer, 39–40):

> Lanificium continet omnia texendi, consuendi, retorquendi genera, quae fiunt manu, acu, fuso, subula, girgillo, pectine, alibro, calamistro, chilindro, sive aliis quibuslibet instrumentis, ex quacumque lini vel lanae materia et omni genere pellium erasarum vel pilos habentium, cannabis quoque, vel suberis, iuncorum, pilorum, floccorum, aut alia qualibet re huiuscemodi, quae in usum vestimentorum, operimentorum linteorum sagorum, sagmatum, substratoriorum, cortinarum, matularum, filtrorum chordarum, cassium, funium, redigi potest. stramina quoque ex quibus galeros et sportulas texere solent homines. haec omnia studia ad lanificium pertinent.

Hugh's account of commerce (*navigatio*) is especially striking. The praise he bestows contrasts sharply with the more typical clerical suspicion of business as an immoral and disruptive activity:[47]

Commerce contains every sort of dealing in the purchase, sale, and exchange of domestic or foreign goods. This art is beyond all doubt a peculiar sort of rhetoric—strictly of its own kind—for eloquence is in the highest degree necessary to it. Thus the man who excels others in fluency of speech is called a *Mercurius*, or mercury, as being a *mercatorum kirrius* (*kyrios*)-a very lord among merchants. Commerce penetrates the secret places of the world, approaches shores unseen, explores fearful wildernesses, and in tongues unknown and with barbaric peoples carries on the trade of mankind. The pursuit of commerce reconciles nations, calms wars, strengthens peace, and commutes the private good of individuals into the common benefit of all.[48]

Hugh's descriptions of the mechanical arts serve to support his underlying concept of the role of technology in human life. Unlike earlier classifications, the rubric *artes mechanicae* is explicitly defined by Hugh as a generic term for *all* crafts, which, he says, we see in "infinite varieties" around us.[49] His list of the arts is clearly designed to be comprehensive without violating the logical and rhetorical necessity for naming seven arts to match the seven liberal arts. "Armament" is a broad group which includes not only weaponry but also architecture, carpentry and metal-working; "hunting" includes food gathering, cookery and the selling and serving of food and drink; and "theatrics" refers to all sorts of entertainments and games.[50] These rubrics are clearly intended to be categories of arts, rather than simply referring to a single craft.

To what extent does Hugh's description of the mechanical arts reflect

---

[47] On conflicting attitudes toward commerce, see Chenu, *Nature, Man and Society*, 224 and Le Goff, "Licit and Illicit Trades," in *Time, Work and Culture*, 58–70; "Trades and Professions as Represented in Medieval Confessors' Manuals," in *Time, Work and Culture*, 107–121; "Merchant's Time and Church's Time in the Middle Ages," in *Time, Work and Culture*, 29–42. See also Georges Duby, *The Three Orders: Feudal Society Imagined*, trans. Arthur Goldhammer (Chicago and London: The University of Chicago Press, 1980), 322–353 and John W. Baldwin, *Masters, Princes and Merchants: The Social Views of Peter the Chanter and his Circle* (Princeton: Princeton University Press, 1970), 1:261–311.

[48] Hugh of St. Victor, *Didascalicon* 2.23, Taylor, 76–77 (Buttimer, 41):

Navigatio continet omnem in emendis, vendendis, mutandis, domesticis sive peregrinis mercibus negotiationem. haec rectissime quasi quaedam sui generis rhetorica est, eo quod huic professioni eloquentia maxime sit necessaria. unde et hic qui faciundiae praeesse dicitur, Mercurius, quasi mercatorum kirrius, id est, Dominus appellatur. haec secreta mundi penetrat, litora invisa adit, deserta horrida lustrat, et cum barbaris nationibus et linguis incognitis commercia humanitatis exercet. huius studium gentes conciliat, bella sedat, pacem firmat, et privata bona ad communem usum omnium immutat.

[49] Hugh of St. Victor, *Didascalicon* 1.9, Taylor, 56 (Buttimer, 17): "Hac eadem pinendi, texendi, sculpendi, fundendi, infinita genera exorta sunt, ut iam cum natura ipsum miremur artificem."

[50] Hugh of St. Victor, *Didascalicon* 2.22, 2.25, 2.27, Taylor, 76, 77–78 (Buttimer, 40–41, 42–43, 44).

the actual technological development of the early twelfth century? In part because of his theoretical and philosophical orientation, Hugh has been accused of relying overmuch upon literary convention and of being overly metaphorical and "bookish," especially with reference to his account of commerce.[51] While it is true that Hugh makes no mention of "state-of-the-art" technology, such as the stirrup, heavy plow, windmill, etc. and some of his discussion undeniably is drawn from the written word rather than personal observation, his descriptions of ordinary, every-day products and tools, such as the description of textile-making and carpentry quoted above, are specific, knowledgeable and, as far as is presently known, his own.[52] At least some of the information Hugh presents on crafts may very well have come from what he saw about him in the abbey of St. Victor or the nearby city of Paris. His approval of commerce, while certainly couched in rhetorical language, may also reflect Hugh's awareness of the rise in the status of the merchant in the twelfth century and the gradual shift from a predominantly rural and agricultural society to a more urban and commercial one.[53] Hugh's pragmatic and observant attitude, moreover, is not at odds with his religious and philosophical concerns but a part of them. The convergence of his interests, as well as his awareness of maritime commerce is illustrated by some of his comments in a discussion of Noah's ark. Prior to his discussion of the spiritual meaning of the Ark, in which he remarks on its literal shape, Hugh argues against Origen's contention that the Ark was built in the shape of a pyramid on the basis of contemporary ship design: "for it is indisputable that so massive a structure, laden with so many and such large animals, and also with provisions, could not possibly keep afloat when the waters came, unless the greater portion of its bulk were at the bottom; this fact we can put to the proof today with ships that carry heavy loads."[54] Hugh also displays some technological imagination when he suggests that chambers open to the sea on one side were constructed on the outer surface of the ark to accommodate

---

[51] Guy H. Allard, "Les arts mécaniques aux yeux de l'idéologie médiévale," in *Les arts mécaniques au moyen âge*, Cahiers d'études médiévales 7 (Montreal: Bellarmin, 1982), 21–22; Andre Vermeirre, "La navigation d'après Hugues de Saint-Victor et d'après la pratique au XIe siècle," in *Arts mécaniques*, 51–61 and Chenu, *Nature, Man and Society*, 44, n. 94. Cf. M.-D. Chenu, "Civilisation urbaine et théologie: L'École de Saint-Victor au XIIe siècle," *Annales* 29 (1974):1253–1263, in which Chenu cites the *Didascalicon*, including the passage on commerce, as evidence of response to medieval society's shift from rural and seigneurial to more commercial and urban.

[52] Taylor, ed., *Didascalicon*, 205–206, has identified those sections of Hugh's discussion which are quotations. They are largely from Isidore's *Etymologiae* and the *Isagoge* of Johannitius to Galen.

[53] Chenu, "Civilisation urbaine et théologie," 1254, 1263.

[54] Hugh of St. Victor, *De arca Noe morali*, 12 in *Selected Spiritual Writings*, 60 (*PL* 176:626–627): "Cui sententiae plura refrageri videntur, primum quod haec forma ad natandum non videtur esse idonea. Constat namque tantae molis machinam, tot et tantis onustam animalibus, atque cibariis, nequaquam ita potuisse supernatare venientibus aquis, ut non ex magna parte sui deorsum premeretur; cuius rei experimentum adhuc capere possumus in navibus magna gestantibus onera."

animals such as the otter and the seal which live both in the water and the dry land.[55]

Hugh, however, is not a craftsman and his concern is clearly more with a theoretical justification of technology than with techniques themselves. His importance lies in the history of ideas about technology—an importance which becomes increasingly apparent as his relationship to earlier approaches to craft is clarified. Hugh's conception of the mechanical arts did not appear in a vacuum but developed out of a specific philosophical milieu. His pragmatic, literal approach is strongly reminiscent of early medieval attitudes toward crafts and some of Hugh's descriptions of the mechanical arts are drawn from Isidore's *Etymologies*.[56] The skeleton concept of seven mechanical arts paralleling the seven liberal arts originated, as we have seen, in the ninth century.[57] The identification of the mechanical arts as "adulterine" has been traced to the tenth-century scholar, Martin of Laon.[58] Many of the arts included as mechanical arts by Hugh were earlier described by Isidore of Seville, including the unusual *theatrica*.[59] Hugh also quotes verbatim, without acknowledgment, the Isidorian definition of *mechanica*.[60] Hugh, in addition, was profoundly influenced by Augustine. Not only did Hugh adapt general Augustinian ideas to support his concept of the mechanical arts, but he may have also derived his specific listing of these arts from Augustine.[61] Jerome Taylor's assessment of the *Didascalicon* as "both a summary and an extension of this didactic tradition . . . bound to it in most of its materials and in aspects of its form, yet providing a new synthesis of the materials, a synthesis remarkable for its originality and its wholeness" is particularly apt for Hugh's treatment of the mechanical arts.[62] Hugh, however, goes much further toward a comprehensive understanding of technology as a distinct sphere of human activity than do any of his known sources. In Books I and II of the *Didascalicon* Hugh presents a careful case in defense of the dignity of

---

[55] Hugh of St. Victor, *De arca Noe morali*, 12 in *Selected Spiritual Writings*, 60 (*PL* 176:616).

[56] Taylor, ed., *Didascalicon*, 206, n. 74.

[57] See above Chapter III. Since John the Scot does not name the mechanical arts individually, the source of Hugh's names is a problem. Alessio, "Filosofia e le 'artes mechanicae,'" 114–116 has suggested Augustine, *City of God* 22.24 as Hugh's source and Sternagel, *Artes Mechanicae*, points to a late ancient Greek-Latin glossary, the *Hermeneumata*, which is known to exist in ninth- and tenth-century manuscripts (76–77). Another possibility is Isidore of Seville's *Etymologiae*; see note 59, below.

[58] Taylor, ed., *Didascalicon*, 191 n. 64.

[59] For the table of contents to Isidore of Seville, *Etymologiae*, ed. Lindsay, see above Chapter III, n. 46.

[60] Hugh of St. Victor, *Didascalicon* 2.20, Taylor, 75 (Buttimer, 39): "Mechanica est scientia ad quam fabricam omnium rerum concurrere dicunt."

[61] For Hugh's dependence on Augustine for his ideas on knowledge see Kleinz, *The Theory of Knowledge of Hugh of St. Victor*, 16–31 and Taylor, *Didascalicon*, 11–14. Alessio, "Filosofia e la 'artes mechanicae,'" 114–116 suggests Augustine, *City of God* 22.24 as the source for the names of Hugh's seven mechanical arts; however, see discussion of this passage above, Chapter II, and below pp. 97–98.

[62] Taylor, ed., *Didascalicon*, 3–4.

crafts and their inclusion as a part of philosophy through the reworking of more traditional ideas, using them as building blocks to emphasize the importance of the mechanical arts.

Underlying Hugh's concept of the mechanical arts and philosophy is his conception of man as both a physical and a spiritual being. Hugh's thought here has parallels with other twelfth-century thinkers who emphasized the combination of the corporeal and incorporeal in man's nature.[63] Hugh, however, is unusually forceful in his transference of an awareness of the physical life of man to the province of philosophy. Philosophy seeks to restore the connection between the human soul and Divine Wisdom.[64] But because philosophy conforms to the whole of human nature, it must include those actions men take to "cherish and conserve" their mortal part.[65]

The purpose of philosophy, moreover, is governed by Hugh's vision of fallen man, damaged in all aspects of his nature.[66] For Hugh, the Fall is the central fact of man's historical and present condition. Original sin has stupefied the mind, corrupted and infected human nature. Men, living in "a great chaos of forgetfulness" find themselves ignorant of wisdom, desirous of evil, and their flesh sickened with mortality.[67] We are restored, however, through knowledge to our natural, pre-lapsarian condition. The three evils of ignorance, vice and physical weakness can be countered by the three remedies of the theoretical sciences, the practical arts and the mechanical arts.

> The intention of all human action is resolved in a common objective: either to restore in us the likeness of the divine image or to take thought for the necessity of this life, which, the more easily it can suffer harm from those things which work to its disadvantage, the more does it require to be cherished and conserved.[68]

The work of restoration therefore encompasses all aspects of human life and involves the relief of our physical deficiencies as well as the purification and sharpening of the mind and will.

In its general outlines, Hugh's understanding of the Fall and restoration through the arts has its roots in patristic and, especially, Augus-

---

[63] Chenu, *Nature, Man and Society*, 24–26.

[64] Hugh of St. Victor, *Didascalicon* 1.1, Taylor, 46 (Buttimer, 4).

[65] Ibid., 1.7, Taylor, 54 (Buttimer, 15).

[66] Ibid., 1.1, Taylor, 47 (Buttimer, 6). Kleinz, *The Theory of Knowledge of Hugh of St. Victor*, 16–20, discusses the relationship of the Fall and knowledge in Hugh's *De sacramentis*.

[67] Hugh of St. Victor, *Epitome* 2.164, ed. Baron, 193–194.

[68] Hugh of St. Victor, *Didascalicon* 1.7, Taylor, 54 (Buttimer, 15): "ex quo colligi potest id quod supra dictum est, quod videlicet omnium humanarum actionum ad hunc finem concurrit intentio, ut vel divinae imaginis similitudo in nobis restauretur, vel huius vitae necessitudini consulatur, quae quo facilius laedi potest adversis, eo magis foveri et conservari indiget."

tinian, thought.[69] Hugh takes from Augustine the fundamental ideal of human life as progress toward the vision of God and education as an essential ingredient in this journey.[70] More specifically, Hugh owes to Augustine his sense of the Fall as a pervasive and disastrous event casting its shadow over man's existence and his reading of Genesis as a kind of blueprint or standard for past and future human behavior.[71] Augustine, unlike other Church Fathers, could conceive of a Paradise in which Adam and Eve not only had a sexual nature but performed physical labor and practiced the craft of agriculture.[72] Yet Augustine, like the other patristic writers, regarded restoration as an exclusively spiritual task. Insofar as the body was regarded as antithetical to man's true nature, Adam, the true man, lived a completely spiritual life and a return to the pre-lapsarian condition could only be accomplished by shedding bodily needs and desires.[73] For Hugh, however, the work of restoration included the repair of man's physical life, not by reducing that life to a minimum or attempting to eliminate it entirely, but by using the opportunity to invent "better things" for himself. Moreover, through its relationship to man's final end, the pursuit of the mechanical arts acquired religious and moral sanction.

In support of his conception of philosophy as encompassing the totality of life, and specifically in support of the mechanical arts, Hugh incorporates a discussion of cosmology into Book 1 of the *Didascalicon* (chapters 6, 7 and 8). As Jerome Taylor has pointed out, these actions serve to place the mechanical arts in a universal setting, connecting their function with that aspect of human nature which is part of the temporal, sublunary world and subject to necessity.[74] Immediately following this discussion, Hugh, in a remarkable chapter which deserves to be quoted in full, brings together facets of the relationship of the mechanical arts to the human condition, nature and God:

---

[69] For the idea of restoration in patristic thought, see Gerhart B. Ladner, *The Idea of Reform: Its Impact on Christian Thought and Action in the Age of the Fathers*, revised ed. (Cambridge, Mass.: Harvard University Press, 1959, rpt. New York, Evanston and London: Harper and Row, Harper Torchbooks, 1967).

[70] Ladner, *Idea of Reform*, 153–203, 373, 377; see, also, Peter Harte Baker, "Liberal Arts as Philosophical Liberation: St. Augustine's *De Magistro*," in *Arts libéraux et philosophie au moyen âge; Actes du quatrième Congrès international de Philosophie Médiévale* (Paris: Libraire Philosophique J. Vrin, 1969), 469–479.

[71] Taylor, ed., *Didascalicon*, 11–15.

[72] Augustine, *City of God* 14.26, *Sancti Aurelii Augustini episcopi De civitate Dei*, ed. B. Dombart (Leipzig: B. G. Teubner, 1928), 2:53–55; *De Genesi ad litteram* 8.8 and 8.10 in *Oeuvres de Saint Augustin*, 7th series, 49, *La Genèse au sens littéral en douze livres*, ed. and trans. P. Agaesse and A. Solignac, 34, 42. There is an interesting illustration of the *City of God*, c. 1100, in which the City of Cain is depicted as a battlefield and the City of God as a pastoral scene of plowing and sowing; Evans (*Medieval Drawings*, pl. 47). The plow is a carefully drawn representation of a swing or heavy plough.

[73] Augustine's idea of reform and restoration is more centered on man's terrestrial life and less contingent on a withdrawal from the world than that of the Greek Fathers but remains exclusively spiritual and moral in content; Ladner, *Idea of Reform*, 106–107, 153–167, 190–191.

[74] Taylor, ed., *Didascalicon*, 10.

Now there are three works—the work of God, the work of nature, and the work of the artificer, who imitates nature. The work of God is to create that which was not, whence we read, "In the beginning God created heaven and earth"; the work of nature is to bring forth into actuality that which lay hidden, whence we read, "Let the earth bring forth the green herb," etc.; the work of the artificer is to put together things disjoined or to disjoin those put together, whence we read, "They sewed themselves aprons." For the earth cannot create the heaven, nor can man, who is powerless to add a mere span to his stature, bring forth the green herb. Among these works, the human work, because it is not nature but only imitative of nature, is fitly called mechanical, that is adulterate, just as a skeleton key is called a "mechanical" key. How the work of the artificer in each case imitates nature is a long and difficult matter to pursue in detail. For illustration, however, we can show the matter briefly as follows: The founder who casts a statue has gazed upon man as his model. The builder who has constructed a house has taken into consideration a mountain, for, as the Prophet declares, "Thou sendest forth springs in the vales; between the midst of the hills the waters shall pass"; as the ridges of mountains retain no water, even so does a house require to be framed into a high peak that it may safely discharge the weight of pouring rains. He who first invented the use of clothes had considered how each of the growing things one by one has its proper covering by which to protect its nature from offense. Bark encircles the tree, feathers cover the bird, scales encase the fish, fleece clothes the sheep, hair garbs cattle and wild beasts, a shell protects the tortoise, and ivory makes the elephant unafraid of spears. But it is not without reason that while each living thing is born equipped with its own natural armor, man alone is brought forth naked and unarmed. For it is fitting that nature should provide a plan for those beings which do not know how to care for themselves, but that from nature's example, a better chance for trying things should be provided to man when he comes to devise for himself by his own reasoning those things naturally given to all other animals. Indeed, man's reason shines forth much more brilliantly in inventing these very things than ever it would have, had man naturally possessed them. Nor is it without cause that the proverb says: "Ingenious want hath mothered all the arts." Want it is which has devised all that you see most excellent in the occupations of men. From this the infinite varieties of painting, weaving, carving, and founding have arisen, so that we look with wonder not at nature alone but at the artificer as well.[75]

---

[75] Hugh of St. Victor, *Didascalicon* 1.9, Taylor, 55–56 (Buttimer, 16–17):

Sunt etenim tria opera, id est, opus Dei, opus naturae, opus artificis imitantis naturam. opus Dei est, quod non erat creare. unde illud: In principio creavit Deus caelum et terram. opus naturae, quod latuit ad actum producere. unde illud: Producat terra herbam virentem etc. opus artificis est disgregata coniungere vel coniuncta segregare. unde illud: Consuerunt sibi perizomata. neque enim potuit vel terra caelum creare, vel homo herbam producere, qui nec palmum ad staturam suam addere potest. in his tribus operibus convenienter opus humanum, quod natura non est sed imitatur naturam, mechanicum id est, adulterinum nominatur, quemadmodum et clavis subintroducta mechanica dicitur. qualiter autem opus artificis imitetur naturam, longum est et onerosum prosequi per singula. qui statuam fudit, hominem intuitus est. qui domum fecit, montem respexit. quia enim, ut ait propheta, qui emittis fontes in convallibus, intra medium montium perstransibunt aquae. eminentia montium aquas non retinet. ita domus in altum quoddam cacumen levanda fuit, ut irruentium tempestatum molestias tuto excipere posset. qui usum vestimentorum primus adinvenit, consideravit quod singula quaeque nascentium propria quaedam habeant munimenta quibus naturam suam ab incommodis defendunt. cortex ambit arborem, penna tegit velucrem piscem squama operit, lana ovem induit pilus iumenta et feras vestit, concha tes-

The broad context of this passage, together with the two chapters preceding it, is the classical *topos* of the nature and dignity of man. Although Hugh's version is severely condensed, he echoes some of the common themes which typically appeared in classical and patristic discussions of human dignity, including man's unique possession of body and soul and the importance of the arts both as an expression of human ingenuity and power and as a remedy for man's physical infirmities. The expression of these ideas is in some respects representative of twelfth-century humanism and appears in the work of Bernard Silvestris and the author of the *Philosophia* attributed to William of Conches and others.[76] Hugh's discussion, however, is unusual in its emphasis on the technological. If we break this passage up into its component parts, we find an intricate reworking of classical and patristic themes, juxtaposed with each other so as to emphasize man's capacity for technological invention as an essential and unique characteristic of human nature.

The comparison of the three works of man, nature and God is drawn from Chalcidius's commentary on the *Timaeus*. Chalcidius meant by the "work of nature" the ordering power of the *anima mundi*; by the work of the artificer, who imitates nature, generally any human activity reflecting that order.[77] In Hugh's interpretation the three works become three different levels of artistic production, which he illustrates, appropriately, with quotations from Genesis.[78] The reference to Genesis serves not only to help explain human, divine and natural production, but also to locate human production in Christian history. Hugh ties the facts of

tudinem excipit, ebur elephantem iacula non timere facit. nec tamen sine causa factum est quod, cum singula animantium naturae suae arma secum nata habeant, solus homo inermis nascitur et nudus. oportuit enim ut illis, quae sibi providere nesciunt, natura consuleret, homini autem ex hoc etiam major experiendi occasio praestaretur, cum illa, quae ceteris naturaliter data sunt, propria ratione sibi inveniret. multo enim nunc magis enitet ratio hominis haec eadem inveniendo quam habendo claruisset. nec sine causa proverbium sonat quod:

"Ingeniosa fames omnes excuderit artes."

hac equidem ratione illa quae nunc excellentissima in studiis hominum vides, reperta sunt. hac eadem pingendi, texendi, sculpendi, fundendi, infinita genera exorta sunt, ut iam cum natura ipsum miremur artificem.

[76] R. W. Southern, *Medieval Humanism and Other Studies* (New York: Harper and Row, Harper Torchbook, 1970), 39–43, finds the expression of the dignity and nobility of man very common in the the twelfth century. The 'Philosophia' is discussed below, pp. 105–106.

[77] Chalcidius, *Commentary* 1.23 in *Timaeus; A Calcido translatus commentarioque instructus*, ed. J. H. Waszink in association with P. J. Jensen, Vol. 4 in *Plato Latinus* (London: Warburg Institute, 1962; Leiden: E. J. Brill, 1962), 73–74.

[78] Taylor, ed. *Didascalicon*, 27, 190 n. 59 discusses differences between Chalcidius's meaning and Hugh's. For Hugh's general tendency to readapt heterodox tests for his own purposes, see Taylor, *Didascalicon*, 19–28. In his *In Ecclesiasten homiliae, 14* (*PL* 175: 215–216) Hugh speaks of four works, distinguishing between the "work of the artificer with nature" and the "work of the artificer alone without nature." A comparison of the three works also appears in William of Conches's commentaries on Boethius's *Consolation* and Plato's *Timaeus* in Joseph-Marie Parent, *La doctrine de la création dans l'école de Chartres* (Paris: Libraire Philosophique J. Vrin, 1938), 127–128, 147–148 and *Glosae super Platonem: Texte critique*, ed. Edouard Jeauneau (Paris: Librairie Philosophique J. Vrin, 1965), 104–105. The significance of this theme in the twelfth century is discussed in Chenu, *Nature, Man and Society*, 40–41.

history, for which the Bible was a key source, to a religious framework yet at the same time he never lost a sense of the literal significance of events.[79] The process of restoration has, for him, a concrete, factual dimension in part expressed in the invention, development and practice of the arts, which have not only their theoretical origins in the conditions of the post-lapsarian world but their historical origins as well. Hence Hugh explicitly identifies the mechanical arts with the first act of Adam and Eve in the fallen world—the making of clothing—and elsewhere in the *Didascalicon*, which, it should be remembered, is a guide for the study of philosophy as well as a classification of knowledge, gives a capsule history of the arts and their important authors and texts.[80]

The relationship of the work of the artificer to that of nature is one of imitation. Yet, while Hugh does not reject the idea that the powers of art are inferior to those of nature, he also suggests that the artisan can rival nature: "We look with wonder not at nature alone but at the artificer as well." Moreover, whereas the original Aristotelian meaning of art imitating nature referred to the *process* by which each imposed form upon matter, Hugh means the intelligent observation of nature by the artisan in order to make an analogous *product*.[81] The example of nature gives guidance for human effort to surpass what nature alone can provide.

The dignity of the mechanical arts lies finally in the way in which they provide an occasion for the exercise of human reason and superiority. In *Didascalicon* 1.9 Hugh uses a time-honored *topos* contrasting man's inferior physical condition "naked and unarmed" with his unique possession of both hands and reason which together render him capable of the arts. This figure, which was often part of the broader theme of the dignity of man, provides a valuable *locus* for ideas about technology

[79] On Hugh's sensitivity to history and his insistence, in contrast to Augustine, on "temporal realism" in discussion of Genesis, see Chenu, *Nature, Man and Society*, 165–173. See also the discussion of Augustine and Hugh of St. Victor in A. G. Molland, "Medieval Ideas of Scientific Progress," *Journal of the History of Ideas* 39 (1978):562–564.

[80] Hugh of St. Victor, *Didascalicon* 3.2, Taylor, 83–86 (Buttimer, 49–52). For the tradition behind Hugh's information on the inventors of the arts, see Brian P. Copenhaver, "The Historiography of Discovery in the Renaissance: The Sources and Composition of Polydore Vergil's 'De inventoribus rerum,' vols. 1–3," *Journal of the Warburg and Courtauld Institutes* 41 (1978):193–222. Hugh, unlike Arnold of Bonneval, Rupert of Deutz and Godfrey of St. Victor (see n. 18 and n. 19 above), ascribes the invention of most of the mechanical arts to pagan authors.

[81] There is a discussion comparable to Hugh's on how the artisan imitates nature in William of Conches's commentary on the *Timaeus* in *Glosae super Platonem*, ed. Jeauneau, 104–105; Parent, *Doctrine de la création*, 104. For Aristotle's understanding of art imitating nature, see M. J. Charlesworth, *Aristotle on Art and Nature*, Auckland University College Bulletin No. 50, Philosophy Series no. 2 (Auckland: Auckland University Press, 1957). Crombie, *Robert Grossteste*, translates "qualiter autem opus artificis imitetur naturam, longum est et onerosum prosequi per singula" (Hugh of St. Victor, *Didascalicon*, Buttimer, 16) as "but how the work of the artificer imitates nature is by long and burdensome pursuit of particulars."

from antiquity through the Renaissance, and its history illustrates some of the complexity of Western attitudes.[82]

In classical literature, the *topos* goes back at least to Plato and Aristotle, in whom the kernel of later classical and medieval versions is already apparent.[83] The "man unarmed" figure, which is also used by Epictetus and Pliny, reached its fullest development in antiquity in Galen's *De usu partium* and Cicero's *De natura deorum,* in which crafts exemplify the power, ingenuity and adaptability of the human race.[84]

Hugh's use of this theme, however, does not represent a straightforward reworking of these classical texts. The sources possibly available to him were, with the exception of Pliny's *Natural History*, entirely works of the Church Fathers.[85] In its patristic versions the "dignity of man" theme, as well as the narrower *topos* of "man unarmed," seems to have been more skeptical about the value of crafts. Ideas of human dignity were complicated, on one level, by Genesis 1:26, "And God said, Let us make man in our image, after our likeness," and 1:28, man's mandate of dominion over the animals, and, on a deeper level, by Judeo-Christian ideas on man's fallen condition and the process of restoration to his true, pre-lapsarian nature.[86] As Charles Trinkaus has pointed out (he

---

[82] For the concept of the dignity of man and bibliography on the subject, see Charles Trinkaus, *"In Our Image and Likeness": Humanity and Divinity in Italiian Humanist Thought* (Chicago: University of Chicago Press, 1970), 2 vols., the article by Trinkaus in *Dictionary of the History of Ideas: Studies of Selected Pivotal Ideas,* s.v. "Renaissance Idea of the Dignity of Man," and for patristic and early medieval authors, Eugenio Garin, "La 'dignitas hominis' e la litteratura patristica," *La Rinascita* 1 (1938):102–146. The figure of man "naked and unarmed" is noted in passing by Trinkaus, "In Our Image and Likeness," 2:104, 280–281 and by Gerhart Ladner, "The Philosophical Anthropology of Saint Gregory of Nyssa," *Dumbarton Oaks Papers* 12 (1958):68.

[83] Plato, *Protagoras* 320d–321d, Loeb Classical Library, 128–132; Aristotle, *Parts of Animals* 4.10, Loeb Classical Library, 373.

[84] Galen, *De usu partium* 1.2–3.6, ed. C. G. Kuhn in *G. Claudii Galeni Opera Omnia* (Leipzig: Teubner, 1822; rpt. Hildesheim: Georg Olms Verlagsbuchhandlung, 1964), 3:3–9; Cicero, *De natura deorum* 2.150–163, ed. Arthur Stanley Pease (Cambridge, Mass.: Harvard University Press, 1958), 939–964. Epictetus, *Moral Discourses.* 1.16, 1–2, Loeb Classical Library (London: Heinemann, 1925), 108–110.

[85] The sources possibly accessible to Hugh include Nemesius of Emesa, *De natura hominis* in the eleventh-century translation by Alfanus, (*Nemesii Episcopi Premnon physicon sive περὶ φύσεος ἀνφρώπου liber a n. Alfano Archiepiscopo Salerni*, ed. Carolus Burkhard (Leipzig: Teubner, 1917), Gregory of Nyssa, *De hominis opificio* in the ninth-century translation by John the Scot, under the title *Sermo de imagine,* or the late fifth-century translation by Dionysius Exiguus (*PL* 67:347–408), and Pliny, *Natural History* 7.1–5, Loeb Classical Library, 2:506–509. For the history of these texts and their availability in the early twelfth century, see Theodore Silverstein, "Guillaume de Conches and Nemesius of Emessa: On the Sources of the New Science of the Twelfth Century," in *Harry Austryn Wolfson Jubilee Volume* (Jerusalem: American Academy for Jewish Research, 1965), 2:719–734; M. L. W. Laistner, *Thought and Letters in Western Europe A.D. 500 to 900*, 2nd ed. (Ithaca, New York: Cornell University Press, Cornell Paperbacks, 1966), 247; Trinkaus, *"In Our Image and Likeness,"* 1:185–188. John the Scot's *Sermo de Imagine* has not been printed but excerpts are embedded in his *De divisione naturae* (these excerpts do not include the "man unarmed" chapter); see M. Cappuyns, *Jean Scot Érigène: sa vie, son oeuvre, sa pensée* (Brussels: Culture et Civilisation, 1964), 172–178.

[86] Trinkaus, article in the *Dictionary of the History of Ideas,* s.v. "Renaissance Idea of the Dignity of Man."

is referring to the Italian humanists, but the point has equal validity for the Church Fathers) if man's dignity lay in his creation in the image and likeness of God, this could be interpreted *either* as meaning that man could and should transcend the limitations of his mere image-likeness and, as much as possible, leave behind the physical, *or* that man could act "like a God" with respect to the sub-human, natural world.[87] If interpreted with the second meaning, crafts retain their function as an emblem of human glory and dignity. If interpreted in the first sense, however, crafts clearly become at best a distraction and at worst an insidious and dangerous temptation.

Hugh's comparison of the natural defenses of animals with man's "unarmed" state resembles those made by Nemesius of Emessa, the late fourth-century bishop and apologist, in his *De natura hominis* and by Gregory of Nyssa in his own work on the same subject, *De hominis opificio*.[88] Nemesius's text may have been accessible to Hugh in an eleventh-century translation by Alfanus, bishop of Salerno, and Gregory's in translations by Dionysius Exiguus and John the Scot.[89] Nemesius, who draws upon Aristotle, Posidonius and Galen, includes many standard elements: man is the link between the physical and incorporeal worlds; all other creatures are made for his use; man's indigence and nakedness lead him to practice all the arts—clothing, the preparation of food, building, medicine and city life.[90] The account concludes with a eulogy to the arts, which, he says, expresses the preeminence of man's place in the universe. But his final words, in which he reminds us that such things must be seen in the context of eternal blessedness and should not be bartered for "a brief season of pleasure," show an underlying ambivalence.[91] However much Nemesius may have been influenced by Stoic and other classical authors toward a more positive assessment of crafts, in this context, at least, he ultimately sees a basic opposition between attention to technology and eternal salvation. Unlike Hugh, who defines the mechanical arts as an essential part of the human effort to recover and restore humanity's true nature, Nemesius considers crafts potentially alienating from that task. This view is reinforced by a curious account of the Fall in which the eating of the fruit of the tree of knowledge was forbidden not because it would confer

[87] Trinkaus, article in the *Dictionary of the History of Ideas*, s.v. "Renaissance Idea of the Dignity of Man."

[88] Nemesius of Emesa, *De natura hominis* (*PG* 40:503–816); Gregory of Nyssa, *De hominis opificio* (*PG* 44:137–256); see n. 85 above.

[89] Silverstein, "Guillaume de Conches and Nemesius of Emessa," 727.

[90] Nemesius, *De natura hominis* 1 (*PG* 40:517–524); Alfanus, *Premmon physicon* 1, Burkhard, 14–15. There are a modern commentary and translation of this section, William Telfer, *Cyril of Jerusalem and Nemesius of Emesa*, Library of Christian Classics, 4 (Philadelphia: Westminster Press, 1955), 242–244. See also Alberto Siclari, *L'Antropologia di Nemesio di Emesa* (Padua: Editrice "La Garangola," 1974), 254–257.

[91] Nemesius, *De natura hominis* 1 (*PG* 40:533–536); Alfanus, *Premmon physicon* 1, Burkhard, 22–23; see also Telfer, *Cyril of Jerusalem and Nemesius of Emesa*, 254–257.

knowledge of good and evil but because it would impart full awareness of human physical weakness, causing people to devote all their concern to the care of the body (i.e. technology) and to neglect their souls.[92]

Gregory of Nyssa's version, which depends upon many of the same sources as Nemesius's, has a more positive tone on the arts and, as Gerhart Ladner has pointed out, Gregory links man's upright posture and the function of his hands to the origin of language, man's spiritual life, and his mastery of creation.[93] Gregory describes how the apparent deficiency of the human body is in fact a means for obtaining dominion over the animals, which supply us with wool, labor, leather for armor and shoes, and feathers for our arrows.[94] Yet Gregory refers to human art or craft only in the relatively limited context of weapons and the domestication of animals and, in the end, finds the possession of hands important not so much for their usefulness in making or handling of instruments, as because they free the body for an upright posture and the mouth for speech.[95] Hugh's treatment of crafts in the "man unarmed" *topos* and dignity of man theme, in contrast, comes from a wider perspective and implies a far broader role for crafts.

The sole classical source accessible to Hugh, Pliny's *Natural History*, contains an unusually negative version of the "man unarmed" figure. For Pliny, man's lack of natural defenses is a sign of his misery. Of all the animals man alone at his birth is nude; even trees have bark, but man is born naked on the naked ground to weep and wail and alone must depend upon borrowed resources.[96]

The most pointed contrast with Hugh's views, however, is in Augustine's *City of God*. The profound influence of Augustine on Hugh makes their divergence on the value of crafts all the more striking. Augustine, who never entirely loses his interest in the material world, at times, as we have seen, shows an appreciation of crafts. Yet Augustine's comments are often tempered by the same moral suspicion we have seen in Nemesius and, in other contexts, in Plato. This is nowhere clearer than in chapter 24 of book 22 of the *City of God*, which comprises a short treatise on the dignity of man, written with direct reference to the account of the same subject in Cicero's *De natura deorum*.[97] Franco Alessio has suggested that Hugh derived the names of his seven mechanical

---

[92] Nemesius, *De natura hominis* 1 (*PG* 40:514–516); Alfanus, *Premmon physicon* 1, Burkhard, 12.

[93] Ladner, "Anthropology of Gregory of Nyssa," 68.

[94] Gregory of Nyssa, *De hominis opificio* 8.1, 8, (*PG* 44:144); Dionysius Exiguus, *De creatione hominis*, (*PL* 67:354–355).

[95] Gregory of Nyssa, *De hominis opificio* 8.1, 8, (*PG* 44;144); Dionysius Exiguus, *De creatione hominis*, (*PL* 67:354–355).

[96] Pliny, *Natural History* 7.1–5, Loeb Classical Library, 2:506–509.

[97] Augustine, *De civitate Dei*, 22.24, ed. B. Dombart, revised by A. Kalb (Leipzig: Teubner, 1928), 2:609–616. On the relationship of the ideas in this passage to Cicero's *De natura deorum*, see Maurice Testard, *Saint Augustin et Cicéron*, (Paris: Études Augustiniennes, 1958). For Augustine's ideas on craft, see above Chapter II, pp. 49–50, 52–55.

arts from the catalogue of the arts and sciences given here by Augustine and that Cicero, Augustine and Hugh form a continuing tradition in praise of human power and art.[98] It is very likely that Hugh considered this chapter, which has often been assumed to be a straightforward panegyric on the arts, a context for his discussion of man's dual mortal and immortal nature and man's reason expressed through art. The congruence between some of the arts catalogued by Augustine and Hugh's list of the mechanical arts in the *Didascalicon*, pointed out by Alessio, is indeed striking.[99] Yet the tone of the two accounts is very different. Augustine's point is that God in his infinite mercy has provided us with certain consolations in our mortal existence, even though this existence is unhappy, depraved and, ultimately, condemned to sin.[100] For Augustine, the arts at once exemplify the "natural genius" of man and are "superfluous, perilous and pernicious":

> And, quite apart from those supernatural arts of living in virtue and of reaching immortal beatitude which nothing but the grace of God which is in Christ can communicate to the sons of promise and heirs of the kingdom, there have been discovered and perfected, by the natural genius of man, innumerable arts and skills which minister not only to the necessities of life but also to human enjoyment. And even in those arts where the purposes may seem superfluous, perilous and pernicious, there is exercised an acuteness of intelligence of so high an order that it reveals how richly endowed our human nature is. For, it has the power of inventing, learning and applying all such arts.[101]

---

[98] Alessio, "Filosofia e la 'artes mechanicae'," 114–116, 128–129. Modern interpretations of this passage in *City of God* 22,24 have varied widely. Glacken, *Traces on the Rhodian Shore*, 199, finds this passage "surprising" because it "generously praises human intelligence, skill and creativity." Ernest L. Fortin, "Augustine, the Arts and Human Progress," in *Technology and Theology: Essays in Christian Analysis and Exegesis*, ed. Carl Mitcham and Jim Grote (Lanham, New York and London: University Press of America, 1984), 200, says that the passage "expatiates in rhapsodic terms on the resourcefulness of the human mind and the splendor of its accomplishments" and Ovitt, "Status of the Mechanical Arts," 95, n. 33 describes the passage as the "*locus classicus* for the salvationary efficacy of the works of the hands." On the other hand, White, "Cultural Climates," 196, says, "At the end of *De civitate Dei*, Saint Augustine discusses technology in a mood of complete ambivalence." Maurice de Gandillac, "Place et signification de la technique dans le monde médiéval," in *Tecnica e casistica* (Padua: Casa Editrice Dott. Antonio Milani, 1964), 273, remarks that if the Victorines were inspired by this text, it is clear that they gave it another sense than Augustine's original one, and Karl Morrison, *The Mimetic Tradition of Reform in the West* (Princeton: Princeton University Press, 1982), 76, characterizes the passage as "ambiguous." Serge Lusignan, "Les arts mécaniques dans le *Speculum Doctrinale* de Vincent de Beauvais," in *Cahiers d'études médiévals*, 7:39, also connects this passage in the *City of God* with the *Didascalicon*, but apparently finds no great difference in the meaning of the two texts. See also the discussion of the passage in Robin Attfield, "Christian Attitudes to Nature," *Journal of the History of Ideas* 44 (1983):377.

[99] Alessio, "Filosofia e le 'artes mechanicae,'" 115–116.

[100] Augustine, *City of God* 22.24, *De civitate Dei*, ed. Dombart, 2:609.

[101] Augustine, *De civitate Dei* 22.24, *The City of God*, trans. Gerald G. Walsh and Daniel J. Honan, *The Fathers of the Church: A New Translation*, 24 (Washington, D.C.: The Catholic University of America Press, 1954), 484 (Dombart, 2:612):

> Praeter enim artes bene vivendi et ad inmortalem perveniendi felicitatem, quae virtutes vocantur

Augustine's list of the arts, examined carefully, includes not only architecture, the manufacture of clothing, agriculture, navigation, sculpture, medicine, cookery, rhetoric, geography, arithmetic, music and philosophy but also hunting, the making of theaters, poisons, weapons, and war machines, and "lastly the brilliance . . . displayed by both pagan philosophers and Christian heretics in the defense of error and falsehood."[102] Throughout the chapter, he repeats, not without irony, that he is speaking only of man's mortal being, not of faith, truth or eternal life.[103] His presentation is, in fact, an elegant statement of profound ambivalence toward crafts which draws upon both the classical and the Christian critique of technology.

Nemesius, Gregory of Nyssa, Augustine and Hugh all see technological arts as in some sense a remedy for the physical discomforts of man's post-lapsarian life. Yet while Nemesius and Augustine consider this remedy a necessary evil to be carefully limited and controlled and Gregory sees a useful but very restricted role for the arts, the tone and working of Hugh's presentation of the "man unarmed" theme, as well as the first two books of the *Didascalicon* in general, suggest a far more positive understanding:

For it is fitting . . . that from nature's example, a better chance for trying things should be provided to man when he comes to devise for himself by his own reasoning things naturally given to all other animals . . . Indeed, man's reason shines forth much more brilliantly in inventing these things then ever it would have had man naturally possessed them . . . Want it is which has devised all that you see most excellent in the occupations of men . . . we look with wonder not at nature alone but at the artificer as well.[104]

---

et sola Dei gratia, quae in Christo est, filiis promissionis regnique donantur, nonne humano ingenio tot tantaeque artes sunt inventae et exercitae, partim necesssariae partim voluptariae, ut tam excellens vis mentis atque rationis in his etiam rebus, quas superfluas immo et periculosas perniciosasque appetit, quantum bonum habeat in natura, unde ista potuit vel invenire vel discere vel exercere, testetur?

[102] Augustine, *De civitate Dei* 22.24, trans. Walsh and Honan (ed. Dombart, 2:612–613): ". . . erroribus et falsitatibus defendis quam magna claruerint ingenia philosophorum atque haereticorum . . ."

[103] Augustine, *De civitate Dei* 22.24, ed. Dombart, 2:609–616.

[104] Hugh of St. Victor, *Didascalicon* 1.9, Taylor, 56 (Buttimer, 17). See above, n. 75 for the Latin text. The "man unarmed" figure also appears in Adelard of Bath, *Quaestiones naturales*, ed. Martin Muller in *Beiträge zur Geschichte der Philosophie des Mittelalters* 31 (1934):19–21 (translated in *Dodi Ve-nechdi the work of Berachya Hanakden . . . to which is added the first English translation from the Latin of Adelard of Bath's Quaestiones naturales*, trans. Hermann Gollancz (London: H. Milford, 1920, 106–108) and Thomas Aquinas, *Summa theologiae* la. 91.3, ed. Blackfriars, 13:29, although neither of these passages focuses as clearly on technology as does Hugh's version. The figure also appears in Petrarch's *De remediis utriusque fortunae* 2.93, a version strikingly close in meaning and language to the *Didascalicon* 1.9, and Benedetto Morandi's *Of Human Happiness*; see Trinkaus, "In Our Image and Likeness," 1:294, 280–282. Brian Stock, *Myth and Science in the Twelfth Century: A Study of Bernard Silvester* (Princeton: Princeton University Press, 1972), 225, suggests the *Asclepius* as a source for the *Didascalicon*; cf. Taylor, *Didascalicon*, 184, n. 32, who notes that, although Hugh knows the *Asclepius*, there are essential differences between Hugh's conception of the mechanical arts and the arts for the tending of the earth as they appear in the *Asclepius*.

The mechanical arts are presented as part of a divine plan which includes both man's need and capacity to develop technology. Carefully justifying the mechanical arts as an expression of reason and as part of the religious quest for salvation, Hugh gives technology both intellectual and moral sanction. He thus begins to resolve the ambivalence toward technology which troubled many Western thinkers since the time of Plato and Aristotle.

Hugh's method of resolution grew out of and reflects his own intellectual roots. From Augustine, Hugh drew the basic idea that knowledge, properly conceived and used, must direct men toward salvation. In this sense, for both him and Augustine, all knowledge, even the theoretical sciences, is ultimately functional, for the value of knowledge lies not in its existence for its own sake but in its efficacy in promoting man's supernatural end. From the early Middle Ages, Hugh inherited the skeleton idea of the mechanical arts, a pragmatic attitude toward learning and the acceptance of concrete and practical information as part of the content of philosophy. Building upon these roots, Hugh outlined a definition and justification of the mechanical arts which established them as fully legitimate parts of philosophy more thoroughly and thoughtfully than had earlier writers. He thus went a long way toward answering the charges of irrationality and immorality which had been commonly leveled against crafts. As we shall now see, his contemporaries and later medieval thinkers, recognizing his achievement, enthusiastically adopted the *artes mechanicae* and the ideas associated with them and made crafts a regularly accepted category of knowledge.

The "artes mechanicae" in the Late Twelfth and Thirteenth Centuries

The importance of Hugh of St. Victor's conception of the *artes mechanicae* is clear not only from the originality and cohesiveness of his work but also in the status accorded him by historians of science and technology: in almost every treatment of medieval ideas about technology, Hugh is given a major place.[105] Perhaps as an unintended consequence of this enthusiasm, Hugh's work has often been tacitly presented as if it were an isolated effort which had little effect on medieval thought as a whole. Few studies cite more than one or two examples of authors who followed Hugh's lead, and little attention has been paid to evaluating the overall position of the mechanical arts in the late twelfth and thirteenth centuries.[106] Yet even as Hugh's ideas depended upon,

---

105 See above pp. 17, 18, 20, 83.

106 The exception is Sternagel, *Artes Mechanicae*, 85–102, which provides an excellent and thorough survey of authors and texts influenced by Hugh; Sternagel, however, gives little analysis of the ideas presented in these works. Ovitt, "The Status of the Mechanical Arts," 97, n. 40, refers to a Victorine legacy, but discusses the influence of Hugh only on Bonaventure and Robert Kilwardby. Ovitt, *Restoration of Perfection*, 120–121, also mentions

and grew out of, a long-standing early medieval tradition, he himself contributed to the formation of new patterns of thought about technology. As we shall see below, numerous quotations and adoptions of his conception of the mechanical arts appeared throughout the high and late Middle Ages and into the Renaissance. This influence, moreover, was widespread, surfacing in authors from a great variety of philosophical orientations. Not only were there over twenty-four separate instances of the direct or indirect quotation or paraphrasing from Hugh on the mechanical arts in the twelfth and thirteenth centuries alone but distant echoes of his theological rationale for technology reappear even into the modern era.[107]

Hugh and his followers did not, of course, entirely overcome the deep-seated heritage of suspicion toward technology in classical and medieval thought. Traces of this distrust remain in Hugh's work itself, most notably in his designation of the mechanical arts as "adulterine." Although the negative connotations of this tag do not predominate in Hugh or most of his followers, the identification was more often repeated than rejected. As Peter Sternagel has suggested, in a few cases the implication of impurity or falsity was explicitly reinforced.[108] Furthermore, the mechanical arts, even if included within philosophy, were often ranked last among the parts of knowledge and were sometimes considered, in contrast with physics, mathematics or grammar, in a certain sense "servile."[109] Outside the specific arena of classifications of knowledge, also, negative attitudes toward technological arts persisted. Despite significant changes in the way the Church and society viewed professions, Bernard of Clairvaux, Peter the Chanter, Pope Innocent III, Berthold of Regensburg and others eloquently preached the vanity and superfluousness of technological endeavors.[110] Although merchants seemed to

---

Godfrey of St. Victor. Alessio, "Filosofia e le 'artes mechanicae,'" 121–125, mentions Kilwardby, Richard and Godfrey of St. Victor, Radulfus Ardens and several unedited manuscripts as containing Hugh's classification of the mechanical arts but concentrates on the first half of the twelfth century. Even less comprehensive are De Gandillac, "Place et signification," 272–273, which emphasizes the importance of Richard of St. Victor; Beaujouan, "Réflexions," 439, 441, and Pedersen, "Du quadrivium à la physique," 115, which single out Hugh of St. Victor and Domingo Gundisalvo and give little indication of their influence; Lynn White, "Cultural Climates," 198, which mentions only Hugh and, briefly, Richard of St. Victor and "Medieval Engineering," 11, which cites Hugh and "several of his contemporaries," as attempting to give an intellectual status to technology.

107 Sternagel, *Artes Mechanicae*, 85–102, has collected most of the examples of the use of Hugh's classification of the mechanical arts in the twelfth and thirteenth centuries; I have located several additional instances. Francis Bacon at the end of the *Novum Organum, Aphorism* 42, expresses a conception of technology as made necessary by the Fall and as a divinely sanctioned part of man's efforts to restore and repair himself, which is remarkably similar to Hugh's. See below, p. 126.

108 Sternagel, *Artes Mechanicae*, 89–91. See also Allard, "Les arts mécaniques," 15–19.

109 Thomas Aquinas, *Summa theologiae* la2ae, 57, 3.3, ed. Blackfriars, 23:48; Bonaventure, *De reductione artium ad theologiam*, 2, ed. Sister Emma Therese Healy, *Saint Bonaventure's De reductione artium* (Saint Bonaventure, N.Y.: Saint Bonaventure College, 1939), 38.

110 Probably the most famous example is Innocent III's diatribe *De contemptu mundi* 14, in which he surveys human activities, including travel, metallurgy, weaving, carpentry,

have gained a considerable degree of social status in the twelfth, thirteenth and fourteenth centuries, this advance was only briefly, if at all, shared by small artisans and laborers.[111] Moreover, as Lynn White and others have pointed out, the new classifications of learning did not affect the curriculum actually taught at schools and universities.[112]

The persistence of a certain ambivalence, however, should not obscure the thoroughness with which the mainstream of medieval thought absorbed Hugh of St. Victor's ideas on the mechanical arts. The *Didascalicon*, continually read from its appearance in 1130, had an influence both "immediate and penetrating."[113] By the end of the twelfth century, the rubric *artes mechanicae* had become the normal term for technological arts, even among authors who otherwise followed the Aristotelian-Arabic classifications of the sciences, and these arts were a regular and expected part of knowledge.[114] Over the next century, authors associated with such diverse schools as Chartres, the philosophical circle around Abelard, the mystical theologians at St. Victor, and the followers of Gilbert de la Porrée, dubbed the Porretani, adopted Hugh's vision of the mechanical arts. By the end of the thirteenth century, many of the most important classifiers of the arts and sciences, including Albertus Magnus, Bonaventure, Robert Kilwardby and Vincent of Beauvais, had used Hugh's ideas. Toward the close of that century personifications of the mechanical arts named by Hugh began to appear in church sculpture and manuscript illuminations.[115] Widely-read epitomes of philosophy such as the *Speculum vitae humanae* (c. 1475) and the *Margarita philosophica* (1504) reproduced Hugh's cycle of the arts and show that the mechanical

---

agriculture, milling, hunting, commerce and warfare, ending with the quotation from Ecclesiastes 2:11 "All is vanity." The text is in *PL* 207:707–708 and it has been translated along with Giannozzo Manetti's answer, by Bernard Murchland, *Two Views of Man* (New York: Frederick Ungar Publishing Co., 1966). For criticism of contemporary building and architecture as extravagant, superfluous, and immoral by Bernard of Clairvaux, Peter the Chanter, and others, see Baldwin, *Masters, Princes and Merchants*, 1:66–69. See also M.-D. Chenu, "Arts 'mécaniques' et oeuvres serviles," *Revue des sciences philosophiques et théologiques* 29 (1940):313–315, and Allard, "Les arts mécaniques," 24–29 and, especially, Ovitt, *Restoration of Perfection*, 150–160 for monastic criticisms of manual labor as outside the primary concerns of the religious life.

[111] Le Goff, "Licit and Illicit Trades in the Medieval West," 69–70.

[112] White "Medieval Engineering," 13–14 and Weisheipl, "Classification of the Sciences," 66.

[113] Taylor, ed., *Didascalicon*, 4, where Taylor also discusses the survival of almost one hundred manuscripts of the *Didascalicon* dating from the twelfth to the fifteenth centuries.

[114] Those works in which Hugh's classification of the *artes mechanicae* appears are discussed in the present chapter; those which use Aristotelian or Arabic classifications of technological arts, even though they may also be influenced by Hugh, are discussed below, Chapter V. There are, in addition, authors who simply use the term *artes mechanicae* without an explicit classification of crafts, such as John of Salisbury, and Otto of Freising and for these, see Sternagel, *Artes Mechanicae*, 54, 58, 90, 94.

[115] Van Marle, *Iconographie de l'art profane*, 2:252–260; Mâle, *The Gothic Image*, 64–75; Evans, *Medieval Drawings*, pl. 89. See however Michael Evans, "Allegorical Women and Practical Men: The Iconography of the *artes* Reconsidered," in *Medieval Women*, ed. Derek Baker (Oxford: Blackwell, 1984), 324–328, who argues that illustrations of the Victorine cycle of the mechanical arts did not appear until the fifteenth century.

arts as named and conceived by Hugh were still part of European culture into the fifteenth and sixteenth centuries.[116]

This tradition, moreover, was not a static one. The interaction between changing currents of thought on the nature and function of knowledge, especially the enormous impact of Aristotle and his Arabic commentators, and increasing awareness of the social and environmental effects of technological growth, produced a constant reworking and revising of Hugh's original scheme. For some authors, revision was confined to the problem of which arts properly belonged to the *artes mechanicae*. No art named by Hugh entirely escaped criticism and some, in particular *navigatio, medicina* and *theatrica,* aroused considerable comment. More fundamental changes occurred when thinkers brought to bear their own philosophical orientations and developed or emphasized different elements in Hugh's thought. In the last half of the thirteenth century, for example, there was a marked tendency to reconcile or, at least, combine Hugh's Augustinian view of knowledge with the new Aristotelian and Arabic scientific learning. Throughout the twelfth and thirteenth centuries thinkers not only repeated Hugh's ideas and list of the mechanical arts but were actively engaged in defining and redefining technological arts as a part of human knowledge. If we look at some of these works more closely, we can see the continuing vitality of this tradition.

THE TWELFTH CENTURY. Hugh's scheme quickly appeared in works of the middle and late twelfth century and was as quickly revised. The introduction to a partial translation of Euclid's *Elements* (the so-called Abelard Version III, a work of uncertain provenance), for example, divides *mechanica* into Hugh's seven arts, but positions them, along with ethics and the liberal arts, as the parts of practical knowledge.[117] A commentary on the *Aeneid,* long attributed to the eclectic poet, philosopher and humanist, Bernard Silvestris, but recently shown to be more probably by an unknown master associated with Chartres or Tours, also repeats the seven mechanical arts but included them after *sapientia, eloquentia* and *poesis* as the fourth part of philosophy.[118] The same master

[116] The *Speculum vitae humanae* by Bishop Roderigo of Zamora (Ruy Sánchez de Arévalo) (Augsburg: Gunther Zainer, 1471); G. Reisch, *Margarita philosophica* (Freiburg: Opera Joannis Schotti, 1504). The classification of the sciences in the *Margarita philosophica* is reproduced in Lisa Jardine, *Francis Bacon: Discovery and the Art of Discourse* (Cambridge: Cambridge University Press, 1974), 103. See also Evans, "Allegorical Women," 325, for an example from the seventeenth century.

[117] See Marshall Clagett, "King Alfred and the *Elements of Euclid,*" *Isis* 45 (154):274 for the text.

[118] Bernard Silvestris (?), *Commentum super sex libros Eneidios Virgilii* 6, Julian Ward Jones and Elizabeth Frances Jones, *The Commentary on the first Six Books of the "Aeneid" of Vergil Commonly Attributed to Bernardus Silvestris* (Lincoln, Nebraska and London: University of Nebraska Press, 1977), 32. The work has been translated by Earl G. Schreiber and Thomas E. Maresca, *Commentary on the First Six Books of Virgil's "Aeneid"* (Lincoln, Nebraska and London: University of Nebraska Press, 1979) and is discussed by J. Reginald O'Donnell, "The Sources and Meaning of Bernard Silvester's Commentary on the Aeneid," *Medieval Studies* 24 (1962) 233–259. For the authorship of the work see Jones and Jones, *Commentary on the "Aeneid,"* ix–xi and Stock, *Myth and Science,* 36–37, who agree that probably neither this commentary nor the one on Martianus Capella discussed below are by Bernard.

is also most likely the author of a commentary on Martianus Capella's *Marriage of Mercury and Philology*, which describes *mechanica* as made up of wool-working, architecture, the making of arms, navigation, hunting, agriculture, medicine and magic.[119]

Such revision of the names of the individual mechanical arts was common. Alessio cites an anonymous twelfth-century tract on the divisions of the sciences which substitutes painting (*pictura*) for *theatrica*.[120] An anonymous early twelfth-century introduction to theology, the *Ysagoge in theologiam* by an author associated with the school of Abelard, reduces the mechanical arts to five by omitting theater and medicine and also substitutes architecture for *armatura*.[121] The *Ysagoge*, like the commentary on the *Aeneid* attributed to Bernard Silvestris, places *mechanica* as the fourth category of knowledge, after *sapientia, eloquentia* and *poesis*[122] and, like it, defines mechanics as "in truth, the knowledge of human works serving corporeal necessities."[123]

A late twelfth- or early thirteenth-century didactic poem, the "Ordo artium," also follows the four-fold division of knowledge of the *Ysagoge* and the *Aeneid* commentary. The author, however, perhaps influenced by Hugh's incidental reference to "infinite varieties" of crafts, greatly expands the field of the mechanical arts of which, he says, "there is no closed number of kinds."[124] His examples combine some of Hugh's list (*armatura, medicine, navigatio*) with new arts (*mercatura*, magic, *ars Tripolemi* and *ars Cereris* or agriculture, *ars Vulcani* or forging, pottery and shoemaking).[125] Another work of the same period, a commentary on Alain de Lille's *Anticlaudianus* by his disciple, Raoul de Longchamps, also suggests that there are "infinite kinds" of mechanical arts, but he names only seven, using Hugh's list with the exception of *chirurgia*, which he substitutes for medicine.[126] His brief descriptions of the seven

---

[119] An excerpt on the divisions of knowledge from this work is printed in Jones and Jones, ed., *Commentary on the "Aeneid,"* Appendix C, 131–133.

[120] Alessio, "Filosofia e le 'artes mechanicae,'" 124.

[121] *Ysagoge in theologiam* 1, *Écrits théologiques de l'école d'Abélard*, ed. Arthur Landgraf, Spicilegium Sacrum Lovaniense, Études et documents, 14 (Louvain: Spicilegium Sacrum Lovaniense, 1934), 72–73.

[122] *Ysagoge in theologiam* 1, *Écrits théologiques*, ed. Landgraf, 72.

[123] *Ysagoge in theologiam* 1, *Écrits théologiques*, ed. Landgraf, 72; *Commentary on the "Aeneid,"* ed. Jones and Jones, 32: "Mechanica vero est scientia humanorum operum corporeis necessitatibus obsequentium." The manuscript of the *Ysagoge* contains a note substituting magic for theater and adding architecture. See Landgraf, 72.

[124] The text of the poem (c. 1200) is edited in Ludwig Gompf, "Der Leipziger 'Ordo artium,'" *Mittel-Lateinisches Jahrbuch* 3 (1966) 94–128, 114: "Sunt mechanicorum/Nullo clauso numero species laborum." For Hugh's remark, see above, p. 86.

[125] *Ordo artium*, ed. Gompf, 113–114.

[126] Raoul de Longchamps, *Commentary on the Anticlaudianus of Alanus de Insulis*, ed. Jan Sulovsky (Warsaw: Zaklad Narodowy im. Ossolinskitch, 1972), 44. The switch from medicine to surgery as one of the mechanical arts may reflect the maneuverings of medical professors seeking prestige for their discipline by associating medicine itself with natural philosophy, as suggested by Darrel W. Amundsen, "Medicine and Surgery as Art or Craft: The Role of Schematic Literature in the Separation of Medicine and Surgery in the Middle Ages," *Transactions and Studies of the College of Physicians of Philadelphia* 1 (1979):124–125.

arts explain how each expels a defect or difficulty; wool-working, for example, expels cold. Navigation, hunting and agriculture expel poverty and theater lessens dislike by encouraging attentiveness and delight.[127]

Many of these treatises, as well as others, adopted not only Hugh's classification of the *artes mechanicae* but also his definition of the branches of knowledge as specific remedies for the difficulties of the human condition. The *Ysagoge in theologiam*, the commentaries on the *Aeneid*, and Martinaus Capella, and Raoul de Longchamp's commentary on the *Anticlaudianus*, like the *Didascalicon*, define the arts and sciences as means to counter the evils of ignorance, vice and physical infirmity which resulted from the Fall.[128] At least ten other authors of the twelfth and thirteenth centuries, the most important of whom are discussed below, also use the formula of corresponding intellectual, moral and technological remedies derived from Hugh as the philosophical basis for their approach to knowledge.[129] The conception of knowledge as a remedy for the ills of man's post-lapsarian life was, as we have seen, not new in the twelfth century; its long history extends back at least to the Church Fathers. The expansion of the idea to include technology as a restorative to the body, just as philosophy healed the soul, however, reflects the broadening horizons of the twelfth and thirteenth centuries, and, in particular, the growing preoccupation with the possibility of mastering the physical world. Other thinkers of the period, for example, Bonaventure and Roger Bacon, use similar ideas also developed from Augustinian roots to underscore the common function of knowledge, including technological expertise, as handmaiden to theology.[130] For all these thinkers, God-given knowledge is necessary in order to survive the present problems of our fallen life and, further, the solutions to these problems were assumed to feed the religious quest. The diffusion of these ideas clearly helped to open the door to acceptance of the mechanical arts. For how could the mechanical arts be rejected when they, like all knowledge, serve the ultimate remedy of salvation?

This seminal idea took different forms as authors related it to their

---

[127] Raoul de Longchamps, *Commentary on the Anticlaudianus*, ed. Sulovsky, 44. Medicine appears as "terrestrial physics" and is subdivided into theoretical and practical, 41.

[128] *Ysagoge in theologiam* 1, *Écrits théologiques*, ed. Landgraf, 70–71; Bernard Silvestris (?), *Commentary on the "Aeneid,"* ed. Jones and Jones, 36; Bernard Silvestris (?), *Commentary on Martianus Capella*, ed. Jones and Jones, Appendix C, 131; Raoul de Longchamps, *Commentary on the Anticlaudianus*, ed. Sulovsky, 39.

[129] L. M. de Rijk, "Some Notes on the Twelfth Century Topic of the Three (Four) Human Evils and of Science, Virtue, and Techniques as Their Remedies," *Vivarium* 5 (1967): 8–15, has collected nine authors (Richard of St. Victor, ps.-William of Conches, Ralph of Beauvais, ps.-Bernard Silvestris, Raoul de Longchamps, and the authors of four unedited manuscripts) who use this formula, all ultimately traceable to Hugh of St. Victor (9). The formula is also used in the *Ysagoge in theologiam* and the *Commentary on Martianus Capella*, as noted above, n. 128 and by Radulfus Ardens and Vincent of Beauvais; see below pp. 105–106, 110, 116. The terms for the evils and their remedies vary; see de Rijk, "Notes on the Topic of the Evils and Their Remedies," 15.

[130] See below, pp. 112–114, 125–126.

own thought and preoccupations. One of the earliest works to turn Hugh's ideas in a new direction was the *Philosophia*, a compendium of philosophy which has been attributed both to William of Conches (1080–1154) and to Hugh of St. Victor, but has more recently been reassigned to a disciple of William's.[131] The author, like Hugh, regards the arts, including crafts, as remedies for the evils created by the Fall and, also like Hugh, is concerned with placing the classification of knowledge in a broad philosophical setting. Unlike Hugh, however, he is less interested in outlining the content of philosophy than in determining how philosophy related to the structure of the universe. The first book of the *Philosophia* covers the divisions of knowledge and, without naming its source, includes extensive quotations from the *Didascalicon* on the mechanical arts and the defense of these arts explicated in the *Didascalicon* (1.4,8 and 9 and 2.20); the second book discusses God, the Trinity, demons and the *anima mundi*.[132] Hugh's account of the "three works" of God, nature and man and his use of the "man unarmed" *topos* to demonstrate the appropriateness of the human need for technology appear almost *verbatim* in the *Philosophia*, where they fit smoothly into the naturalistic viewpoint of the work.

The additions made by the author also might be seen to reflect the perspective of a student of natural philosophy. He borrows, for example, Hugh's description of the parts of magic but, while he admits that magic is remote from philosophy, he considerably softens Hugh's condemnation of its practice. The author of the *Philosophia* not only discards Hugh's remark that magic lies about the truth, infects men's minds, seduces them from divine religion and impels people to criminal indulgence, but also attaches the history of magic to a legend usually associated with the liberal arts (according to which two columns, one of stone and one of brick, were inscribed with all known knowledge in order to preserve this knowledge from destruction in the Flood).[133]

Other details also suggest a thoughtful revision of Hugh's *Didascalicon*. To Hugh's explanation of the mechanical arts as "adulterine" because they imitate nature, the author adds the further comment that these arts also deliberate first in reason and later manifest themselves in a work.[134] *Armatura* is imaginatively expanded to include "defense" by clerics, and

---

[131] The work known as the *Philosophia* is edited under the name of William of Conches, *Un brano inedito della "Philosophia" di Guglielmo di Conches*, Carmelo Ottaviano, ed. (Naples: Alberto Morano Editore, 1935). For the question of authorship see Lemay, *Abu Ma'shar*, 160–161, and Gregory, *Anima mundi*, 28–40, who concludes that the work is by a disciple of William. The *Philosophia* is also discussed in Southern, *Medieval Humanism*, 42–44. It should not be confused with the *De philosophia mundi*, authentically by William.

[132] Ps.-William of Conches, *Philosophia*, ed. Ottaviano, 25, 31. The discussion of the three evils and their remedies is on 22–23.

[133] Ibid., 35–36; Hugh of St. Victor, *Didascalicon* 6.15, Taylor, Appendix B, 154–155, Buttimer, 132. For the legend of the inscribed columns, see Cora Lutz, "Remigius' Ideas on the Origin of the Seven Liberal Arts," *Medievalia et Humanistica* 10 (1956):41, 43–49.

[134] Ps.-William of Conches, *Philosophia*, ed. Ottaviano, 31.

the author makes a point of justifying theater or games on the grounds that they were discovered to refresh the body and soul through delight and activity, two things most necessary to human life.[135]

Most importantly, however, the author of the *Philosophia*, as suggested by his association of the Church with defense mentioned above, links his plan of knowledge closely to a comparable plan of society. This sociological aspect, almost completely lacking in Hugh's thought, is brought out in the opening sections of the work in which the author describes an analogy between the excellences of the human body and the body politic: as the head is the citadel, so the arms represent soldiers guarding the whole, the stomach and knees represent artisans and workers (*opifices*), the bones and blood, business men (*negotiatores*) and the feet, farmers.[136] A similar comparison appears in the commentary on the *Aeneid* attributed to Bernard Silvestris and in John of Salisbury's *Policratus*. The striking aspect of the version in the *Philosophia*, however, is its positive emphasis on commerce and the mechanical arts, which together occupy the greater part of the community. In comparison, the *Aeneid* commentary leaves out artisans and styles merchants as *cuppedinarii*, associating them with cupidity and avarice, while John of Salisbury lumps farmers and all the mechanical arts together as "the feet who discharge the humbler offices."[137] Moreover, the author of the *Philosophia* immediately reinforces his view by repeating Hugh's notion of the three evils and their remedies, but with the significant addition of the corresponding professions which practice these remedies. Wisdom, which guards against ignorance, he says, is pursued by men of learning; virtue, which guards against vice, is pursued by men of religion; and conveniences (*commoda*) which guard against infirmity are sought by businessmen of the world (*negotiatores mundani*).[138] The mechanical arts, therefore, like other branches of knowledge, do not exist in an intellectual vacuum but are an essential part of human life and society to be practiced as well as studied.

Like the author of the *Philosophia*, Hugh's successors at St. Victor, Richard and Godfrey, incorporate the *artes mechanicae* into the pattern of their own thought. Although both were better known as theologians and mystics, they both, nevertheless, produced major encyclopedic works which included a discussion of the content and divisions of phi-

---

[135] Ibid., 32, 34.

[136] Ibid., 21.

[137] Bernard Silvestris (?), *Commentary on the "Aeneid,"* ed. Jones and Jones, 23; John of Salisbury, *Policraticus* 6.20, *Ioannis Saresberiensis episcopi Carnotensis Policraticus sive de nugis curialium et vestigiis philosophorum libri VIII*, ed. Clemens C. I. Webb (Oxford: Oxford University Press, 1909), 2:58–59: "Pedes quidem qui humiliora exercent officia. . . ." The use of the figure in the commentary on the *Aeneid* attributed to Bernard is discussed in O'Donnell, "Bernard Silvester's Commentary," 242–243.

[138] Ps.-William of Conches, *Philosophia*, ed. Ottaviano, 23.

losophy.[139] Richard's *Liber exceptionum* (c. 1158–1160) describes the parts of philosophy and each of the seven mechanical arts in quotations taken directly from the *Didascalicon*.[140] In harmony with Richard's general tendency to tie philosophy closely to issues of faith, the *Liber exceptionum* opens with an unusually detailed account of the sciences as post-lapsarian substitutes for the three original goods bestowed by God, man's creation in the image of God, his similitude to God and the immortality of his body.[141]

Godfrey of St. Victor (c. 1125–1194), even more than Richard, made the mechanical arts his own. In a short poem, the *Fons philosophiae*, Godfrey briefly describes the divisions of the sciences and calls the fountain of the mechanical arts a "dirty gymnasium" for frogs.[142] Yet, some nine years later, his far more substantial work, the *Microcosmus*, vindicates crafts as legitimate and, above all, moral activities.[143]

Godfrey's view of the mechanical arts differs in several ways from Hugh's. Like the "Ordo artium" and Raoul de Longchamps, he finds that there are a large number of mechanical arts, but, he says, it suffices to enumerate seven; he also leaves out theater, considers *armatura* and *fabricatura* as two separate categories and changes the name of *navigatio* to *mercatura* (commerce).[144] Like the author of the *Philosophia*, he is interested in the practitioners of the arts as well as the arts themselves and remarks that arms were the invention of soldiers, commerce of merchants, agriculture of men of the country, building of artificers, wool-working of wool-workers, hunting of huntsmen and medicine of doctors, adding that there is no one who does not continuously know through experience all the effects of the mechanical arts.[145] The most significant development of Hugh's original conception, however, is Godfrey's extraordinary emphasis on the intrinsic goodness of technology.

---

[139] The religious thought of Richard of St. Victor is discussed by Smalley, *The Study of the Bible in the Middle Ages*, 106–111. The critical editions of both encyclopedias are accompanied by extensive commentary; Richard of Saint Victor, *Liber exceptionum: Texte critique avec introduction, notes et tables*, ed. Jean Chatillon, Textes philosophiques du moyen âge, 5 (Paris: J. Vrin, 1958); Godfrey of Saint Victor, *Microcosmus: texte établi et présenté*, ed. Philippe Delhaye, Mémoires et travaux publiés par les professeurs des Facultés Catholiques de Lille, 56 and 57 (Lille: Facultés Catholiques, 1951; Gembloux: J. Duculot, 1951).

[140] Richard of St. Victor, *Liber exceptionum* 1.6, 14–21, ed. Chatillon, 106, 109–111. De Gandillac, "Place et signification," 272–273, particularly emphasizes the importance of Richard for the establishment of a Christian view of the world which included technology.

[141] Richard of St. Victor, *Liber exceptionum* 1.1–5, ed. Chatillon, 104–106; Smalley, *The Study of the Bible in the Middle Ages*, 106–111.

[142] Godfrey of St. Victor, *Le Fons philosophiae de Godefroy de Saint-Victor*, ed. Pierre Michaud-Quantin, Analecta mediaevalia Namurcensia, 8 (Namur: Éditions Godenne, 1956), 36: "ranarum Palastria Sordidatus limo." Godfrey's poem has been translated, *The Fountain of Philosophy: A Translation of the Twelfth-Century Fons philosophiae of Godfrey of Saint Victor*, tr. Edward A. Synan (Toronto: The Pontifical Institute of Mediaeval Studies, 1972).

[143] On Godfrey's life and the dates for the *Fons philosophiae* and the *Microcosmus*, see Delhaye, *Microcosmus*, Mémoires et travaux, 57:13–33.

[144] Godfrey of St. Victor, *Microcosmus* 1.57, ed. Delhaye, Mémoires et travaux, 56:74.

[145] Ibid.

Godfrey begins by bracketing the mechanical arts with ethics. Spinning an extended analogy based on Genesis 1:11 ("And God said, Let the earth bring forth grass, the herb yielding seed, and the fruit tree yielding fruit after its kind, whose seed is in itself, upon the earth") Godfrey describes the mechanical and practical arts in terms of an earthly paradise.[146] The two kinds of arts are two rivers. The first, the mechanical arts, irrigates the lower earth; the second, the practical arts, waters the upper earth. The first river of the mechanical arts divides itself into many parts so that "it might fill up all parts of the earth in the microcosm and cause it to be covered everywhere with green plants, by which not only the animals of the world are nourished but in truth the earth itself is made lovely."[147] In like fashion, the river of the practical arts also flows through many parts of the earth, bringing fruit-bearing trees to germination.

In keeping with what Philippe Delhaye calls Godfrey's "humanistic point of view," Godfrey values mankind's earthly activities despite his conviction that man's final end is a supernatural one.[148] Godfrey describes the practical and mechanical arts equally as necessary to human like, both because they are useful and honorable in their own right and because they serve as part of humanity's spiritual education. In a curious echo of Eusebius and Arnold of Bonneval, Godfrey states that not only ethics but the mechanical arts have their origins in the law of Moses.[149] Together they are part of the external discipline or rules which help direct and control the faulty movements of the irrational part of the soul toward proper goals.[150] Appropriately, Godfrey rejects the labeling of the mechanical arts as "adulterine." While it may have happened, he says, that the mechanical arts obtained this name on account of their abuse, for many men have indeed misused them for pleasure, it is more correct that they be called practical on account of their good and proper use which consists in exterior actions.[151] He explicitly insists upon the moral dimension of technology. In a radical revision of Augustine's view of crafts as expressed in *City of God* 22.24, Godfrey finds *all* crafts both moral and necessary, and relegates their use for pleasure or immoral activities to a *misuse*, revealing not their true nature but a perversion:

For out of arms peace and calm is brought forth by the soldiers into our land.

---

[146] Ibid., 1.53–56, (ed. Delhaye, 56:72–73).

[147] Ibid., 1.56, (ed. Delhaye), 56:73: "Quorum primum quidem in multa se flumina subdividit ita ut universas partes terre microcosmi impleat, eamque virentibus herbis undique cooperiri faciat, quibus, non solum animalia terre pascuntur, verum etiam ipsa terra venustatur."

[148] Delhaye, ed., *Microcosmus*, Mémoires et travaux, 57:115, 118.

[149] Godfrey of St. Victor, *Microcosmus* 1.52, ed. Delhaye, Mémoires et travaux, 56:72; on Eusebius and Arnold of Bonneval, see above, pp. 78–79 and n. 19.

[150] Godfrey of St. Victor, *Microcosmus* 1.52, ed. Delhaye, Mémoires et travaux, 56:71–72; see, also, Delhaye's commentary, Mémoires et travaux, 57:115–116.

[151] Godfrey of St. Victor, *Microcosmus* 1.55, ed. Delhaye, Mémoires et travaux, 56:73.

For even though the abuse of armed force is the source of hatred and ill-will, nevertheless the aim of its proper use is nothing but peace and calm. And that which has good as its aim is itself also good. Out of the exchanges of merchants, the poverty of lands is aided by goods transported from region to region. But also what need is there to recall the usefulness of farmers, by whose labors and services every living being is nourished? Nor is there a lesser utility provided by wool-workers who not only provide wools so that we might not be weakened by nudity or cold but also in truth bring a wonderful decoration to human life. Next lofty cities, castles, villas and marvelous edifices of houses made from stone, wood and metal demonstrated how useful are the building arts. Among these things indeed the exercise of hunting is not ignoble, as is shown on the more opulent table of the wealthy. Finally, the many advantages resulting from their "experiments" demonstrate how much the many-sided power of doctors (*medici*) can do. But all these things are not unsuitably compared to the sprouting of herbs because they only outwardly display the seasonal vigor of our earth, for, as emerging outwardly, they transmit nothing of their own to the interior man.[152]

A very different work by a contemporary of Godfrey's, Radulfus Ardens, brings a contrasting development to the idea of the mechanical arts in the twelfth century. Radulfus, a follower of Gilbert de la Porrée, produced a *Speculum universale* (1193–1199), the opening sections of which have been described in some detail by Martin Grabmann and edited in an unpublished thesis by Michele Le Paul.[153] Although the entire work has not yet been published and a full assessment is not possible without access to the complete text, these accounts are enough

---

[152] Ibid., 1.57, (ed. Delhaye, 56:74):

> Siquidem ex armatura militie in terra nostra pax et quies gignitur. Nam etsi abusus militie fomes odii et inuidie sit, boni tamen usus eius finis nonnisi pax et quies est. Cuius autem finis bonus est, ipsum quoque bonum est. Ex commerciis autem mercatorem merces suas de terris in terras transportantium adiuuatur inopia terrarum. Sed et agricultorum quid opus est utilitatem commemorare, quorum laboribus et obsequiis omnis anima pascitur? Nec minor apparet utilitas lanificium qui non solum ne feda nuditate uel frigoribus afficiamur agunt, uerum etiam mirum decorem humane uite conferunt. Porro fabriles artes quid prosint, urbes excelse, castra, uille et domorum miranda edificia ex lapide, ligno, metallo facta probant. Inter hec etiam non degener est usus uenandi, sicut probat lautior mensa diuitum. Denique quid possit uirtus plurima medicorum, multa experimentorum commoda docuerunt. Sed hec omnia non incongrue uirentibus herbis comparantur quia temporalem uirorem tantum terre nostre prestant, dum foris apparentia nichil de suo ad interiorem hominem transmittunt.

Note the changing meanings attached to *armatura* as one of the mechanical arts; cf. the views of Hugh of St. Victor above, p. 85f. and John of Dacia and Robert Kilwardby, below.

[153] Martin Grabmann, *Die Geschichte der scholastischen Methode* (Freiburg: Herder'sche Verlag, 1909; rpt. Graz: Akademische Druck- u. Verlagsanstalt, 1957), 1:252–254, has transcribed the opening chapters of the *Speculum universale* of Radulfus Ardens which discuss the division of the sciences; a summary of the work of Michele de Paul, *Étude du Speculum universale: Édition du premier livre* is given in École Nationale des Chartes. Positions des thèses soutenues par les élèves de la promotion de 1951 (Paris: École des Chartes, 1951), 107–109. The table of contents only of the entire work is given by Johannes Grundel, *Das "Speculum Universale" des Radulfus Ardens* (Munich: Max Hueber, 1961), which also provides bibliography on Radulfus, 3. For Radulfus as one of the *porretani* or followers of Gilbert de la Porrée, see P.H. Vicaire, "Les Porrétains et l'Avicennisme avant 1215," *Revue des sciences philosophiques et théologiques* 26 (1937):449–450.

to show that the work both belongs to the tradition begun by Hugh of St. Victor and significantly expands upon it. The *Speculum universale* begins with the theme of the corresponding evils, remedies and sciences, demonstrating its connection to the tradition begun by Hugh of St. Victor.[154] In the outline of the divisions of knowledge which follows, Radulfus describes the mechanical arts with intelligent attention to their content and scope. He divides them into *victuria* (nourishment), *lanificaria, architectoria, suffragatoria* (supports), *medicina, negotiatoria* (business) and *patrocinia* (defenses).[155] The arts listed under wool-working and architecture are quite similar to the arts in Hugh's descriptions but the remainder differ considerably. Insofar as it can be judged from Grabmann's diagram, Radulfus's scheme shows unusual detail, superior organization and an awareness of the breadth of contemporary technological involvement. *Victuria* combines Hugh's categories of agriculture and hunting, a more logical and concise arrangement. He expands "defenses" to include the means of guarding not only one's country but also one's religion, laws and personal authority ("tueri unicique ius suum") and separates it from architecture, a more precise and inclusive arrangement than Hugh's. Navigation, perhaps in response to the growth of commerce and trade, has been broadened to business and, in addition to Hugh's examples of buying, selling and exchange, Radulfus lists borrowing (*mutuationem*) and adjusting (*accommodationum*). Medicine includes purging, strengthening, moderating and preserving the body. The introduction of a group of "supports," or beasts of burden, tools, equipment and vehicles, is a striking recognition of contemporary technology.

By the end of the twelfth century, therefore, Hugh of St. Victor's idea of the mechanical arts had been absorbed into the mainstream of medieval thought. The immediate success of the *artes mechanicae* probably owes much to the cohesiveness and persuasiveness of Hugh's original scheme, yet also certainly reflects a widespread need for a method to incorporate technology within the sphere of legitimate and valued knowledge. This sustained interest in the mechanical arts, which led to new developments and variations of Hugh's ideas, continued through the thirteenth century.

THE THIRTEENTH CENTURY. Prior to the second half of the thirteenth century a clear demarcation existed between authors whose classifications of the arts and sciences incorporated Hugh of St. Victor's vision of the nature and purpose of the mechanical arts and those, such as Domingo Gundisalvo and Michael Scot, who were influenced by Aristotelian and Arabic thought on the place of crafts in the ordering of knowledge. As

---

[154] Radulfus Ardens, *Speculum universale* 1.1 in Grabmann, *Scholastischen Methode,* 1:252–253.

[155] Radulfus Ardens, *Speculum universale* 1.1; the names and parts of the mechanical arts according to Radulfus are diagrammed in Grabmann, *Scholastischen Methode,* 1:254.

we shall see in more detail in Chapter V, these thinkers did not place crafts in a discrete category, as did Hugh and his followers, but considered them under the rubrics of mathematics, physics and the economic arts as the practical aspects of these theoretical sciences. Moreover, for most of these thinkers the emphasis was less on how technology might contribute toward salvation than on how crafts functioned as adjuncts to the various sciences. Although one may note isolated cross-currents, as, for example, Gundisalvo's use of the term *artes mechanicae* as well as *fabriles artes,* by and large in the twelfth and early thirteenth centuries these two quite divergent conceptions of crafts existed side by side without influencing each other.[156]

By the mid-thirteenth century, however, this situation had begun to change. Discussions of the classification of knowledge lost much of their earlier individual and idiosyncratic character and became more rigorous, systematic and comprehensive. The new focus on orderly presentation reflected not only the growing standardization of education but also the availability of the full corpus of Aristotle's works which supplied a complex system of ordering knowledge and helped fill in the content of many areas of knowledge.[157] The often detailed and precise treatment of crafts in the Arabic tradition also provided an alternative to Hugh's classification and some degree of blending of Augustinian or Victorine, Arabic and Aristotelian ideas on crafts became the characteristic approach by the last half of the thirteenth century.[158] In the background the tension between the Augustinian view of knowledge as finally and ultimately dependent upon the soul's pursuit of God, and the Aristotelian view, which gave philosophy an autonomous, even if often subordinate, value, provided a fundamental touchstone for ideas on the value and nature of technology. It is important to recognize that while the impact of Aristotle and Arabic philosophy was immense, it was not overwhelming. The view of crafts as necessary aids to salvation developed by Hugh and his twelfth-century followers continued to be influential and, even though modified in terms of Aristotelian and Arabic thought, retained its particular strength as a divinely-ordained sanction for the pursuit of technology.

Hugh's classification of the mechanical arts appeared over the last half of the thirteenth century in the works of Bonaventure (1221–1274), Vincent of Beauvais (d. 1264), Robert Kilwardby (d. 1279), Albertus Magnus (1206–1280), John of Dacia (fl. 1280), Nicholas of Paris (fl. mid-thirteenth century), John Duns Scotus (c. 1265–1308) and Raymond Lull (c. 1235–

[156] Domingo Gundisalvo (Dominicus Gundissalinus), *De divisione philosophiae,* ed. Ludwig Baur, *Beiträge zur Geschichte der Philosophie des Mittelalters,* 4.2–3 (Münster: Druck und Verlag der Aschendorffschen Buchhandlung, 1903), 139.

[157] Weisheipl, "Classification of the Sciences," 68.

[158] Weisheipl, "Classification of the Sciences," 68–69, 75, 80–81. Weisheipl emphasizes that many thirteenth-century thinkers interpreted Aristotle's works in the light of a Platonism derived either from Augustine or Arabic Neoplatonism (80–81).

1315).[159] All these authors, with the exception of Bonaventure, show the marked influence of Aristotelian or Arabic ideas about the place of crafts in divisions of knowledge, yet all also retain the Victorine conception of the mechanical arts. Vincent of Beauvais's *Speculum doctrinale*, the second volume of his monumental encyclopedia, the *Speculum maius*, and Robert Kilwardby's *De ortu scientiarum*, for example, in quite different ways represent a fulfillment of Hugh's ideas through a synthesis with the "new science." Although less comprehensive in scope, the remaining authors also adapt the *artes mechanicae* to the new intellectual atmosphere.

Least touched by Aristotelian and Arabic thought was Bonaventure, whose ideas on the divisions of knowledge are contained in his *De reductione artium ad theologiam* and *Collationes in Hexaëmeron*.[160] Bonaventure, a strong proponent of Augustinianism, here and elsewhere defends the necessity of subordinating philosophy to Sacred Scripture and the demands of faith; without faith, philosophy for him is at best a dangerous distraction and, at worst, brought men to the edge of the "infinite precipice."[161] At the same time, Bonaventure believes that both the sensible things of the world and the mind's response to them through the illumination of the intellect reflect and manifest the divine.[162] Like Augustine, Bonaventure oscillates between distrust of philosophy's claims and appreciation for the way philosophy, properly used, leads the human mind toward God. It is significant that within these boundaries, however, Bonaventure, unlike Augustine, finds no more difficulty in including the mechanical arts within the sphere of divinely sanctioned knowledge than he does in including natural or moral philosophy. Although the mechanical arts are "in a certain sense, servile" and are of a lower nature than philosophy proper, they equally have their origin in divine illumination, their function in the service of

---

[159] All of these authors, with the exception of Nicholas of Paris, are discussed below. Nicholas of Paris's work on the division of the sciences has not been published but according to Martin Grabmann, *Mittelalterliches Geistesleben* (Munich: M. Hueber, 1926), 1:242–244 he followed Hugh of St. Victor on the mechanical arts.

[160] Bonaventure, *Saint Bonaventure's De reductione artium ad theologiam: A Commentary with an Introduction and Translation*, ed. and tr. Sister Emma Therese Healey (Saint Bonaventure, N.Y.: Saint Bonaventure College, 1939); Bonaventure, *Collationes in Hexaëmeron*, ed. R.P. Ferdinandus Delorme (Florence: Ad Claras Aquas, 1934); for a general discussion of Bonaventure's ideas on the division of knowledge see, especially, Bonaventure Hinwood, "The Division of Human Knowledge in the Writings of Saint Bonaventure," *Franciscan Studies*, n.s. 38 (1978):220–259.

[161] Bonaventure, *Collationes in Hexaëmeron* 1.3, ed. Delorme, 11; on the relationship of theology and philosophy in Bonaventure's thought, see John Francis Quinn, *The Historical Constitution of St. Bonaventure's Philosophy*, Studies and Texts, 23 (Toronto: Pontifical Institute of Mediaeval Studies, 1973), 811–816.

[162] Bonaventure, *Itinerarium mentis in Deum* 1–4, *Itinéraire de l'esprit vers Dieu: texte de Quaracchi*, trans. Henry Dumery (Paris: J. Vrin, 1960), 26–31; *The Mind's Road to God*, trans. George Boas (New York: The Liberal Arts Press, 1953); J.M. Bissen, *L'exemplarisme divin selon Saint Bonaventure* (Paris: J. Vrin, 1929).

human welfare, and their final purpose in the manifestation of Divine Wisdom.[163]

Bonaventure takes both his conception of the purpose of the mechanical arts and the list of these arts from Hugh of St. Victor, whom, as he says, he much admired.[164] Perhaps in indirect reference to Augustine's discussion, at the end of the *City of God,* of the arts as part necessary, part pleasurable God-given consolations for the distress of our fallen life, Bonaventure considers how each mechanical art is intended for human consolation or comfort, and how each banishes want by supplying a necessity or removing an impediment, or, alternatively, benefits and delights.[165] In his *Sermones de decem praeceptis* Bonaventure discusses which mechanical arts can be performed on the Sabbath and divides them into those necessary for the conservation of life and health (which are therefore approved insofar as they are necessary and prohibited insofar as they are servile), those entirely servile and therefore prohibited on the Sabbath, and those for pleasure, which are permitted on account of our weakness. Unfortunately, he does not tell us which arts fit into which category.[166] Bonaventure emphasizes the post-lapsarian function of the mechanical arts in other ways, also. Thus, for example, he strongly expresses the idea that the whole corporeal world, including the animals, was created to serve mankind and that after the Fall this service was specifically directed toward satisfying man's physical needs for clothing, food, and labor.[167]

Bonaventure, unlike Hugh, is further interested in the analogical spiritual meaning of the arts. Here Bonaventure uses Aristotelian definitions to help explain how the *artes mechanicae* exemplify divine art through analogy. The mechanical arts, like other kinds of knowledge, manifest Divine wisdom and can be reduced to the light of Sacred Scripture. Thus the artificer's use of a mental image to produce an artifact exemplifies by analogy the process by which the Invisible becomes visible and the Word was made incarnate; the artificer's desire to produce a work that is beautiful, useful and enduring corresponds to the three elements of life, knowledge which produces beauty, the will which renders an object useful and perseverance which renders it lasting; and, finally, the artificer's desire for praise, benefit and delight exemplifies the soul's three-

---

163 Bonaventure, *De reductione artium* 2:11–13. (Healy, 39–41, 52–55).

164 Ibid., 5 (Healy, 46).

165 Augustine, *City of God* 22.24, (Dombart, 612); Bonaventure, *De reductione artium* 2 (Healy, 38–41).

166 Bonaventure, *Sermones de decem praeceptis. Sermo* 4, in *Opera omnia,* ed. A. C. Peltier (Paris: L. Vivès, 1864), 2:243: "Illa vero, quae sunt merae jucunditatis, sunt permissa, non prohibita, quia propter parvitatem nostram permittentur ab Ecclesia." Bonaventure's list of the mechanical arts here differs slightly from that in *De reductione artium* in that he names *fabricatio* in place of *armatura.* The mechanical arts are also briefly mentioned in *Collationes in Hexaëmeron,* 34., ed. Delorme, 200.

167 See Alexander Schaefer, "The Position and Function of Man in the Created World according to Saint Bonaventure," *Franciscan Studies,* n.s. 20 (1960):261–316, and, especially, 326.

fold activity, to praise, serve and find delight in God.[168] The mechanical arts serve humanity not only by providing necessary physical consolations and benefits but in the larger purpose of demonstrating God's "footprints" in the world; they, like other kinds of knowledge, which in their own ways are "reduced" to theology, draw the mind toward the divine.

Bonaventure's treatment of the mechanical arts differs from Hugh's in certain respects, but, nevertheless, retains both the precise list of arts given in the *Didascalicon* and the fundamental Augustinian premise that the pursuit of technology was a part of the fallen soul's progress toward God. More often late thirteenth-century discussions of the mechanical arts show a stronger Aristotelian influence. Albertus Magnus, for example, despite his overall dependence on Aristotelian and Arabic schemes of knowledge, may have known Hugh's descriptions of the seven mechanical arts.[169] Although he also uses the rubrics *factibilia* and *apotelesmata* derived from the Aristotelian tradition, Albertus's favorite term for technological arts is *artes mechanicae*; other echoes of Hugh include the labeling of the mechanical arts as "adulterine" and, perhaps, the frequent pairing of liberal and mechanical arts as analogous sets of disciplines.[170] John Duns Scotus, on the other hand, avoids the use of the term *artes mechanicae* altogether and lists wool-working, wood-working, soldiering, navigation, agriculture, medicine and the art of construction as the "practical arts which are concerned with making."[171] Duns Scotus here combines a definition of technological arts ultimately derived from the Aristotelian tradition of the productive arts, or arts which made a product, with a specific list of arts clearly descended from Hugh of St. Victor.[172] John of Dacia also places the *artes mechanicae* in an Aristotelian framework. He opens his discussion of the division of the sciences with the premise, ascribed to Aristotle, that all men have

---

[168] Bonaventure, *De reductione artium* 11–14 (Healy, 52–55).

[169] Albertus Magnus, *Liber de apprehensione* 7.22 in *Opera omnia*, ed. Augustus Borgnet (Paris: L. Vivès, 1841), 5:631 lists and briefly defines the seven mechanical arts but does not mention Hugh of St. Victor's name; while keeping to Hugh's categories, Albertus also gives alternative names in some cases, for example, he refers to "lanificium sive vestitiva," "navigatio vel mercatura," and "venatio seu cibativa." For discussion of Albertus' classification of the arts and sciences in the Arabic pattern, see below Chapter V, pp. 136–9.

[170] Albertus Magnus, Commentary on Aristotle's *Physics*, Book. 2, Tract.1, ch. 10–11, in *Opera omnia*, 3:112–115; Commentary on Aristotle's *Ethics*, Book 1, Tract. 3, ch. 1–2, 8 in *Opera omnia*, 7:29–33, 40–41; Commentary on Aristotle's *Politics*, Book 1, ch. 2 in *Opera omnia*, 8:20–21; Commentary on Aristotle's *Metaphysics* Book 1, tract. 1, ch. 6, 10, Book 1, tract. 2, ch. 7, 9 in *Opera omnia* ed. Bernard Geyer (Cologne: Monasterium Westfalorum in Aedibus Aschendorff, 1960), 9, 15, 24, 26.

[171] Johannes Duns Scotus, *Quaestiones in tertium librum Sententiarum* Dist. 34, qu. 1, Scholium in *Opera omnia*, nova ju. ed. Wadding (Paris: L. Vivès, 1894), 15:494–495: "Habitus etiam practicus acquisitus dividitur in eum, qui est circa agibile, et in eum qui est circa factibile." The names of the arts, sometimes abbreviated, are given as "lana., nemus., miles, navigatio, rus., medicina, ars fabrilis."

[172] Aristotle (*Metaphysics* 2.1 993b and 11.7 1064a) distinguishes practical arts, or arts expressed in action and productive arts, or arts which made some product or object; see above Chapter II, p. 35.

been given a natural desire to remove the many imperfections of both body and soul under which they suffer.[173] The mechanical arts were discovered to satisfy these physical needs and free men to pursue the liberal arts.[174] After briefly contrasting magic, which is useless and prohibited, with the useful and necessary liberal and mechanical arts, John names the mechanical arts as they are listed in the *Didascalicon*.[175] He alters their definitions, however, to fit more closely his concept of their function. *Lanificium*, for example, includes methods of repelling cold and inducing its opposite, decoration and all business involving wool or flax; *armatura* refers to the means by which injuries to the body and accidental death are avoided; medicine, he points out, belongs to the mechanical arts only insofar as it consists of works concerned with the human body.[176] Raymond Lull, who uses Aristotelian terminology to explain the function of the arts as skills, calling them "habits mecans e liberalis," pairs the seven liberal arts with the seven mechanical arts, named as iron-working, carpentry, textile-working, agriculture, commerce, navigation and cavalry.[177] Lull places an interesting emphasis on feudal warfare as a mechanical art not only by including cavalry but also by describing carpentry as the art which produces the lance used by the knight and the trebuquet, as well as building, the plow and the rudder of a ship.[178]

The most substantial single treatments of the division of the sciences in the middle and late thirteenth century, Vincent of Beauvais's *Speculum doctrinale* and Robert Kilwardby's *De ortu scientiarum*, offer a more thorough and comprehensive synthesis of the *artes mechanicae* with the new scientific learning. Vincent explicates the content and scope of the individual arts in greater detail than earlier authors, as well as expanding upon the Augustinian and Victorine tradition which tied knowledge, including the mechanical arts, to the mandate given to the human race to restore itself to its pre-lapsarian condition. Kilwardby, on the other hand, outlines a novel justification of Hugh's mechanical arts as practical *sciences*, replacing the religious sanction for technology with one based

[173] John of Dacia, *Divisio scientiae* in *Johannis Daci opera*, ed. Alfred Otto, *Corpus philosophorum Danicorum Medii Aevi*, 1 (Hauriae: Apud Librarium G. E. C. Gad, 1955), 3.

[174] Ibid., 20.

[175] Ibid., 20–21, The discussion of magic, 18–20, is also derived from Hugh of St. Victor, (*Didascalicon* 6.15 [Buttimer, 132–133]).

[176] John of Dacia, *Divisio scientiae* in *Opera*, ed. Otto, 20–21. The definitions of the individual arts bear a certain resemblance to those in the commentary on Martianus Capella attributed to Bernard Silvestris, *Commentary on the "Aeneid,"* ed. Jones and Jones, Appendix C, 133. Cf. Raoul de Longchamps, *Commentary on the Anticlaudianus*, ed. Sulovsky, 44, which is also similar.

[177] Raymond Lull, *Arbre de ciència* 5.5 in *Obres essencials*, ed. Armand Llinarès (Barcelona: Editorial Selecta, 1957), 629–630. Lull gives the names of the mechanical arts as *ferreria, fusteria, sartoria, agricolia, mercaderia, marineria, cavalleria*; medicine and law are described after the liberal arts and preceding philosophy, 632. See Ovitt, *Restoration of Perfection*, 133–135, for a general discussion of Lull's conception of the relationships among the sciences.

[178] Lull, *Arbre de ciència* 5.5b (ed. Llinarès, 629).

on the Aristotelian and Arabic concept of natural philosophy and mathematics as composed of a dual theoretical and practical aspect. Almost diametrically opposed in their treatments of technology as a branch of knowledge, together these two works sum up much of the current development of medieval thought on the mechanical arts.

While characteristic of thirteenth-century thought in its push toward encyclopedic synthesis, Vincent's *Speculum doctrinale* is also very much in the spirit of the *Didascalicon*, both in its underlying principles and in its attention to concrete detail. That Vincent's conception of learning is imbued with the Augustinian and Victorine ideal of knowledge as divinely planned restoration is clear from the very beginning of the work. It starts with an account of the Fall, drawn from Augustine, Hugh of St. Victor and Richard of St. Victor; the natural goods provided to man by God; the evils resulting from the Fall; and their corresponding remedies in the arts and sciences.[179] Like Hugh, Vincent regards the mechanical arts as a fully-fledged category of knowledge. He quotes extensively from the *Didascalicon* on the necessity for including mechanics among the parts of philosophy.[180] Recapitulating the development of Augustinian ideas on the status of technology, Vincent begins the section on the *artes mechanicae* by quoting the provocative and ambivalent passage on the arts in Augustine's *City of God* and immediately follows it with Hugh of St. Victor's answer in the *Didascalicon* (1.9) which shows the mechanical arts to be the expression of human dignity and power.[181] Yet since he wishes to present a complete digest of up-to-date knowledge, he also incorporates aspects of Aristotelian and Arabic learning. His discussion of the classification of knowledge, for example, includes alternative schemes by Michael Scot and Aristotle which also emphasize technological arts. In Michael Scot's classification, for example, which follows the Arabic prototype, medicine, agriculture, navigation and alchemy are described as parts of practical physics and business, carpentry, construction, shoemaking and similar arts are part of practical mathematics.[182] In Vincent's description of Aristotle's classification, philosophy is divided into *mechanica*, which repels the indigence of the body, and the liberal arts, which repel the indigence of the soul, or,

[179] Vincent of Beauvais, *Speculum quadruplex sive speculum maius*, vol. 2, *Speculum doctrinale* (Graz: Akademische Druck- u. Verlagsanstalt, 1965), 1.1–9. This is a photo-reproduction of the 1624 edition by Douai, cols. 1–10; on the *Speculum maius*; see Serge Lusignan, "Préface au *Speculum Maius* de Vincent de Beauvais: réfraction et diffraction," *Cahiers d'études médiévales* 4 (1979):95–110 and Lusignan, "Les arts mécaniques dans le *Speculum Doctrinale* de Vincent de Beauvais," *Cahiers d'études médiévales* 7 (1982):33–48.

[180] Vincent of Beauvais, *Speculum doctrinale* 1.15 (Douai, col. 15).

[181] Ibid., 11.1 (Douai, col. 993). Vincent also quotes the section on the arts from the *City of God* 22.24 in *Speculum doctrinale* 1.8 (Douai, col. 8) in his description of the natural goods of the soul given to man. Whether deliberately or, more probably, because of a copyist's or printer's error, Augustine's division of the arts into "part necessary, part pleasurable (*voluptariae*)" has become in the *Speculum doctrinale* "part necessary, part voluntary (*voluntariae*)."

[182] Vincent of Beauvais, *Speculum doctrinale* 1.16 (Douai, col. 16).

alternatively, into theory or speculative philosophy and practice, divided into the operations of the soul (morals) and the operations of the body (*mechanica*).[183]

Vincent of Beauvais's major contribution to the medieval concept of technology is the fleshing out of the content and scope of each of the mechanical arts. The plan of the *Speculum doctrinale* follows the *Didascalicon* and, except for the substitution of alchemy for medicine, also borrowed from the Arabic tradition, Vincent uses Hugh's names for the mechanical arts. When Vincent treats each art in detail, his varied use of sources amounts to a synthesis of classical and medieval learning on the crafts.[184] Vincent's discussion of *armatura*, for example, includes a brief description taken from Richard of St. Victor's *Liber exceptionum*, excerpts from Isidore of Seville's *Etymologiae* on naval warfare, the parts of buildings, and triumphs, and lengthy quotations from Vitruvius's *De architectura* and Vegetius's *De re militari.*[185] The section on navigation similarly combines Isidore on ships with Cicero on the relative worth of retail and wholesale trade and the discussion of agriculture ranges from Richard of St. Victor, to Cicero and Augustine on the personal delights of gardening and agriculture, to technical advice taken from Palladius's *De agricultura* and, finally, to Isidore on farming tools.[186] Vincent's inclusion of alchemy as the last mechanical art is a departure from his earlier dependence on the Victorine tradition. The description of alchemy, drawn from the important sources available in the thirteenth century, covers material, instruments and procedures and points out the usefulness of alchemy for medicine and construction.[187]

The *Speculum doctrinale* in many ways fleshes out the description of the mechanical arts in the *Didascalicon*. Monumental in scope, it explores in detail the connections between man's Fall and his need for knowledge, the place of technology among the parts of philosophy and the available learning on each of the *artes mechanicae*. If Vincent's approach is concerned more with booklearning than actual practice of the arts, more with religious purpose than philosophical or scientific rigor, these

[183] Ibid., 1.18, (Douai, col. 17). Here Vincent gives yet another derivation of the term *mechanica*, which he asserts is from the Greek *maecha* or servant.

[184] For a more detailed and quantitative assessment of these chapters, see Lusignan, "Arts mécaniques," 37, 40, 44.

[185] Vincent of Beauvais, *Speculum doctrinale* 11.13–91, (Douai, cols. 1001–1043).

[186] Ibid., 11.98–100 (Douai, col. 1048–1050) on navigation; 11.102–104 (Douai, cols. 1051–1053 on agriculture).

[187] Ibid., 11.105–133 (Douai, cols. 1053–1082); Vincent removes medicine from the mechanical arts because it consists less in manual operation than in mental speculation, ibid., 11.104 (Douai, col. 1053), and, one suspects to make room for alchemy. Vincent's connection between alchemy, medicine and construction, ibid., 11.105 (Douai, cols. 1053–1054), as well as his inclusion of alchemy as a mechanical art is emphasized by Lusignan, "Arts mécaniques," 44–46 as demonstrating an interest in contemporary practical problems lacking in the remainder of Vincent's discussion of the mechanical arts. For bibliography on alchemy in the Middle Ages, see Claude Gagnon, "Recherche bibliographique sur l'Alchimie médiévale occidentale," in *La Science de la nature: Théories et pratiques*, Cahiers d'études médiévales, 2 (Montreal: Bellarmin, 1974; Paris: J. Vrin, 1974), 155–199.

qualities are also characteristic of the *Didascalicon* and of one strand of medieval thought on technology. A quite different view of crafts, yet one still within the Victorine tradition, is provided in Robert Kilwardby's *De ortu scientiarum*.

Robert Kilwardby's full-scale treatise on the divisions of philosophy has been called the culmination and completion of the Victorine tradition of classification and "the most ambitious and astute consideration" of the classification of the sciences in the thirteenth century.[188] Its importance for the history of ideas about technology lies less in the newness of Kilwardby's conceptions than in his successful redefinition of the Victorine notion of the *artes mechanicae*, which harmonizes with Aristotelian and Arabic concepts of scientific knowledge. Written around 1250,[189] the *De ortu scientiarum* draws upon Aristotelian and Arabic Neoplatonic sources, as well as Latin works with an Augustinian ambiance, in particular the *Didascalicon*, and presents a cohesive, philosphically rigorous reworking of current traditions on the nature of crafts as a part of knowledge.[190]

Kilwardby begins his treatment of the mechanical arts by systematizing the Victorine categories under which crafts are subsumed. Writing as he does at the end of a long line of revisions of Hugh's original scheme, Kilwardby modifies the list of the mechanical arts along what had become conventional lines but in an unusually explicit and thorough manner. Like Godfrey of St. Victor and others, he places mechanics with ethics as the practical sciences of the body and soul respectively.[191] In keeping with his systematic approach, Kilwardby first gives an account of the mechanical arts according to Hugh, then identifies the relevant sections of Isidore of Seville's *Etymologiae* and follows with his own improvements.[192] First, as in many other revisions of Hugh, theater is eliminated. Kilwardby, however, adds the explanation that theater ought to be greatly detested and repudiated by Catholics.[193] The playing

---

[188] Ovitt, "The Status of the Mechanical Arts," 101; Weisheipl, "The Nature, Scope and Classification of the Sciences," in *Science in the Middle Ages*, ed. Lindberg, 479. For Kilwardby's ideas on the nature and classification of mathematics, metaphysics, ethics and language, see D.E. Sharp, "The *De ortu scientiarum* of Robert Kilwardby," *The New Scholasticism* 8 (1934):1–30 and Weisheipl, "Classification of the Sciences," 75–78. The only substantial discussion of Kilwardby on the mechanical arts is Ovitt, "The Status of the Mechanical Arts," 101–104, and *Restoration of Perfection*, 127–130.

[189] On the date, see Crombie, *Robert Grossteste*, 138.

[190] For Kilwardby's use of Arabic Neoplatonism, see Weisheipl, "Classification of the Sciences," 75; Sharp, "The *De ortu scientiarum*," 2, however, rejects any influence of Neo-Platonism on Kilwardby, but suggests that Kilwardby used both Aristotelian and Augustinian ideas as they suited his own view.

[191] Kilwardby, *De ortu scientiarum* 34 and 35, ed. Albert G. Judy (Oxford: Clarendon Press, 1976), 123–126.

[192] Ibid., 39 and 40 (ed. Judy, 129–133). Ovitt, "The Status of the Mechanical Arts," 101–102, overestimates the degree of originality in Kilwardby's revisions of the list of mechanical arts; most of Kilwardby's changes had been anticipated in the twelfth century; see above, pp. 103–4, 105–6, 107.

[193] Kilwardby, *De ortu scientiarum* 40.373, ed. Judy, 131.

of instruments is permissible, but only because this falls under medicine.[194] Second, again typically, Kilwardby points out that this omission permits architecture to be separated from arms or defense.[195] Third, he suggests that several of Hugh's names for the categories of mechanical arts are inappropriate. Thus what Hugh calls *lanificia* would more properly be called *arte vestitivam* (art of garments) or *coopertivam* (coverings) because these terms are more general, and, similarly, navigation should be *mercatura*, agriculture *terraecultus*, hunting *cibativa* (food science) or *nutritiva* (nutrition) or some name of this sort.[196] The jettisoning of theater also allows a closer approximation to the liberal arts than Hugh had suggested, for now *terraecultus, cibativa* and medicine, which all pertain to the inner body, can be associated with the *trivium* and *vestitiva, armatura, architectura* and *mercatura*, which pertain to the exterior of the body, can be associated with the *quadrivium*.[197]

Kilwardby's pragmatic attitude comes through in the closing passage of the chapter:

On the subject of subtle division of these arts through their immediate [objects], their proper definitions, materials and ends, I do not think one ought to be concerned at present, first so as not to wander uselessly among those subjects which modern philosophers consider of little importance; then because their materials and ends rather become known to operators by hand work than to philosophers who consider truth alone while unfamiliar with operations, and we are incompetent in these [materials, ends]; finally, because mechanical arts could be distinguished in [so] many various ways, and in [so] many diverse numbers. For I see no other compelling reason why about so countless an array of arts we should number them precisely as seven, save for a certain superficial correspondence with the seven liberal arts.[198]

Kilwardby's importance and originality for the history of medieval conceptions of technology, however, lie primarily in the subsequent section of his work in which he takes up, perhaps in deliberate contrast to the "modern philosophers" referred to in the passage quoted above, the question of how the mechanical arts pertain to philosophy. Kilwardby had begun the *De ortu scientiarum* by distinguishing among:

---

194 Ibid., 40.373 (ed. Judy, 132).

195 Ibid., This and many of the other changes made by Kilwardby described here seem to reflect the variations made by Godfrey of St. Victor; see above, p. 107.

196 Ibid., 40.374–377 (ed. Judy, 132–133).

197 Ibid., 40.378 (ed. Judy, 133).

198 Ibid., 40.378 (ed. Judy, 133):

De istarum artium subtili divisione per immediata et definitionibus earum propriis materiisque ac finibus non reputo ad praesens esse sollicitandum, tum ne inutiliter evagemur ad ea quae moderni philosophi parum considerant, tum quia materiae earum et fines magis manu operatoribus innotescere habent quam philosophis solam veritatem speculantibus et nos operationum expertes sumus et in eisdem inexperti, tum quia mechanicae variis modis distingui possent et in variis numeris. Nullam enim video necessitatem quare in tam innumerabilibus artibus ponamus praecise septenarium nisi quandam congruentiam apparentem ad septenarium artium liberalium.

knowledge or science necessary to salvation (that is, Sacred Scripture); science which is superstitious, injurious and to be avoided (magic); and science which teaches truths about things or about honorable conduct, which is catholic, useful and to be esteemed (philosophy).[199] Having quietly abandoned the Augustinian ideal that all knowledge must serve salvation, even while keeping intact Hugh's principle of classification of the mechanical arts, Kilwardby must substitute a justification of the *artes mechanicae* as science based on a reworking of Aristotelian and Arabic ideas.

The essential difficulty for Kilwardby is that, according to Aristotle, true science, including physics, must be concerned with universals, but ethics and mechanics, because they proceed from human acts and works, are concerned with the singulars or contingencies which are products of human will.[200] As has been recently and insightfully pointed out by George Ovitt, Kilwardby attacks this dichotomy from several directions.[201] Physics does not itself always argue from necessary truths, he remarks, and the diversity of opinions about natural things testifies to this.[202] More importantly, Kilwardby argues that although a distinction between operative and contemplative sciences must be maintained, nevertheless, the speculative sciences are practical and the practical sciences speculative:

> In as much as we have said something separately concerning the speculative part of philosophy and something about the practical part, now it is important to say something about them in comparison with each other. I ask therefore in what way they are distinguished according to their degree of speculative philosophy and praxis, since those which are practical are, indeed, speculative—it is important certainly that one consider first by speculative virtue what one ought to perform in practical virtue—and, conversely, the speculative sciences are not without praxis. Does not, in fact, arithmetic teach how to add numbers to each other and to subtract them from each other, to multiply and divide and draw out their square roots, all of which things are operations? Again does not music teach to play the lute and flute and things of this sort? Again does not geometry teach how to measure every dimension, through which both carpenters and stoneworkers work? Again, does not one know the time for navigation and planting and things of this sort through astronomy? It seems therefore that every single science said to be speculative is also practical. It seems, therefore, that the speculative sciences are practical and the practical speculative.[203]

---

[199] Ibid., 1.2 (ed. Judy, 9). For a background of the problem of truth and the organization of knowledge in the thirteenth century, see Steven P. Marrone, *William of Auvergne and Robert Grosseteste: New Ideas of Truth in the Early Thirteenth Century* (Princeton: Princeton University Press, 1983), 3–23.

[200] Kilwardby, *De ortu scientiarum* 41.379 (ed. Judy, 134).

[201] Ovitt, "The Status of the Mechanical Arts," 102–103, and *Restoration of Perfection*, 128–130.

[202] Kilwardby, *De ortu scientiarum* 41.389 (ed. Judy, 136–137).

[203] Ibid., 42.393 (ed. Judy, 138):

Kilwardby is not content to rest here but attempts to establish more precisely the relationship of the practical sciences. On the one hand, he arranges the sciences in a hierarchy of increasing universality and status. Metaphysics is the highest science because of the dignity of its subject, followed by mathematics, because of its certainty, physics, ethics and, finally, mechanics.[204] Mechanics and ethics, however, are related to each other through their common character as practical or operative sciences, and, although mechanics cannot be considered a subdivision of ethics, corporeal good, aimed at by mechanics, should be ordered toward spiritual good and, therefore, mechanics can aid one to lead a more virtuous life more easily.[205] On the other hand, Kilwardby explores how the practical sciences are connected directly to the speculative sciences through the relationship of subalternation or subordination. Not only do the theoretical sciences also teach practical operations but the different mechanical arts make use of various theoretical sciences according to their particular materials or aims. The relationship of subalternation is further governed by the speculative sciences' demonstration of *propter quid* or the "reason for something being as it is" and the mechanical arts' explanation *quia* or "that something is."[206]

. . . so it seems to me that all the mechanical arts are subalternate to the speculative sciences, although occasionally the condition of subalternation is found more completely in some, less completely in others. Under physics, indeed, are medicine and alchemy, which [itself] is not incongruously reduced to commerce, which itself is the science of wealth-getting. In the same way, wool-working, the making of arms, architecture, agriculture and food science, which examine with respect to their object, are much supported by physics, and physics makes known the *propter quid* of many things about which they make known the *quia sunt*. Similarly, navigation, which pertains to commerce, and agriculture are much aided by astronomy because of their concern with seasons and movements of the heavens, and they make use of many things which astronomy and astrology make known the *propter quid*. Similarly, the art of numbering, which because of its computations is well reduced to commerce, is under arithmetic

---

Postquam aliquid de parte philosophiae speculativa et aliquid de parte practica seorsum diximus, nunc oportet de earum ad invicem comparatione aliquid dicere. Quaero igitur quomodo distinguantur penes speculationem et praxim, cum illae quae practicae sunt sint etiam speculativae—oportet enim prius virtute speculativa contemplari quod virtute practica debemus operari—et e converso speculativae non sine praxi sunt. Nonne enim arithmetica docet numeros addere ad invicem et subtrahere ab invicem, multiplicare et dividere et radices eorum extrahere, quae omnia sunt operationes? Item nonne musica docet citharizare et canere tibia et huiusmodi? Item nonne geometria docet mensurare omnem dimensionem unde et carpentarii et caementarii per eam operantur? Item nonne per astronomiam scitur tempus navigandi et seminandi et huiusmodi? Videtur igitur quod unaquaeque dictarum speculativarum sit etiam practica. Videtur ergo quod et speculativae sint practicae et practicae speculativae.

[204] Ibid., 41.392 (ed. Judy, 137).
[205] Ibid., 43.406 (ed. Judy, 142).
[206] On this distinction in Aristotle and medieval thought, see Crombie, *Robert Grosseteste*, 25–27, 52–57.

and the instrumental art of harmony, which can be reduced to medicine, is under the mathematics of proportions. Similarly, architecture, construction, and arms-making with respect to their method of operating are under geometry because geometry makes known the *propter quid* of many things about which they make known only the *quia*. Similarly, I think that wool-making is with respect to its method under arithmetic and geometry. It examines indeed the number and texture of threads and the measurement and form of the warp, affirming in each of these things that it *is* this way or that way, while the causes of these same things pertain to arithmetic or geometry. Again, medicine is aided not only by physics but by astrology, and consequently, by astronomy, without which astrology is not able to be known. Similarly, in other mechanical arts everywhere you find that they are under some speculative science or sciences. . . .[207]

Kilwardby here reinforces his earlier point about the interdependence of the speculative and practical sciences by exploring how crafts provide empirical knowledge of physical conditions, the causes of which can then be explained by the theoretical sciences. Thus, although the mechanical arts are not themselves concerned with universals and cannot supply fully certain knowledge, they are, nevertheless, part of philosophy through their close relationship to such sciences, as physics and mathematics. Moreover, as part of philosophy, the mechanical arts have their origin in the human soul's natural desire to seek the good of the body, and take their value from the assistance they offer to human efforts to live virtuously or to understand the physical world.[208]

Kilwardby's work in many ways reflects the unifying and systematizing tendencies of thirteenth-century thought in general. His view of knowledge as both theoretical and operative or practical, as well as the specific linkages he makes between medicine, agriculture and physics, commerce and arithmetic, and construction and geometry, shows the strong influence of Arabic ideas, as we will see in the following chapter. Similarly, his view that philosophy as a whole teaches one to live well

[207] Kilwardby, *De ortu scientiarum* 43.401 (ed. Judy, 139–140):

Ut mihi videtur, quod omnes mechanicae subalternantur scientiis speculativis, quamvis alicubi inveniatur in eis plenior ratio subalternationis, in aliquibus minus plena. Sub physica enim sunt medicina et alchimia, quae non incongrue reducitur ad mercaturam quae ditativa est. Eodem modo lanificium et armatura et architectonica et agricultura et cibativa, ratione eorum quae considerant, multum iuvantur a physica, et physica habet dicere *propter quid* multorum de quibus istae dicunt *quia sunt*. Similiter navigatio, quae ad mercaturam pertinet, et agricultura multum iuvantur ab astronomia propter considerationem temporum et motuum astrorum et multa supponunt quorum astronomia vel astrologia habet dicere *propter quid*. Similiter ars numerativa, quae propter computationes bene reducitur ad mercaturam, sub arithmetica est, et ars harmonicae instrumentalis, quae bene potest reduce ad medicinam, sub harmonica mathematica est. Similiter architectonica, fabrilis et armatura quoad modum operandi sub geometria sunt, quia ipsa habet dicere *propter quid* multorum de quibus ipsae dicunt tantum *quia*. Similiter lanificium quoad modum puto esse sub arithmetica et geometria. Numerum enim et texturam filorum et mensuram telarum et formam considerat dicens in omnibus quia sic est vel sic, cum eorundem causae ad arithmeticam vel geometriam spectent. Item medicina non tantum a physica iuvatur sed ab astrologia, et per consequens ab astronomia, sine qua nequit sciri astrologia. Similiter in aliis mechanicis ubique invenies quod ipsae sint sub aliqua speculativa vel aliquibus.

[208] Ibid., 37.358 (ed. Judy, 127).

but has no direct relation to salvation is clearly Aristotelian rather than Augustinian in inspiration. At the same time, Kilwardby's treatment of the mechanical arts as a distinct category and his consideration by name of each of the mechanical arts as named by Hugh (with the single exception, carefully justified, of theater) place Kilwardby squarely within the Victorine tradition. Kilwardby's concern to harmonize these different strands of thought, and his success in doing so, demonstrate both his own originality and the power and adaptability of Hugh of St. Victor's concept of the *artes mechanicae.*

Conclusion

This survey confirms the continuing importance of Hugh of St. Victor's vision of the mechanical arts through the last half of the thirteenth century from its origin in the early twelfth century. The *artes mechanicae* clearly helped to fill a wide-spread need to encompass technology within the sphere of legitimate knowledge. Whereas in the ancient world and the early medieval period crafts appeared only peripherally, when at all, in discussions of the parts of knowledge, from the mid-twelfth century the vast majority of such discussions gave an important place to crafts, most in terms derived from Hugh of St. Victor. Even if, as has been suggested by George Ovitt, medieval classifications of learning in general were defined and informed by a "convention of list-making," and entrenched hierarchical principles, or, as suggested by Guy Allard, they were influenced by a literary tradition,[209] the classification of the arts and sciences surveyed here was also an aspect of a genuine intellectual response to contemporary technological growth and innovation. Kilwardby's insistence on the close relationship of crafts and theoretical physics and mathematics, as well as his casual remark that artisans who work with their hands know more about the mechanical arts than philosophers, suggests that an empirical, scientific approach was hardly incompatible with the concept of the *artes mechanicae.* The frequent revision of the arts tells us that the Victorine tradition was neither entirely "literary" and divorced from actual practice nor copied by rote, but reflected changing ideas about the nature and content of knowledge, which, in turn, reflected, however distantly, contemporary social conditions. The addition of magic (the commentary on Martianus Capella, the "ordo artium"), the "defenses" of clerics (the *Philosophia*), cavalry (Raymond Lull) and alchemy (Vincent of Beauvais) to the list of the mechanical arts tells us something about the interests and attitudes of twelfth- and thirteenth-century thinkers, as does the frequent exclusion of theater (commentary on Martianus Capella, *Ysagoge in theologiam*, the "ordo artium," Godfrey of St. Victor, Radulfus Ardens, Kilwardby). The association of medicine with alchemy (Vincent of Beauvais) or with

[209] Ovitt, *Restoration of Perfection*, 136; Allard, "Les arts mécaniques," 20–21.

music and astrology (Kilwardby) may add to our knowledge of how medieval medical knowledge was conceptualized. One can also note the several instances in which medicine is detached from the mechanical arts and placed in another category of knowledge (Vincent of Beauvais, Raoul de Longchamps, Raymond Lull). The impact of technological and economic development can be seen in the expansion of Hugh's category of navigation to commerce (Godfrey of St. Victor, Raymond Lull, Kilwardby) or to business (the *Philosophia*, Radulfus Ardens) and in the references to transport, tools and animal power (Radulfus Ardens) and weapons (Raymond Lull). There is also a persistent individual emphasis on the moral purposes of the mechanical arts, expressed, for example, in Godfrey of St. Victor's remarkable defense of the intrinsic goodness of the mechanical arts, including warfare, the presentation by the anonymous author of the *Philosophia* of businessmen as productive members of the body politic, along with scholars and clergymen, and Kilwardby's reference to the mechanical arts as aids to the virtuous life.

The tradition of the *artes mechanicae*, moreover, also helps explain an important aspect of the process by which technology was assimilated into the European world-view. The intellectual suspicion of technology inherited by the Middle Ages from the classical world was in part based upon a radical distinction between *scientia*, or theoretical knowledge, pursued for its own sake and valued for itself as truth, and crafts, by their very nature directed toward a useful corporeal end and subordinate to other kinds of knowledge for their final ends and purposes. This difference was preserved, for example, by Thomas Aquinas, who often emphasizes the theoretical, non-utilitarian character of natural philosophy in such a way as sharply to separate crafts and manual arts from philosophy and render them servile.[210] For Aquinas, as for Aristotle, the inferiority of manual labor and craftsmanship lies in part in their orientation toward the production of an artifact without knowledge of the use to which the artifact is to be put; thus, the navigator, for example, who uses the completed ship is superior to the shipbuilder and the carpenter.[211] Consequently, despite his interest in the autonomous value of the natural world and human understanding of that world, and, indeed, perhaps, because of it, Aquinas shows relatively little interest in the mechanical arts and, far more than most of his contemporaries, labels them servile and degrading.[212] The dichotomy could be overcome, as it was by Robert Kilwardby and others, by stressing the interdependence of practical and theoretical science. This approach which bypassed the specifically Christian emphasis on the Fall, as we

---

[210] Francis J. Kovach, "Divine Art in Saint Thomas Aquinas," in *Arts libéraux et philosophie au Moyen Âge*, 665.

[211] Thomas Aquinas, *Commentary on the Metaphysics of Aristotle* 1.26, trans. John P. Rowan (Chicago: Henry Regnery, 1969), 14.

[212] See, for example, Aquinas, *Summa Theologiae* 1a2ae. 57,3.3 (ed. Blackfriars, 23:48); *Commentary on the Metaphysics* 1.16 and 3.59.

shall see, became important in the latter part of the thirteenth century among Latin writers influenced by Aristotle and his Arabic commentators. To integrate fully the mechanical arts and natural philosophy, however, stretched the perimeters of contemporary scientific knowledge and, ultimately, required the complete overthrow of Aristotelian science.[213] A simpler and more easily assimilated way of bridging the gap between speculative philosophy and technology was provided by the Augustinian or Victorine view of knowledge. In this view, *all* knowledge is conceived of as finally subordinate to, or "for," the higher purpose of the soul's progress toward God. Although this conception of knowledge could be used, as it is by Augustine himself, to diminish the value of technology as irrelevant or destructive to spiritual values, in the hands of many twelfth- and thirteenth-century philosophers and theologians the ideal of knowledge as preparatory to salvation serves instead to bring technology into the fold of philosophy by subsuming both under the same function and, in effect, defining both philosophy and technology as means to a higher end rather than as ends in themselves. Technology, therefore, like other branches of knowledge, was seen to serve a precise religious and historical function as an aid to recovery from the effects of original sin. This principle is central in the thought of Hugh of St. Victor, Godfrey and Richard of St. Victor, Bonaventure, Vincent of Beauvais and others. Its unique strength as a device or rationale for the incorporation of technology into philosophy should not be underestimated or dismissed as "unmodern."[214] Far from being intrinsically hostile to technology, the view that knowledge is in the service of religion was often expressed by thinkers, such as Roger Bacon (1214–1292) and that eloquent spokesman for modernity, Francis Bacon (1561–1626), who most valued technological progress.

Roger Bacon, significantly, has been praised as one of the most forward-looking and "modern" of medieval thinkers, precisely because of his interest in technology.[215] Bacon based his classification of the arts and sciences and his conception of science on Arabic models; this aspect of his thought will be treated below in Chapter Five. He also, however, often couched his remarks on the nature and purpose of knowledge in terms taken from an Augustinian framework. Thus Bacon argues that all knowledge has been given to man "by one God, to one world, for one purpose" and natural philosophy and experimental science, no less

---

[213] Paolo Rossi, *Philosophy, Technology and the Arts in the Early Modern Era*, trans. Salvator Attanasio and ed. Benjamin Nelson (New York, Evanston, and London: Harper and Row, Harper Torchbooks, 1970), 14–61, 137–146.

[214] Ovitt, "The Status of the Mechanical Arts," 103–104 suggests that Kilwardby was more "characteristically 'modern'" because he began to reject the salvationary function of science.

[215] Allard, "Arts mécaniques," 28 finds Bacon's interest in practical science "strange and new," in comparison with Hugh of St. Victor and most other medieval thinkers and, according to A.G. Molland, "Scientific Progress," 571, Bacon, more than other medieval thinkers, was aware of and appreciated technical progress.

than theology and canon law, are important aids to faith and part of the wisdom of God.[216] Philosophical knowledge was revealed to the saints and prophets at the time of Sacred Scripture and this knowledge, now largely lost, must be recovered and increased.[217] The bulk of Bacon's work is, indeed, a plea for this recovery and a method of accomplishing it. Much of Bacon's personal interest is in the technological devices he expects to recover, or rediscover—the burning glasses, incendiary substances, medicines, flying machines, and other wonderful instruments—which will remedy the ills of the Church and Christians.[218] Although his method of experimental science depends upon Arabic alchemical, optical and astrological science, Bacon's view of the purpose of knowledge and technology's role must be included within the Augustinian and Victorine traditions.[219]

Any full consideration of Francis Bacon is clearly beyond the scope of this study, yet certain obvious affinities between Bacon's ideas about technology and Hugh of St. Victor's can be briefly noted. For Bacon, as well as Hugh, technological knowledge is a remedy for human deficiencies caused by the Fall and provides a means of return to mankind's original paradisical state:

> For man by the Fall fell at the same time from his state of innocency and from his dominion over creation. Both of these losses, however, can even in this life be in some part repaired; the former by religion and faith, the latter by arts and sciences. For creation was not by the curse made altogether and for ever a rebel, but in virtue of that charter "In the sweat of thy face shalt thou eat bread," it is now by various labours (not certainly by disputations or idle magical ceremonies, but by various labours) at length and in some measure subdued to the supplying of man with bread; that is, to the uses of human life.[220]

The essential idea developed by Hugh of St. Victor and henceforth associated with the mechanical arts was that technology possesses a moral value. Although this value is not inherent to technology, it was conferred upon it by God who provided mankind with the means to recover, at least in part, his lost natural condition. The latent ambiguity

---

216 Roger Bacon, *Opus maius* 2.1, trans. Robert Belle Burke (New York: Russell and Russell, 1962), 2:36 (ed. J.H. Bridges, Supplementary Volume, 36), ". . . quoniam ab uno Deo data est tota sapientia et uni mundo, et propter finem unum."

217 Bacon *Opus maius* 2.15 (Bridges, Supplementary Volume, 67–68).

218 Bacon *Opus maius* 6. Ex. 2–3 (Bridges, 2:204–222).

219 On the sources of Bacon's science, see Stewart Copinger Easton, *Roger Bacon and his Search for a Universal Science: A Reconsideration of the Life and Work of Roger Bacon in the Light of His Own Stated Purposes* (Oxford: Basil Blackwell, 1952; rpt. New York: Russell and Russell, 1971), 70, 177, and Jeremiah M. Hackett, "The Meaning of Experimental Science (*Scientia experimentalis*) in the Philosophy of Roger Bacon," Ph.D. diss.: University of Toronto, 1983.

220 Francis Bacon, *Novum Organum*, Aphorism 42, in *The Works of Francis Bacon*, ed. James Spedding (London: Longmans and Co., 1870; rpt. New York: Garett Press, 1968), 4:297–298.

whether technology belonged more truly to man's pre-lapsarian condition or to his fallen condition was (and still is) unresolved,[221] but this seems to have mattered little to the twelfth- and thirteenth-century thinkers who gave the mechanical arts moral, and hence, intellectuual legitimacy as part of the human search for perfection. This reassessment is perhaps underestimated in the twentieth century, which only very recently has begun again to question the assumption of the inherent goodness of technological progress. Yet in comparison to the classical philosophical tradition, which consistently, if not monolithically, emphasized the neutrality or moral dangers of technology, it was a step of major significance.

[221] See, for example, the opposing views of Wilhelm E. Fudpucker, "Through Christian Theology to Technological Christianity," in *Theology and Technology: Essays in Christian Analysis and Exegesis*, ed. Carl Mitcham and Jim Grote (Lanham, New York and London: University Press of America, 1984), 56–57, who believes that Adam in Paradise was given a divine command to "subdue" the earth through technology and Jacques Ellul, "Technique and the Opening Chapters of Genesis,"in *Theology and Technology*, 135, who concludes that technology is uniquely part of the fallen world only.

TRANS. AMER. PHIL. SOC.
VOL. 80 PT. 1, 1990

V. The Mechanical Arts and the Aristotelian Tradition

The integration of crafts into classifications of knowledge did not occur solely within the religious or "salvationary" framework developed by Hugh of St. Victor and his followers. A second tradition, in which crafts were assigned a more purely secular function as practical parts of theoretical science, became important among many writers influenced by the body of Aristotelian and Arabic thought introduced into the West during the twelfth and thirteenth centuries.[1] This tradition, however, was far more diverse than that begun by Hugh, in part because the vast corpus of Aristotelian and Arabic works assimilated into medieval philosophy during this period contained several quite different strands of thought on the nature and value of technology as a category of knowledge. In particular, Aristotle's view of the relationship between theoretical science and crafts often diverged considerably from that implicit in Arabic classifications of knowledge, many of which were based on a synthesis of Aristotelian and Neoplatonic principles.

Aristotle, like Augustine, left a double-edged legacy for ideas on the values of crafts. On the one hand, Aristotle frequently expressed attitudes and ideas which left little room for a positive evaluation of manual arts. For Aristotle, scientific knowledge, that is, metaphysics, mathematics and physics, is properly speculative and deals with the contemplation of unchanging truth; science (*scientia*) therefore is clearly distinct both from the productive arts, which deal with the making of a product according to rational rules, and from the practical arts, which deal with actions.[2] Since science is concerned with universals, it is of more value than art, which is concerned with the particular and contingent. Aris-

---

[1] For the impact of Aristotle and the Arabic philosophers see, especially, Richard Lemay, *Abu Ma'shar and Latin Aristotelianism in the Twelfth Century: The Recovery of Aristotle's Natural Philosophy through Arabic Astrology*, American University of Beirut, Publications of the Faculty of Arts and Sciences, Oriental Series, 38 (Beirut: American University of Beirut, 1962) and Fernand van Steenberghen, *Aristotle in the West: The Origins of Latin Aristotelianism*, trans. Leonard Johnston, 2nd ed. (Louvain: Nauwelaerts Pub. House, 1970). For general background, see Maurice De Wulf, *Histoire de la philosophie médiévale* (Louvain: Institut Supérieur de Philosophie, 1924). For medieval science in this period, including the impact of the translating movement, see David C. Lindberg, ed., *Science in the Middle Ages* (Chicago: University of Chicago Press, 1978) and additional bibliography in Edward Grant, *Physical Science in the Middle Ages* (Cambridge: Cambridge University Press, 1977), 91–115.

[2] On Aristotle's division of the sciences, see Joseph Mariétan, *Problème de la classification des sciences d'Aristote à St. Thomas* (Paris: Felix Alcan, 1901), 11–48 and above, Chapter II, pp. 34–36.

totle's emphasis on the theoretical sciences as separate and autonomous fields of inquiry, further, tends to minimize the connections between these sciences and other kinds of knowledge. Aristotle also often describes the exercise of crafts as satisfying merely utilitarian ends and therefore as degrading to the body and mind. Passages in the *Politics, Ethics,* and *Metaphysics,* for example, condemn manual labor as inferior and contemptible.[3] These passages served for some medieval authors as texts to reinforce a conception of crafts as unworthy, servile or vulgar.

At the same time, although crafts play only an inconspicuous part in Aristotle's classification of the arts and sciences, his discussion of art and nature and his account of the divisions of knowledge contain great potential for relating crafts to each other and to the higher sciences. His scattered comments on mechanics as a more physical part of mathematics, on the theoretical and practical aspects of economics and on the relationship of subalternate or subordinate arts to more general or higher arts, for example, if vague and unsystematic, could nevertheless be developed into devices for integrating crafts into philosophy.[4] Moreover, the very comprehensiveness of Aristotle's division of knowledge into theoretical, practical and productive may have indirectly encouraged exploration of how crafts could be fitted into this overall picture of knowledge.

The medieval West in the twelfth and thirteen centuries inherited both of these implicit approaches to the value of technology, not only through the direct reading of Aristotle himself but also through the reading of the works of Arabic philosophers and scientists who had themselves read Aristotle in the light of their own intellectual interests. Islam, unlike early medieval Europe, had maintained continuous contact with the entire Aristotelian corpus; Arabic thinkers, however, often interpreted Aristotle according to a sophisticated philosophical tradition heavily colored with Neoplatonism.[5] One result of this complex process was the production of elaborate, highly precise classifications of the arts and sciences which gave a major place to crafts and other arts related to technology.

Arabic classifications of knowledge tend to modify Aristotle's original scheme in characteristic ways.[6] First, these classifications often introduce

---

[3] On Aristotle's view of crafts as degrading, see above, Chapter II, pp. 28–29.

[4] See above, Chapter II, pp. 34f.

[5] See especially, F. E. Peters, *Aristotle and the Arabs: The Aristotelian Tradition in Islam* (New York: New York University Press, 1968), 3–17.

[6] On Arabic classifications of the sciences, see Peters, *Aristotle and the Arabs*, 79–87, 105–120; Harry Austryn Wolfson, "The Classification of Sciences in Medieval Jewish Philosophy," in *Hebrew Union College Jubilee Volume (1875–1925)* (Philadelphia: Jewish Publication Society Press, 1926), 263–315, which includes much information on the Arabic classifications; Majid Fakhry, "The Liberal Arts in the Mediaeval Arabic Tradition from the Seventh to the Twelfth Centuries," in *Arts libéraux et philosophie au Moyen Âge; Actes du quatrième Congrès International de Philosophie Médiévale* (Montreal: Institut d'Etudes Médiévales, 1969, Paris: Libraire Philosophique J. Vrin, 1969), 91–97, and Seyyed Hossein Nasr, *Science and Civilization in Islam* (Cambridge, Mass.: Harvard University Press, 1968), 60–64. Excerpts

Neoplatonic elements and, in particular, emphasize the role of mathematics.[7] Second, Aristotle's separation of philosophy into theoretical (speculative) and practical (knowledge expressed in action) is often reinterpreted to mean that philosophy as a whole has theoretical and practical, or operative, branches. Mathematics, for example, is often divided into "rational" mathematics which leads to an understanding of the speculative sciences and "sensible" mathematics which leads to an understanding of the "practical" arts or crafts.[8] Arts which involve the manipulation of matter, such as carpentry or mechanics, therefore, became in the Arabic scheme instances of the application of theoretical sciences through activity, i.e., practical sciences corresponding to speculative knowledge.

Within this framework Arabic classifications, perhaps reflecting contemporary interest in commerce and mechanical devices, typically give considerable attention to a variety of arts we would now include under technology.[9] Al-Farabi (d. 950), for example, whose classification of the sciences served as a model for many later Arabic classifications and was also influential in the Latin West, includes carpentry, stone-working and other crafts under practical geometry, the science of weights (statics) and the science of devices or instruments (*scientia de ingeniis*) as parts of mathematics, and medicine, agriculture, navigation and alchemy under physics.[10] Similarly, other Arabic thinkers including Amiri (992), Nasir al-Din al-Tusi and Ibn Khaldun (fourteenth century) include crafts within the divisions of the sciences, often categorizing medicine, agriculture, carpentry, cooking and other "necessary" activities as derived from natural philosophy.[11]

---

from some of the more important classifications are translated in Franz Rosenthal, *The Classical Heritage in Islam*, trans. Emile and Jenny Marmorstein (Berkeley: University of California Press, 1975), 52–70.

[7] Peters, *Aristotle and the Arabs*, 113, 119–120.

[8] Wolfson, "Classification of Sciences in Medieval Jewish Philosophy," 269–271.

[9] Peters, *Aristotle and the Arabs*, 108; Wolfson, "Classification of Sciences in Medieval Jewish Philosophy," 280, 298, 303; Wolfson also shows that medieval Jewish philosophers also sometimes adopted this pattern.

[10] Al-Farabi wrote two treatises on the classification of the sciences, *De scientiis*, ed. Manuel Alonso Alonso (Madrid: Escuelas de Estudios Arabes de Madrid y Granada, 1954). ed. Clemens Baeumker, *Alfarabi, Über den Ursprung der Wissenschaften*, Beiträge zur Geschichte der Philosophie des Mittelalters, 19.3 (Munster: Aschendorffsche Verlagsbuchhandlung, 1916). For al-Farabi's placement of crafts, see *De scientiis*, ed. Alonso, 86–90, 108–12 and *De ortu scientiarum*, ed. Baeumker, 20. Al-Farabi's classification is diagrammed in Nasr, *Science and Civilization*, 60–62. On al-Farabi's division of the sciences, see James A. Weisheipl, "Classification of the Sciences in Medieval Thought," *Medieval Studies* 27 (1965): 69–70 and Muhsin Mahdi, "Science, Philosophy, and Religion in Alfarabi's Enumeration of the Sciences," in *The Cultural Context of Medieval Learning*, ed. John E. Murdoch and Edith Dudley Sylla, Boston Studies in the Philosophy of Science, 26 (Boston: D. Reidel, 1975), 113–145, and on al-Farabi's ideas on mechanical science, see George Ovitt, "The Status of the Mechanical Arts in Medieval Classifications of Learning," *Viator* 14 (1983): 97. On al-Farabi's influence see Wolfson, "Classification of Sciences in Medieval Jewish Philosophy," 264–265.

[11] See Rosenthal, *Classical Heritage in Islam*, 63–70. For Nasir al-Din al-Tusi see *The Nasirean Ethics*, trans. G. Wickens (London: George Allen, 1962).

Medieval thinkers in turn drew upon various elements of this complex Aristotelian and Arabic tradition according to the texts available to them, and to their own interests, circumstances and intellectual orientation. Some, such as Vincent of Beauvais and Robert Kilwardby, as we have already seen, in various ways attempted to integrate Aristotelian and Arabic views of crafts with Hugh of St. Victor's concept of the *artes mechanicae*. Others, such as Thomas Aquinas, depended almost entirely upon a direct reading of Aristotle. Still others, including Domingo Gundisalvo and Roger Bacon, were profoundly influenced by Arabic views of knowledge. The resultant treatments of crafts in classifications of the arts and sciences, while still in some sense recognizably "Aristotelian" frequently differed considerably from one another. An assessment of twelfth- and thirteenth-century concepts of the nature and value of technology must consider this diversity.

The Twelfth Century

Domingo Gundisalvo's *De divisione philosophiae* (c. 1150) has long been recognized as one of the most important treatises on the classification of the sciences in the twelfth century.[12] Although it lacks originality and, as its editor has shown, is largely composed of quotations from both Arabic and Latin authors, including al-Farabi, whose works on the classification of the sciences Gundisalvo had translated,[13] it effectively introduced the Arabic pattern of classification to the Latin West.[14] Its significance lies, in part, in Gundisalvo's adoption of al-Farabi's conception of crafts as practical sciences.

The underlying structure of the *De divisione philosophiae* is Neoplatonic in that the sciences are arranged hierarchically in descending degrees of concreteness, from the knowledge of God.[15] Yet Gundisalvo also de-

---

[12] Domingo Gundisalvo, *De divisione philosophiae*, ed. Ludwig Baur, Beiträge zur Geschichte der Philosophie des Mittelalters, 4.2–3 (Munster: Druck und Verlag der Aschendorffschen Buchhandlung, 1903). Gundisalvo's treatise is singled out by Olaf Pedersen, "Du *quadrivium* à la physique: Quelques aperçus de l'évolution scientifique au Moyen Age," in *Artes Liberales von der Antiken Bildung zur Wissenschaft des Mittelalters*, ed. Josef Koch, Studien und Texte zur Geistesgeschichte des Mittelalters, no. 5 (Leiden: E. J. Brill, 1959), 115; A. C. Crombie, *Robert Grosseteste and the Origins of Experimental Science, 1100–1700* (Oxford: Clarendon Press, 1953), 36–40, and Franco Alessio, "La filosofia e la 'artes mechanicae' nel secolo XII," *Studi Medievali*, 3rd series, 6 (1965): 129–153. There is a partial translation of the *De divisione philosophiae* by Marshall Clagett and Edward Grant in Edward Grant, ed., *A Source Book in Medieval Science* (Cambridge, Mass.: Harvard University Press, 1974), 59–76.

[13] See Ludwig Baur, ed., *De divisione philosophiae*, 314; for an analysis of Gundisalvo's sources, see Baur's notes, 164–314.

[14] For a discussion of the relationship of the *De divisione philosophiae* to Kilwardby's *De ortu scientiarum*, see D. E. Sharp, "The *De ortu scientiarum* of Robert Kilwardby," *The New Scholasticism* 8 (1934): 2, 22 and Baur, ed. *De divisione philosophiae*, 268–275. See also below, n. 67. For the probable influence on Michael Scot, see below, n. 37.

[15] Weisheipl, "Classification of the Sciences in Medieval Thought," 70–72, emphasizes the Neoplatonic character of the *De divisione philosophiae* in contrast to Baur, ed. *De divisione philosophiae*, 314, who describes it as Aristotelian.

scribes philosophy as divided into *scientia*, or understanding of what is, and practical knowledge, or understanding of what ought to be done or executed.[16] Practical philosophy refers not only to ethics, economics and politics, as in the Aristotelian tradition, but also, following al-Farabi, to the practical disciplines which are part of mathematics. Under mathematics Gundisalvo includes not only the *quadrivium*, but perspective, the science of weights and the science of devices (*de ingeniis*).[17] This latter science teaches "ways of inventing" (*modos excogitandi*) and comprises knowledge of the instruments and methods by which the other sciences can be manifested or put into effect.[18] Gundisalvo's description refers to the instruments used by stone masons which measure bodies, instruments for lifting, musical instruments, weapons, mirrors and other optical devices, instruments used by carpenters and instruments "according to many arts."[19] Although the science of devices, which, as the most concrete, is placed last in the list of mathematical disciplines and may be considered as subordinate to geometry which considers "pure form," all branches of mathematics according to Gundisalvo have a practical or "instrumental" side.[20] Under practical arithmetic, for example, Gundisalvo lists the manipulation of numbers by adding and subtraction, the arithmetic used in business, the use of the abacus and mathematical games, and under practical geometry, surveying, carpentry, iron-working, masonry and the instruments used in these crafts.[21] The remaining branches of mathematics also have their appropriate instruments.[22]

Following al-Farabi, Gundisalvo gives the parts of natural science or physics as medicine, judgments, necromancy, images, agriculture, navigation, mirrors and alchemy.[23] A certain ambiguity exists about whether these sciences, too, are to be regarded as both theoretical and practical. Although each is defined as a speculative science in terms of how each

---

[16] Gundisalvo, *De divisione philosophiae*, Prologue (ed. Baur, 12).

[17] Ibid., 112–114, 121–124.

[18] Ibid., 122: "Sciencie ergo ingeniorum docent modos excogitandi et adinueniendi." On Gundisalvo's concept of the "science of devices," see Ovitt, "Status of the Mechanical Arts," 97–98, who finds it "lack[ing] in precision." For the impact of Arabic science on medieval ideas of the *quadrivium*, see Guy Beaujouan, "The Transformation of the Quadrivium," in *Renaissance and Renewal in the Twelfth Century*, ed. Robert L. Benson, Giles Constable and Carol D. Lanham (Cambridge, Mass.: Harvard University Press, 1982), 463–487. Gundisalvo's description follows that of al-Farabi, *De scientiis*, ed. Alonso, 108–112, very closely.

[19] Gundisalvo, *De divisione philosophiae*, ed. Baur, 112–124.

[20] Weisheipl, "Classification of the Sciences in Medieval Thought," 71.

[21] Gundisalvo, *De divisione philosophiae*, ed. Baur, 103–112.

[22] Ibid., 117, 120–121.

[23] Al-Farabi, *De ortu scientiarum* (ed. Baeumker, 20); Gundisalvo, *De divisione philosophiae* (ed. Baur, 20). For the occult sciences in Gundisalvo's work, see Lynn Thorndike, *History of Magic and Experimental Science* (New York: Columbia University Press, 1923), 2: 78–81. Al-Farabi's list of the eight parts of natural science also appears in Daniel of Morley's *Liber de naturis inferiorum et superiorum*, ed. Karl Sudhoff in *Archiv für die Geschichte der Naturwissenschaften und Technik* 8 (1917): 34.

contributes to an understanding of natural bodies, Gundisalvo describes medicine, the first of the natural sciences, as both theoretical and practical.[24] Practical medicine is said to consist of both natural and artificial instruments.[25] Having described medicine, however, Gundisalvo says that he will not speak about the other parts of physics because he has not yet attained full knowledge of them.[26] Recognizing that medicine, which had traditionally been regarded as connected to both theory and practice,[27] may have been an exception, Gundisalvo's text nevertheless gives the impression that the remaining parts of physics also combined a theoretical and practical aspect.

Gundisalvo also describes crafts, in this context given the collective name of the *fabrilis* or mechanical arts (*fabrilis autem sive mechanice artes*), together with the liberal arts as comprising the art of ruling the family, the second branch of civil life.[28] Here he expands considerably on al-Farabi, who discusses only the sciences of law and eloquence.[29] The mechanical arts provide assistance in the present life by supplying necessities and relieving poverty; they have many kinds according to the material they make use of, whether wood, wool, flax, leather, bone or the various kinds of metal and stones.[30]

For Gundisalvo, unlike Hugh of St. Victor, therefore, the function of crafts or the mechanical arts is secular, to supply goods to the family and appropriate instruments to the sciences. The value of crafts derives entirely from the recognition that crafts provide the means by which different areas of human knowledge can be executed. Yet this utilitarian character does not for Gundisalvo result in crafts being devalued; on the contrary, these practical arts seem to absorb the respect accorded to the theoretical sciences which they sustain.

The Thirteenth Century

Whereas Hugh of St. Victor's definition of the *artes mechanicae* was already well established by the end of the twelfth century, the alternative Aristotelian and Arabic conceptions of crafts as a category of knowledge did not begin to be widely used until the thirteenth. As Greek and Arabic scientific and philosophical texts became more available, however, classifications of the sciences more frequently reflected both the new learning as a whole, and Aristotelian and Arabic views of crafts.

On the other hand, the assimilation of Aristotle and his Arabic in-

---

[24] Gundisalvo, *De divisione philosophiae* (ed. Baur, 20–23, 83–86).

[25] Ibid., 86.

[26] Ibid., 89.

[27] John M. Riddle, "Theory and Practice in Medieval Medicine," *Viator* 5 (1974): 161–184.

[28] Gundisalvo, *De divisione philosophiae* (ed. Baur, 139). For this aspect of Gundisalvo's treatment of crafts, see Alessio, "Filosofia e la 'artes mechanicae,'" 149–152.

[29] Al-Farabi, *De scientiis*, ed. Alonso, 133–140.

[30] Gundisalvo, *De divisione philosophiae* (ed. Baur, 139).

terpreters focused attention on the nature of scientific thought and method; sometimes, if not always, such concerns included discussion of the relationship between speculative science and crafts.[31] In the hands of Robert Kilwardby and Roger Bacon, for example, consideration of the method and scope of the sciences, drawn from a combination of Aristotelian and Arabic sources, became a *locus* for explicating the utility of crafts in supplying information and instruments to the theoretical branches of knowledge. If in some respects foreshadowed in the previous century by Gundisalvo, the views of Kilwardby and Bacon on the value of technology were not only more original but drew upon a more varied and complex body of ideas.

A second result of the increased impact of Aristotle was greater attention to crafts as a basic part of civil life. The mechanical arts, often paired with the *trivium*, and, sometimes, law, were considered the basis for the maintenance of the community. Michael Scot wrote a division of the sciences (c. 1230) which places crafts with civil science as the parts of practical philosophy.[32] Jean of Antioch's introduction to his translation of Cicero's *Rhetoric* (1282)[33] and the slightly later encyclopedia of Brunetto Latini, the *Tresor*, includes the mechanical arts, together with the arts of speech, as a division of politics.[34]

This developing secular view of crafts, however, was sometimes confused by a latent tension between Aristotle's comments on crafts, available directly in the Aristotelian corpus, and the secondary Arabic tradition, exemplified by Gundisalvo, which had grown up around Aristotle's original classification. In particular, Aristotle's negative characterization of crafts as servile contrasted with the more positive evaluation of crafts found in the Arabic tradition.

This conflict is especially clear in Michael Scot's treatise on the division of the sciences, probably written around 1230 but known today only as excerpted in Vincent of Beauvais's *Speculum doctrinale*.[35] Scot offers two

---

[31] The importance of Aristotle, especially his *Posterior Analytics*, for thirteenth-century discussions of scientific method has been shown by Crombie, *Robert Grosseteste*, 35–36, 52–60; that such discussions did not always consider the mechanical arts *per se* is shown by Grosseteste himself, whose concern was with experimental science rather than crafts.

[32] Michael Scot, *Divisio philosophiae*, extant in fragments in Vincent of Beauvais's *Speculum doctrinale*, ed. Douai (1624) and photo-reproduced (Graz: Akademische Druck- u. Verlagsanstalt, 1965), 1.16, col. 16. Bauer, ed. *De divisione philosophiae*, 398–400, has collected these fragments.

[33] Jean of Antioch, *Notice sur la Rhétorique de Cicéron traduite par Maître Jean d'Antioche, ms. 590 de Musée Condé*, ed. Léopold Delisle (Paris: Librairie C. Klincksieck, 1899), 14. Jean places mechanical science, verbal science or grammar, logic and rhetoric, with law as the parts of the civil science or politics.

[34] Brunetto Latini, *Li livres dou Tresor*, ed. Francis J. Carmody (Berkeley: University of California Press, 1948), 21. The mechanical arts, or all works of the hands, are placed with the *trivium* as the parts of politics, "la plus haute science."

[35] On Michael Scot, see Charles Haskins, "Michael Scot and Frederick II," *Isis* 4 (1921): 250–275 and *Studies in the History of Mediaeval Science* (Cambridge: Cambridge University Press, 1924), and Lynn Thorndike, *Michael Scot* (London: Thomas Nelson, 1965).

brief divisions of the sciences. In the first,[36] Scot ascribes to Aristotle the principle that philosophy is divided into theory, which deals with all natural things, and practice, which deals with things having their origin in human will and works, including laws, institutions, armies, wars, and "all artificial things." Practical philosophy then is divided into civil science, which includes the sciences of language, morals and the other sciences which pertain to civil and respectable men, and vulgar arts, for example, shoemaking, building and other arts which pertain to common or unworthy men.

Scot's second division of practical philosophy, however, derives from the Arabic tradition, perhaps by way of Gundisalvo, and carries none of the negative attitudes of the first.[37] Here Scot separates practical philosophy into three parts corresponding to the three parts of theoretical philosophy. The first, which is related to natural science, includes medicine, agriculture, alchemy, necromancy, judgments, mirrors, navigation and "many other things." The second has a resemblance to doctrinal science or mathematics and includes business, carpentry, construction, stone-working, shoemaking and "many others of this sort which look to mechanics and are as it were its practice."[38]

The association of Aristotle with a view of the mechanical arts as servile was made explicit in other texts as well. Vincent of Beauvais, for example, also includes in his *Speculum doctrinale* a classification which he attributes to Aristotle in which philosophy is divided into mechanical and liberal; mechanical philosophy acquired its name because it was used in antiquity by servants.[39] Elsewhere, John of Dacia cites the *Metaphysics* to explain why the mechanical arts are servile with respect to the liberal arts, just as the body is servile with respect to the soul.[40]

The constraints of Aristotle's view of crafts, as well as a range of possible responses, are illustrated by the treatment of the mechanical arts in the commentaries of Albertus Magnus (1206–1280) and his pupil, Thomas Aquinas (1224–1274), on Aristotle's works. While both Albertus and Aquinas adopted a purely Aristotelian organization of the sciencies,[41] and consequently paid little attention to the Arabic Neoplatonic

---

[36] Vincent of Beauvais, *Speculum doctrinale* 1.16 (ed. Douai, col. 16).

[37] Du Wulf, *Histoire de la philosophie médiéval,* 1.313 suggests the connection with Gundisalvo.

[38] Vincent of Beauvais, *Speculum doctrinale* 1.16 (ed. Douai, col. 16): "et aliae huiusmodi multae, que spectant ad Mechanicam, et sunt quasi practica illius."

[39] Ibid., 1.16 (ed. Douai, col. 17). Vincent also excerpted al-Farabi; these fragments are collected in Alonso, 143–162.

[40] John of Dacia, *Divisio scientiae in Johannis Daci opera,* ed. Alfred Otto, *Corpus philosophorum Danicorum Medii Aevi,* 1 (Hauriae: Apud Librarium G. E. C. Gad, 1955), 3, 20.

[41] On the classification of the sciences in Albertus Magnus and Thomas Aquinas, see, especially, Mariétan, *Classification des sciences d'Aristote à St. Thomas,* 156–194 and Weisheipl, "Classification of the Sciences in Medieval Thought," 81–89. For the content of Albertus Magnus's thought on the different areas of knowledge (with the exception of the mechanical arts), see the collected essays in James Weisheipl, ed., *Albertus Magnus and the*

tradition of crafts as practical sciences, Albertus maintained a noticeably more positive attitude than did Aquinas.

James Weisheipl describes the "authentically Aristotelian" outlook of Albertus and Aquinas on the classification of the sciences as characterized by the subordination of mathematics to natural philosophy and the presentation of each science as autonomous in its own sphere.[42] In contrast to the Neoplatonic view, mathematics neither provides the principles of scientific demonstration nor serves as a link between the theoretical sciences and practical arts. Unlike Gundisalvo, and, as we shall see, Robert Kilwardby and Roger Bacon, therefore, Albertus and Aquinas do not attempt to connect crafts to higher branches of knowledge but regard them as a separate and distinct group of arts.

The basic divisions of philosophy for Albertus are those of Aristotle: the theoretical sciences, the practical arts, and arts concerned with making. Albertus's treatment of crafts as a part of philosophy, however, is far from systematic and his views are expressed in scattered comments rather than in any unified discussion. Even his terminology is eclectic. Although he most often refers to the *artes mechanicae,* he also uses the term *artes factivae,* derived from Aristotle's productive arts, and *apotelesmata,* derived from a later Greek tradition.[43] Although a treatise attributed to Albertus by his editors, B. Geyer and A. Borgnet, repeats Hugh of St. Victor's list and descriptions of the seven mechanical arts,[44] the genuine works imply that the mechanical arts consist of a large and unorganized group of arts, for which the examples of bread-making, wool-working, the military art, architecture and "other things of this sort" are given.[45] In another context, Albertus refers to the mechanical

---

Sciences: Commemorative Essays, 1980 (Toronto: Pontifical Institute of Mediaeval Studies, 1980).

42 Weisheipl, "Classification of the Sciences," 41. On Albertus and mathematics see A. G. Molland, "Mathematics in the Thought of Albertus," in *Albertus and the Sciences,* 468–469.

43 Albertus, for example, uses the term *artes mechanicae* in his commentary on the *Metaphysics* 1.1.6, 1.1.10, in *Opera omnia,* ed. Bernard Geyer (Cologne: Monasterium Westfalorum in Aedibus Aschendorff, 1960), 16: 9, 15; however, the same work uses *apotelesmata* and *ars factivum* as synonyms; see 1.1.9, 1.2.1, 1.2.9 and 2.8 (ed. Geyer, 13, 17, 26, 100). Similarly in his *Super Ethica* 1.2, and 1.8, ed. Wilhelmus Kubel in *Opera* (ed. Geyer, 14: 8, 9.43) he refers to *artes apotelesmata, artes factivae* and *artes mechanicae*. For additional examples of Albertus's use of the term *artes mechanicae,* see Peter Sternagel, *Die Artes Mechanicae im Mittelalter: Begriffs- und Bedeutungsgeschichte bis zum Ende des 13. Jahrhunderts* (Kallmung über Regensburg: Lassleben, 1966), 103–111. The origins of the terms *apotelesmata* and *factiva* as applied to crafts are made in the commentary on Aristotle's *Ethics* by Eustratius of Nicaea (fl. c. 1100) which was translated by Robert Grosseteste; the relevant sections are given in Robert Kilwardby, *De ortu scientiarum,* ed. Albert G. Judy (Oxford: Clarendon Press, 1976), 144, notes 1 and 3.

44 Albertus Magnus, *Liber de apprehensione* 7.22, in *Opera omnia,* ed. Augustus Borgnet (Paris: L. Vivès, 1841), 5: 631. On the question of the authenticity of the *Liber de apprehensione,* see Pearl Kibre, "The Boethian *De institutione arithmetica* and the Quadrivium in the Thirteenth Century University Milieu at Paris," in *Studies in Medieval Science: Alchemy, Astrology, Mathematics and Medicine* (London: The Hambledon Press, 1984), 79.

45 Albertus Magnus, commentary on the *Metaphysics* 1.1.10 (ed. Geyer, 16: 15).

arts in terms reminiscent of Gundisalvo as the "sciences of devices" (*scientiae de ingeniis*) which are subalternate to geometry.[46]

Perhaps because of the fragmented character of his views, Albertus's concept of the mechanical arts has not attracted much attention.[47] His Aristotelianism, however, gives coherence to his viewpoint. The mechanical arts, for Albertus, are those concerned with making, which we perform not for their own sake but for the sake of some utility.[48] Albertus's identification of the classical distinction between arts which we perform for some useful product and those (like singing and dancing) which we perform for the sake of themselves, with the distinction between the mechanical and the liberal arts, sometimes leads him to the curious position that animals possess more of the liberal arts than the mechanical.[49] Albertus attempts to refine the philosophical content of his definition by applying Aristotle's concepts of form and matter to the processes used by the mechanical arts. Thus, he divides the mechanical arts into three kinds according to their relationship to their material.[50] The first type considers matter simply and draws material into a completed form, as in ship-building or as the builder of a house considers stones and wood from which he brings out the form of a house. The second type uses an already completed object, as the soldier uses a sword for the common utility of all in the community; this kind includes economics and the military art. And the third type is in the middle between these, such as wool-working which both makes use of wool and produces textiles for the use of all.

This emphasis on utility, however, does not for Albertus, as for Aristotle and, as we shall see, for Aquinas, mean that the mechanical arts are inherently inferior or servile. When Albertus explicates a passage at the beginning of the *Metaphysics* in which Aristotle argues that the inventors of the arts of recreation were naturally more admired than the inventors of useful arts because their arts did not aim at utility (981b13), he emphasizes, as far as possible without distorting the passage, the importance of admiring the mechanical arts; these, like the liberal arts,

---

[46] Albertus Magnus, commentary on the *Posterior Analytics* 1.2.17, in *Opera* (ed. Borgnet 2: 67).

[47] Weisheipl, "Classification of the Sciences in Medieval Thought," does not consider Albertus's view of the mechanical arts; Mariétan, *Classification des sciences d'Aristote à St. Thomas*, 158–160, considers them only very briefly. Sternagel, *Artes Mechanicae*, 103–111, provides references to most of the relevant texts. Ovitt, "Status of the Mechanical Arts," however, does not consider Albertus at all and Guy Allard, "Les arts mécaniques aux yeux de l'idéologie médiévale," in *Les arts mécaniques au Moyen Age*, Cahiers d'études médiévales, 7 (Montreal: Bellarmin; Paris: J. Vrin, 1982), 17, refers to Albertus only very briefly.

[48] Albertus Magnus, commentary on the *Metaphysics* 1.1.6 and 2.8 (ed. Geyer, 16: 9, 100); *De anima* 2.2.2 (ed. Clemens Stroick in *Opera* [ed. Geyer, 7: 85]); *Super Ethica*, 1.1 (ed. Kubel in *Opera*, 14: 6).

[49] Albertus Magnus, *De animalibus* 8.6.2, ed. Hermann Stadler, Beiträge zur Geschichte der Philosophie des Mittelalters, 15 (Munster: Aschendorffsche Verlagsbuchhandlung, 1916), 671–673; commentary on the *Metaphysics* 1.1.6 (ed. Geyer, 16: 9).

[50] Albertus Magnus, commentary on the *Physics* 2.1.11 (ed. Borgnet, 3: 114–115).

are directed toward providing the necessary and useful things of political life.[51] Albertus also remarks in his commentary on Aristotle's *Ethics* that because they consider the reasons behind the production of works, "the mechanical arts ought not to be excluded by the philosopher," as, for example, Vitruvius reported on architecture, Palladius on agriculture, Vegetius on the military art, Razi on surgery and other philosophers on other arts.[52]

Albertus's interest in observing contemporary technological methods and practices is well known; his accounts of iron-smelting, and agricultural techniques such as the building of drainage ditches and cross-plowing to avoid erosion, are accurate and detailed.[53] Little of this personal interest carries over into his discussions of crafts as a part of knowledge, which remain somewhat dry and abstract. Nevertheless, Albertus uses Aristotle creatively in this area as he does in others.

Aquinas, on the other hand, persistently displays a pejorative attitude toward the mechanical arts. He resists, for example, recognizing crafts as the practical part of any division of speculative philosophy, instead arguing that according to the *Ethics* only moral philosophy is appropriately called "practical" and, further, that while medicine, alchemy, agriculture, etc. may be subalternate to physics, they are not parts of physics since "physics in itself and all its parts is speculative."[54] Even in his discussion of the *scientiae mediae*, or the sciences which apply mathematical principles to natural things, where Aquinas might be expected to consider the importance of crafts, he mentions only astrology, music, perspective, and, in one instance, statics.[55]

---

[51] Albertus Magnus, commentary on the *Metaphysics* 1.1.10 (ed. Geyer, 16: 15). See also in the commentary on the *Metaphysics* 1.2.9 (ed. Geyer, 16: 26):

> Licet igitur aliae quaedam sint *magis necessariae* ad vitae regimen, sicut praecipue sunt architectonicae et civilis et medicina, nulla tamen inter omnes est *dignior* quam ista. . . . Illae quae sunt operatrices apotelesmatum, quibus vitae humanae conservatur communicatio, sunt maxime necessariae, quia sine illis aut vita hominis non est aut omnino mala et laboriosa est et ideo sapientiae intendere non potest.

[52] Albertus Magnus, commentary on the *Ethics* 1.3.2 (ed. Borgnet, 7: 32): ". . . et ita ars quae rationes operum considerat, habet sapientiae rationem: propter quod artes mechanicae a Philosopho non sunt refutandae."

[53] Nadine F. George, "Albertus Magnus and Chemical Technology in a Time of Transition," in *Albertus Magnus and the Sciences*, ed. Weisheipl, 235–261; for Albertus's comments on contemporary agricultural techniques, see Clarence J. Glacken, *Traces on the Rhodian Shore: Nature and Culture in Western Thought from Ancient Times to the End of the Eighteenth Century* (Berkeley: University of California Press, 1967), 314–316, 346 and on metallurgy, J. M. Riddle and J. A. Mulholland, "Albertus Magnus on Stones and Minerals," in *Albertus Magnus and the Sciences*, ed. Weisheipl, 221–227.

[54] Thomas Aquinas, *The Division and Methods of the Sciences: Questions V and VI of his Commentary on the 'De Trinitate' of Boethius*, trans. Armand Maurer, 3rd. rev. ed. (Toronto: Pontifical Institute of Mediaeval Studies, 1963), 14–15; *Sancti Thomae de Aquino Expositio super librum Boethii De Trinitate*, ed. Bruno Decker (Leiden: E. J. Brill, 1955), Qu. 5, art. 1, reply 4 and 5, 171: "Et sic relinquitur quod physica secundum se et secumdum omnes partes suas est speculativa quamvis aliquae scientiae operativae subalternentur ei."

[55] Carlos A. Ribeiro do Nascimento, "La statut épistemologique des 'sciences inter-

The mechanical arts not only stand apart from other kinds of knowledge but are markedly inferior because of their corporeal nature.[56] Although these arts, more closely than the liberal arts or the sciences, conform to Aristotle's definition of art as "reason's habit of making external things properly," and correspond precisely to the productive arts,[57] they are necessarily unworthy: "those arts which are ordered to some utility through performing an action are called mechanical, or servile."[58] More consistently than any of his contemporaries, Aquinas points to the utilitarian character of crafts as a sign of their servility. Following Aristotle, his concern with the independent value of speculative science, which is sought only "for itself," leads him to ignore the possible relevance of the mechanical arts.

Even Aquinas, however, was not entirely untouched by contemporary interpretations of the role of the mechanical arts. His examples of medicine, alchemy, agriculture and similar sciences as subalternate to physics recall the Arabic pattern of classification. In his commentary on Aristotle's *Posterior Analytics,* moreover, he acknowledges that those "subordinate sciences, as the mechanical arts, which employ measurements," may apply a demonstration from geometry.[59] Later in the same work he mentions that mechanical engineering, i.e. the art of making machines, is subordinate to stereometry, or the science of measuring bodies.[60] In this limited context, at least, he recognizes a connection between crafts and mathematics. Finally, although Aquinas appears to owe little to Hugh of St. Victor beyond the adoption of the term *artes mechanicae,* he does at least once appear to echo Hugh and imply a positive role for technology when he remarks that man "can equip himself with weapons and covering and the other necessities of life in an infinite variety of ways. . . . And indeed it is far more suitable for a rational

médiaires' selon S. Thomas d'Aquin," in *La science de la nature: Théories et pratiques,* Cahiers d'études médiévales, 2 (Montreal: Bellarmin; Paris: J. Vrin, 1974), 43–46. Although Aquinas does refer to *artes mechanicae, quae utuntur mensuris* (see below n. 57), these are not called *scientiae mediae.* See also Jean Gagné, "Du *quadrivium* aux *scientiae mediae,*" in *Arts libéraux et philosophie au Moyen Âge,* 975–986.

[56] Allard, "Arts mécaniques," 19, 23 emphasizes this point.

[57] Francis J. Kovach, "Divine Art in Saint Thomas Aquinas," in *Arts libéraux et philosophie au Moyen Âge,* 663–669. Also useful for the definition of the mechanical arts in Aquinas is Pierre Conway and Benedict Ashley, "The Liberal Arts in Thomas Aquinas," *Thomist* 22 (1959): 460–532. Sternagel, *Artes Mechanicae,* 103–111, provides additional references. Ovitt, "Status of the Mechanical Arts," does not discuss Aquinas.

[58] Thomas Aquinas, *In I Metaphysicam* 3 ad c, in *Opera omnia,* Leonine edition (Rome: Ex Typographia Polyglotta, 1882), 46: "illae vero, quae ordinantur ad aliquam utilitatem per actionem habendam, dicuntur mechanicae, sive serviles." This work has been translated: *Commentary on the Metaphysics of Aristotle,* trans. John P. Rowan (Chicago: Henry Regnery Company, 1961).

[59] Thomas Aquinas, *In I Posteriora Analytica,* lect. 17, in *Opera omnia,* Leonine Edition, 1: 207: "quod demonstratio geometriae procedit ad scientias inferiores, sicut sunt artes mechanicae, quad utuntur mensuris." This work is translated: *Commentary on the Posterior Analytics of Aristotle,* trans. F. R. Larcher (Albany, N.Y.: Magi Books, 1970).

[60] Thomas Aquinas, *In I Posteriora Analytica,* lect; 25, in *Opera,* Leonine edition, 1: 237: *Commentary,* trans. Larcher, 79–80.

nature, which is capable of endless ideas, to have in this way the ability to equip itself with an endless catalogue of tools."[61]

The intellectual currents which fed into the formation of thirteenth-century views of the definition and status of the mechanical arts, therefore, produced not one picture of technology as a category of knowledge but a variety of attitudes and positions. The problem of formulating a unified picture from these diverse elements, which included not only the Aristotelian "making" arts and the Arabic conception of crafts as practical science but also, as we have seen in the previous chapter, the continued importance of Hugh of St. Victor's definition of the mechanical arts, was a formidable one.

Robert Kilwardby's *De ortu scientiarum* was one attempt to synthesize the various views of the mechanical arts circulating in the thirteenth century. Kilwardby, whose classification of the sciences is discussed in detail in Chapter IV,[62] follows Hugh of St. Victor's seven-fold division of the *artes mechanicae* and retains Hugh's definition of them as a separate and independent group of arts; from this perspective Kilwardby belongs firmly in the Victorine tradition. Kilwardby's organization of the sciences, however, shows the strong influence of Latin Neoplatonism and, as George Ovitt points out, of the Aristotelian concept of scientific demonstration according to the *propter quid* and *quia*.[63] These elements bring Kilwardby also into the Arabic tradition on crafts. In particular, Kilwardby's placement of the mechanical arts with the verbal and practical arts as the human sciences whose purpose is to aid in living well, and his emphasis on the reciprocal relationship of theoretical and practical science strongly suggest the influence of Arabic patterns of classification.[64] Kilwardby is known to have read Gundisalvo's *De divisione philosophiae* and, although he rejects much of Gundisalvo's organization of the sciences,[65] he may well have been influenced by Gundisalvo's description of crafts as practical sciences. In this context, Kilwardby's insistence that "the theoretical sciences are practical and the practical sciences theoretical,"[66] and his account of the seven mechanical arts as the operative or practical side of physics, arithmetic, geometry and astronomy, appear to reflect, at least indirectly, the impact of Arabic concep-

---

[61] Thomas Aquinas, *Summa Theologiae* 1a.91, 3.2. ed. and trans. Edmund Hill, in *Summa theologiae*, ed. Blackfriars (New York: McGraw-Hill; London: Eyre and Spottiswoode, 1961), 28: ". . . quibus potest parare sibi arma et tegumenta et alia vitae necessaria infinitis modis . . . et hoc etiam magis competebat rationali naturae, quae est infinitarum conceptionum, ut haberet facultatem infinita instrumenta sibi parandi."

[62] See above, Chapter IV, pp. 118–123.

[63] Weisheipl, "Classification of the Sciences," 75–78; Ovitt, "Status of the Mechanical Arts," 102–104.

[64] Kilwardby, *De ortu scientiarum* 1.1, 34.346, 36.352, 41.379–409 (ed. Judy, 9, 122, 124–125, 133–143). See above, Chapter IV, pp. 120–122.

[65] Sharp, "The *De ortu scientiarium*," 2.

[66] Kilwardby, *De ortu scientiarum* 42.393 (ed. Judy, 138): "Videtur ergo quod et speculativae sint practicae et practicae speculativae."

tions of crafts.[67] While Ovitt rightfully emphasizes Kilwardby's originality, therefore, the *De ortu scientiarum* is the product not only of the twelfth-century Victorine tradition but also of a long-standing Arabic tradition.[68]

The Arabic influence is far clearer in the work of Roger Bacon (1214–1292). Bacon's enthusiasm for technological marvels such as flying machines, submarines and self-propelled vehicles and his interest in "experimental science" are well known.[69] Far less attention has been paid, however, to the way in which Bacon integrated crafts and technological arts into his classification of knowledge and, consequently, to how he conceived their function as part of philosophy.[70]

Bacon does not seem to have been especially interested in the division of knowledge *per se* and, as far as is known, did not write a work specifically on the classification of the arts and sciencies.[71] Two of his works, however, the *Communium naturalium* and the *Communia mathematica*, are prefaced by outlines of the parts of natural science and mathematics.[72]

Bacon begins the *Communium naturalium* by dividing knowledge into grammar or the study of languages and logic, mathematics, natural sci-

---

[67] For discussion of these passages in the *De ortu scientiarum*, see above. According to Weisheipl, "Classification of the Sciences," 78: "Underlying his [Kilwardby's] discussion of the speculative sciences is the conviction that the science of numerical proportions is the key to understanding all the other sciences. . . . This typically neo-Platonic conviction was undoubtedly due rather to the influence of the Arabic sources."

[68] Ovitt, "Status of the Mechanical Arts," 102–104. Ovitt also somewhat over-emphasizes Kilwardby's originality with respect to the Victorine tradition, see above, Chapter IV, pp. 118–119.

[69] See Thorndike, *History of Magic and Experimental Science*, 2: 616–691 and Stewart Copinger, *Roger Bacon and his Search for a Universal Science* (New York: Russell and Russell, 1971). There is an important Ph.D. thesis by Jeremiah M. Hackett, "The Meaning of Experimental Science (*Scientia experimentalis*) in the Philosophy of Roger Bacon," Ph.D. diss., University of Toronto, 1983. For Bacon's expression of the powers of technology, see Roger Bacon, *Opus maius* 6. Exemplum 3, *The 'Opus maius' of Roger Bacon*, ed. John Henry Bridges (Oxford: Clarendon Press, 1897; rpt. Frankfurt: Minerva, 1964), 2: 217; *Epistola Fratris Rogerii Baconis de Secretis operibus artis et naturae et de nullitate magicae* 4, in *Fr. Rogerii Bacon Opera quaedam hactenus inedita*, ed. J. S. Brewer, Rerum Britannicarum Medii Aevi Scriptores, 11 (London: Longman, Green, Longman and Roberts, 1859), 532–533. On Bacon's ideas of scientific progress, see A. G. Molland, "Medieval Ideas of Scientific Progress," *Journal of the History of Ideas* 39 (1976): 567–571.

[70] Sternagel, *Artes Mechanicae*, does not consider Bacon and Ovitt, "Status of the Mechanical Arts," 99, refers to him only very briefly. Weisheipl, "Classification of the Sciences," 79–81, considers Bacon, but not his treatment of technology. An exception is Allard, "Arts mécaniques," 29, who considers Bacon's ideas on technology "strange and new" because of the high value he gives to the useful sciences. Hackett, "Meaning of Experimental Science," compares Bacon's list of the sciences with Kilwardby's, see *Dissertation Abstracts International*, August, 1984, 45.02: 545-A.

[71] For a list of Bacon's works, see the appendix in A. G. Little, *Roger Bacon Essays* (Oxford: Clarendon Press, 1914).

[72] Roger Bacon, *Communium naturalium* 1, in *Opera hactenus inedita Rogeri Baconi*, ed. Robert Steele (Oxford: Clarendon Press, 1922), fasc 2: 5–9, and *Communia mathematica Fratris Rogeri* in *Opera* (ed. Steele, fasc 16: 38–55). The introduction to the *Communia mathematica*, vii, points out that both works in their present form were put together by an unknown "assembler" from several manuscripts.

ence or physics and metaphysics, to which is attached morals.[73] Since mathematics, according to Bacon, "perfects and regulates" the natural sciences,[74] the parts of physics have a strongly mathematical character: they are perspective, astronomy (judicial and operative), the science of weights, alchemy, agriculture, medicine and experimental science.[75] Bacon defines the subject area of each science, referring each to the appropriate texts by Aristotle, Avicenna, Averroes and others.[76] Experimental science, he says, instructs the other sciences in the production of instruments and works.[77]

The more elaborate division of the sciences in the *Communia mathematica* helps clarify the relationship between mathematics, natural science and instruments. Here Bacon considers the theoretical and practical parts of geometry and arithmetic. Practical geometry is concerned with instruments and various useful works.[78] Its first part is that science of ruling families and states which is called agriculture, followed by the sciences of measurement which are necessary in the building of cities, houses, towers, etc. The fourth part consists of the construction of canals, aqueducts, bridges, ships, etc.; the fifth includes the construction of marvelous instruments, including flying machines, self-propelled vehicles and lifting devices. The sixth division includes the building of weapons. This is followed by a second division of practical geometry which includes the instruments used by all the sciences, including astrology, music, perspective, science of weights, experimental science, medicine and alchemy.[79] Practical arithmetic then includes the use of the abacus and astronomical tables, calendars, weights and measures, the measurement of distances and dimensions, mathematical games and the ordering of all kinds of business by correcting, selling, contracting, leasing, barter, exchange, adjustments, spending and saving.[80]

The format of Bacon's account clearly recalls the Arabic pattern of classification, as exemplified by al-Farabi and Gundisalvo, in which crafts and other technological arts are defined as practical mathematics which supply devices or instruments to the other sciencies. In Bacon, this capacity of the practical sciences to provide the means by which man can exert power over the natural world (or over his fellow man) overshadows what the theoretical sciences can provide by themselves; the aim of science, indeed, is to perform works for the advantage of

[73] Bacon, *Communium naturalium* 1 (ed. Steele, 1). This division is comparable to that in the *Opera maius* except that optics and experimental science are included under physics.
[74] On Bacon's view of the role of mathematics, see Weisheipl, "Classification of the Sciences," 79–80, and N. W. Fisher and S. Unguru, "Experimental Science and Mathematics in Roger Bacon's Thought," *Traditio* 27 (1971): 353–378.
[75] Bacon, *Communium naturalium* 1 (ed. Steele, 5).
[76] Ibid., (ed. Steele, 5–9).
[77] Ibid., (ed. Steele, 9).
[78] Bacon, *Communia mathematica,* 1.3 (ed. Steele, 42–44).
[79] Ibid., (ed. Steele, 44–47).
[80] Ibid., (ed. Steele, 47–49).

individuals or the community. A passage in the *Opus maius* brings Bacon's understanding of the relationship between science and technology into sharper focus:

> All things of such wonderful utility in the state belong chiefly to this [experimental] science. For this science has the same relation to the other sciences as the science of navigation to the carpenter's art and the military art to that of the engineer. For this science teaches how wonderful instruments may be made, and uses them when made, and also considers all secret things owing to the advantages they may possess for the state and for individuals; and it directs other sciences as its handmaids, and therefore the whole power of speculative science is attributed especially to this science.[81]

Thus Bacon begins to bring together the isolated elements implicit in the Arabic classifications of crafts as part of civil science and as the operative side of mathematics into an organic vision of technology as applied science in the service of man's earthly life.

Bacon's relationship to contemporary traditions on the place of crafts in classifications of knowledge is not completely clear. He once refers to the "mechanical arts [which] are wool-making, arms (*armatura*), navigation, hunting, agriculture and medicine" and therefore knew the definition of the mechanical arts according to Hugh of St. Victor or one of his followers.[82] However, although Bacon often couches his discussion of the sciences in Augustinian terms reminiscent of Hugh's concept of the mechanical arts, he was far more concerned with the secular value of technology. The only other instance I have been able to identify in which Bacon uses the term *artes mechanicae* is uncharacteristically pejorative. Citing Aristotle's *Metaphysics*, Bacon identifies the mechanical arts with Aristotle's manual worker who works without knowing the reason for what he does; the art of building, thus, is merely mechanical geometry and is not part of philosophy.[83]

The degree of Bacon's originality with respect to his Arabic sources is uncertain without a full examination of how crafts were treated in Arabic classifications of the sciences, unfortunately beyond the scope of the present study. Within the context of Latin writers, however, Bacon expressed the view that technology provided the instruments by which

---

[81] Bacon, *The Opus Majus of Roger Bacon*, trans. Robert Belle Burke (New York: Russell and Russell, 1962), 2: 633 (ed. Bridges 2: 221):

> Tamen omnia hujusmodi utilitatis mirificae in republica pertinent principaliter ad hanc scientiam. Nam haec se habet ad alias, sicut navigatoria ad carpentariam, et sicut ars militaris ad fabrilem; haec enim praecipit ut fiant instrumenta mirabilia, et factis utitur, et etiam cogitat omnia secreta propter utilitates reipublicae et personarum; et imperat aliis scientiis, sicut ancillis suis, et ideo tota sapientiae speculativae potestas isti scientiae specialiter attribuitur.

Cf. *Opus minus* in *Opera*, ed. Brewer, 2: 321, 324, 328.

[82] Bacon, *Sumule dialectices* in *Opera*, ed. Steele, 15: 193.

[83] Bacon, *Compendium philosophiae* 4 in *Opera*, ed. Brewer 1: 420.

human beings both understand, and exert power over, nature more explicitly and forcefully than any of his contemporaries. As Guy Allard has suggested, Bacon came close to reversing the usual hierarchy of the speculative and useful in medieval thought.[84] Yet, this concept of the value of technology, which Allard describes as "strange and new," appears to be part of a broader tradition. Even if less universalized and explicit, as in al-Farabi and Gundisalvo, or expressed in different terms, as in Kilwardby, comparable ideas flourished among Bacon's contemporaries. Perhaps it might even be said that Bacon, usually regarded as a maverick, was, in this respect at least, more representative than that arbiter of medieval thought, Thomas Aquinas.

[84] Allard, "Arts mécaniques," 29. See also Allard's comparison of Albertus, Aquinas and Bacon in "Réactions de trois penseurs du XIIIe siècle vis-à-vis de l'Alchimie," in *Science de la nature*, 97–106.

TRANS. AMER. PHIL. SOC.
VOL. 80 PT. 1, 1990

VI. Conclusion

By the end of the thirteenth century, medieval thinkers had developed several definitions of craft and craftsmanship which could be integrated into prevailing systems of thought, whether Augustinian or Aristotelian in tenor. The mechanical arts were given moral and intellectual sanction either by placing them within the context of man's efforts to restore himself to his pre-lapsarian condition, as in the Victorine tradition, or by defining them as applied science, as in the Arabic tradition. By the close of the thirteenth century, the mechanical arts had come to be regarded as a necessary and often highly valued category of knowledge.

This new understanding of the mechanical arts represented a substantial and significant change from the classical evaluation of craft and craftsmanship. Classical philosophy had been profoundly ambivalent about technology. While crafts were sometimes implicitly acknowledged as a part of human knowledge and achievement, they were also often regarded as non-rational and therefore as antithetical to mankind's highest and truest ends. For many twelfth- and thirteenth-century thinkers, however, the mechanical arts, if not the highest form of learning, were clearly an essential kind of knowledge which shared in the ultimate aims of natural philosophy or theology.

The interest of medieval thinkers in integrating crafts into philosophy, moreover, was more persistent and thoughtful than has been previously recognized. Scholarly treatment of medieval ideas about technology has tended to single out certain figures as "exceptions" to what has been perceived as a general devaluation of technology by medieval intellectuals. Lynn White, for example, has pointed to Hugh of St. Victor, George Ovitt to Robert Kilwardby and Raymond Lull, and Guy Allard to Roger Bacon as standing apart from their contemporaries in their attitudes toward the mechanical arts. In fact, if we look more closely at medieval classifications of the arts and sciences, it appears that each of these thinkers depended upon and synthesized an earlier body of thought which gave his ideas substance and weight. Without minimizing the importance and originality of Hugh, Kilwardby, and Bacon, they can most usefully be seen not as isolated figures but as representative of a broad interest in articulating the value of technology as a category of knowledge.

Medieval thinkers, therefore, reworked the classical heritage of ideas about crafts and craftsmanship and explored technology's positive place in the relationship of human beings to God and nature within the framework available to them. To what extent, then, did those twelfth- and thirteenth-century ideas anticipate or influence modern attitudes toward technology? The question is an important one, both in itself and because the search for the origins of present-day Western assumptions and technological practices has been a pervasive, if not always explicit, context for much of the discussion about technology in the Middle Ages.

First, the medieval writers discussed here established that crafts and craftsmanship had a normal place among the recognized arts and sciences. Although the precise lines of transmission between thirteenth-century, Renaissance, and early modern classifications of the sciences have yet to be established, it is clear that after the thirteenth century the mechanical arts (as we have seen, a term still current in the early modern period) or their equivalent under the seventeenth-century neologism "technology," were assumed in Western thought to be an integral part of the taxonomy of knowledge.

Second, the history of definitions of the mechanical arts sheds some light on broader issues raised by Lynn White, George Ovitt, and others. Classifications of the sciences, for example, offer little evidence in support of Lynn White's thesis that Latin Christianity "caused" the West to become technologically advanced. Certainly, some aspects of Christian theology supplied important justifications for the pursuit of the mechanical arts for many of these writers, in particular the Victorines. Yet for many others new ideas about the nature and aims of natural science derived from Islamic Arabic thought were more important. On the other hand, contrary to White's assertion that medieval philosophers were blinded by classical prejudice against technology, these treatises show that twelfth- and thirteenth-century intellectuals not only shared in the general interest in technology of the period but actively sought to revise classical ideas in order to accommodate technology within the sphere of legitimate knowledge.

The history of the mechanical arts also offers a parallel and often complementary perspective to the development of monastic attitudes toward labor outlined by George Ovitt. Unlike monastic writings, medieval definitions of the *artes mechanicae* were developed by theologians or theologically-trained scientists within the context of the philosopher's task to categorize or systematize knowledge. The setting was the university or school, not the artist's workshop or the monastery. Their concerns, therefore, were somewhat different from those of the monastic writers with which Ovitt largely deals. The question of the social, moral, and religious value of labor *per se* is largely incidental to these thinkers; their interest is rather in justifying the invention of machines, tools, and techniques as a rational and intellectual enterprise.

Given this different orientation, the thought of monastic writers on the place of manual labor and university writers on the place of the mechanical arts diverges somewhat. Both sometimes share in a certain snobbish attitude toward workers themselves. Yet, if as Ovitt suggests, by the thirteenth century the Church was rejecting an earlier commitment to communal labor and divorcing the work of the hands from the religious life, medieval writers on the mechanical arts seem to be in the process of creating a distinction between purely physical labor and the intellectual work of the inventor, engineer, or mechanician. Whereas monastic writers may have rejected the *opus manuum* and thereby secularized it, writers on the mechanical arts continued to justify these arts on both religious and secular grounds, not as work of the hands but as intellectual work.

This philosophical orientation explains the admittedly abstract quality of medieval discussions of the mechanical arts, which had recourse to intellectual tradition and book-learning rather than hands-on experience. There is little of the immediacy that one finds, for example, in the writings of Palissy or Juan Luis Vives in the sixteenth century. Nor did twelfth- and thirteenth-century thinkers have a clearly worked out view of science as founded on mechanical principles and primarily concerned to manipulate the natural world for the practical benefit of mankind, such as we see in the scientific vision of the sixteenth and seventeenth centuries. In this sense, twelfth- and thirteenth-century thinkers did not "value" the mechanical arts in the way the modern world values technology.

But this is as much to say that the medieval world is not the modern world and that medieval thought is not modern thought. Europe in 1300 was just beginning to enter into the complex social and economic changes which marked the gradual shift from feudalism to capitalism and would sustain the development of a distinctively modern worldview. It would take a Scientific Revolution to overthrow Aristotelian science and provide a new ontology underpinning mechanical philosophy. It would take other revolutions, both political and intellectual, to establish the material world as more important than the spiritual one. Medieval writers on the mechanical arts did not entirely overcome the ambivalence toward technology inherited from antiquity and they did not invent an entirely new way of looking at technology. They did, however, attempt in various ways to fashion a coherent and positive view of technology from the diverse body of thought developed by their contemporaries and predecessors. In doing this, they made an important contribution to the development of Western cultural attitudes toward technology.

TRANS. AMER. PHIL. SOC.
VOL. 80 PT. 1, 1990

Selected Bibliography

Abbreviations

PG = *Patrologiae cursus completus. Series graeca.* Edited by J.-P. Migne. 162 vols. Paris: J.-P. Migne, 1859–87.
PL = *Patrologiae cursus completus. Series latina.* Edited by J.-P. Migne. 221 vols. Paris: J.-P. Migne, 1855–65.

Primary Sources

Adelard of Bath. *Die Quaestiones naturales des Adelardus von Bath.* Edited by Martin Müller. Beiträge zur Geschichte der Philosophie des Mittelalters, 31. Munster: Aschendorff, 1934.
———. *Quaestiones naturales.* Translated by Hermann Gollancz. In *Dodi Ve-nechdi the work of Berachya Hanakden . . . to which is added the first English translation from the Latin of Adelard of Bath's Quaestiones naturales.* London: H. Milford, 1920.
Albertus Magnus. *De animalibus.* Edited by Hermann Stadler. Beiträge zur Geschichte der Philosophie des Mittelalters, 15. Munster: Aschendorffsche Verlagsbuchhandlung, 1916.
———. *Opera omnia.* 38 vols. Edited by Augustus Borgnet. Paris: L. Vivès, 1841.
———. *Opera omnia.* 28 vols. Edited by Bernard Geyer. Cologne: Monasterium Westfalorum, In Aedibus Aschendorff, 1960.
Aldhelm. *De virginitate.* Edited by R. Ehwald. In *Opera, Monumenta Germaniae historica. Auctores antiquissimi,* 15. Berlin: Apud Weidmanos, 1919.
Alexander Neckham. *De naturis rerum libri duo.* Edited Thomas Wright. Rerum Britannicarum Medii Aevi Scriptores, 34. London: Longman, Green, Longman, Roberts and Green, 1863.
Ambrose. *Hexaemeron.* Vol. 1 of *Opera.* Edited by Karl Schenkl. 7 vols. Corpus scriptorum ecclesiasticorum latinorum, 32. Leipzig: G. Freytag, 1896.
Aristotle. *The Ethics of Aristotle.* Edited by John Burnet. New York: Arno Press, 1972.
———. *Metaphysics.* Loeb Classical Library. London: Heinemann, 1933.
———. *Minor Works.* Loeb Classical Library. London: Heinemann, 1936.
———. *Parts of Animals.* Loeb Classical Library. London: Heinemann, 1931.
———. *Physics.* Loeb Classical Library. London: Heinemann, 1929.
———. *Politics.* Loeb Classical Library. London: Heinemann, 1932.
Augustine. *De civitate Dei.* 2 vols. Edited by B. Dombart. Leipzig: Teubner, 1918.
———. *The City of God.* Translated by Gerald G. Walsh and Daniel J. Honan. The Fathers of the Church: A New Translation, 24. Washington, D.C.: The Catholic University of America Press, 1954.
———. *De doctrina christiana.* In *Opera.* Corpus christianorum, series latina, 32. Trunholt: Brepols Editores Pontificii, 1962.
———. *The Literal Meaning of Genesis.* Translated by John Hammon Taylor. Ancient Christian Writers, 42. New York: Newman Press, 1982.
———. *Oeuvres de Saint Augustin. Texte de l'éd. bénédictine, traduction et notes.* Edited by Gustave Bardy. 12 vols. Paris: Desclée de Brouwer, 1950–72.
———. *On Christian Doctrine.* Translated by D. W. Robertson, Jr. Indianapolis: Bobbs-Merrill, 1958.
Bacon, Francis. *Novum Organum.* Vol. 4 of *The Works of Francis Bacon,* edited by James Spedding. London: Longmans and Co., 1870. Reprint. New York: Garett Press, 1968.
Bacon, Roger. *Fr. Rogeri Bacon Opera quaedam hactenus inedita.* Edited by J. S. Brewer. Rerum Britannicarum Medii Aevi Scriptores, 15. London: Longman, Green, Longman and Roberts, 1859.
———. *Opera hactenus inedita Rogeri Baconi.* Edited by Robert Steel. 12 vols. Oxford: Clarendon Press, 1905–40.

———. *Opus Maius*. 2 vols. Translated by Robert Belle Burke. New York: Russell and Russell, 1962.

———. *The 'Opus maius' of Roger Bacon*. Edited by John Henry Bridges. 2 vols. Oxford: Clarendon Press, 1897. Reprint. Frankfurt: Minerva, 1964.

Basil. *Exegetic Homilies*. Translated by Sister Agnes Clare Way. Washington, D.C.: The Catholic University of America Press, 1963.

———. *Homiliae in Hexaemeron*. Vol. 1 of *Opera omnia*, edited by Julian Garnier. Paris: Apud Gaume Fratres Bibliopolis, 1839.

La Bible moralisée, illustrée, condensée à Oxford, Paris et Londres. Reproduction intégrale de manuscrit du XIIIe siècle, accompaynée de planches tirées de Bibles similares et d'une notice par le comte A. de Laborde. 5 vols. Paris: Société Française de Reproduction des Manuscrits à Peintures, 1911–27.

Bernard Silvestris (?). *The Commentary on the First Six Books of the "Aeneid" of Vergil Commonly Attributed to Bernardus Silvestris*. Edited by Julian Ward Jones and Elizabeth Francis Jones. Lincoln, Nebraska: University of Nebraska Press, 1977.

———. *Commentary on the First Six Books of Virgil's "Aeneid."* Lincoln, Nebraska: University of Nebraska Press, 1979.

Bonaventure. *Collationes in Hexaëmeron*. Edited by R. P. Ferdinandus Delorme. Florence: Ad Claras Aquas, 1934.

———. *Itinéraire de l'esprit vers Dieu: texte de Quaracchi*. Translated by Henry Dumery. Paris: J. Vrin, 1960.

———. *The Mind's Road to God*. Translated by George Boas. New York: The Liberal Arts Press, 1953.

———. *Saint Bonaventure's De reductione artium: A Commentary with an Introduction and Translation*. Edited and translated by Sister Emma Therese Healy. Saint Bonaventure, New York: Saint Bonaventure College, 1939.

———. *Sermones de decem praeceptis*. In vol. 2 of *Opera omnia*, edited by A. C. Peltier. Paris: L. Vivès, 1864.

Brunetto Latini. *Li livres dou Tresor*. Edited by Francis J. Carmody. Berkeley: University of California Press, 1948.

Cassiodorus. *Institutiones divinarum et saecularium lectionum*. Edited by R. A. B. Mynors. Oxford: Clarendon Press, 1961.

———. *An Introduction to Divine and Human Readings*. Translated by Leslie Webber Jones. New York: Columbia University Press, 1946. Reprint. New York: Octagon Books, 1966.

———. *The Letters of Cassiodorus*. Translated by Thomas Hodgkin. London: Henry Frowde, 1886.

———. *Variae*. Edited by Å. J. Fridh. Corpus christianorum, series latina, 96. Turnholt: Brepols Editores Pontifici, 1973.

Chalcidius. *Timaeus; A Calcido translatus Commentarioque instructus*. Edited by J. H. Waszink in association with P. J. Jenson. Vol. 4, *Plato Latinus*. London: Warburg Institute; Leiden: E. J. Brill, 1962.

Cicero, *Academica*. Loeb Classical Library. London: Heinemann, 1933.

———. *De natura deorum*. Edited by Arthur Stanley Pease. 2 vols. Cambridge, Mass.: Harvard University Press, 1958.

———. *De officiis*. Loeb Classical Library. London: Heinemann, 1913.

Clemens. *Ars grammatica*. Edited by Johannes Tolkiehn, in *Philologus. Supplementband* 20, fasc. 3 (1928): 3–109.

Daniel of Morley. *Liber de naturis inferiorum et superiorum*. Edited by Karl Sudhoff. In *Archiv für die Geschichte der Naturwissenschaften und Technik* 8 (1917): 6–40.

Diogenes Laertius. *Lives of Eminent Philosophers*. Loeb Classical Library. London: Heinemann, 1925.

Dionysius Exiguus. *De creatione hominis*. *PL* 67: 347–408.

Duns Scotus, Johannes. *Quaestiones in tertium librum Sententiarum*. In vol. 15 of *Opera omnia*, edited nova juxta editionem Wadding: XII tomos continentem a patribus Franciscanis de observantia acurate recognita. Paris: L. Vivès, 1894.

Ecrits théologiques de l'école d'Abélard. Edited by Arthur Landgraf. Spicilegium Sacrum Lovaniense, études et documents, 14. Louvain: Spicilegium Sacrum Lovaniense, 1934.

Epictetus. *Moral Discourses*. Loeb Classical Library. London: Heinemann, 1925.

Ermenrich. *Epistola ad Grimaldum Abbatem*. In *Monumenta germaniae historica Epistolae karolini aevi*, 5. Berlin: 1899.

al-Farabi. *Alfarabi, Über den Ursprung der Wissenschaften*. Edited by Clemens Baeumker.

Beiträge zur Geschichte der Philosophie des Mittelalters, 19.3. Munster: Aschendorffsche Verlagsbuchhandlung, 1916.

———. *De scientiis*. Edited by Manuel Alonso Alonso. Madrid: Escuelas de Estudios Arabes de Madrid y Granada, 1954.

Fulgentius. *Mitologiae*. Edited by R. Helm. Leipzig: Teubner, 1898.

Galen. *De usu partium*. Edited by C. G. Kuhn. Vol. 3 of G. *Claudii Galeni Opera omnia*. Leipzig: Teubner, 1822. Reprint. Hildesheim: Georg Olms Verlagsbuchhandlung, 1964.

———. *Protreptikos*. In *Scripta minora*, edited by Ioannis Marquardt. Leipzig: Teubner, 1893. Reprint. Amsterdam: Hakkert, 1967.

Godfrey of Saint Victor, *Le Fons philosophiae de Godefroy de Saint-Victor*. Edited by Pierre Michaud-Quantin. Analecta mediaevalia Namurcensia, 8. Namur: Editions Godenne, 1956.

———. *The Fountain of Philosophy: A Translation of the Twelfth-Century Fons Philosophiae of Godfrey of Saint Victor*. Translated by Edward A. Synan. Toronto: The Pontifical Institute of Mediaeval Studies, 1972.

———. *Microcosmus: texte, établi et présente*. Edited by Philippe Delhaye. Mémoires et travaux publiés par les professeurs de Facultés Catholiques de Lille, 56, 57. Lille: Facultés Catholiques; Gembloux: J. Duculot, 1951.

Gregory of Nyssa. *Contra Eunomium*. Edited by Werner Jaeger. Leiden: E. J. Brill, 1960.

———. *De hominis opificio*. *PG* 44: 137–256.

Gundisalvo, Domingo. *De divisione philosophiae*. Edited by Ludwig Baur. Beiträge zur Geschichte der Philosophiae des Mittelalters, Texte und Untersuchungen, Band 4, Heft 2-3. Munster: Aschendorffsche Verlagsbuchhandlung, 1903.

Hero of Alexandria. *The Pneumatics of Hero of Alexandria: A facsimile of the 1851 Woodcroft Edition*. London: Macdonald, 1971.

Herodotus. *Persian Wars*. Loeb Classical Library. London: Heinemann, 1921.

Herrade de Landsberg. *Hortus deliciarum*. Edited by Joseph Walter. Strasburg and Paris: F. X. de Roux, 1952.

Hippocrates. *The Art*. Loeb Classical Library. London: Heinemann, 1931.

Honorius Augustodunensis. *De animae exsilio et patria*. *PL* 172: 1241–1246.

———. *De imagine mundi*. *PL* 172: 115–188.

Hugh of St. Victor. *De arca Noe morali*. *PL* 176: 617–680.

———. *The "Didascalicon" of Hugh of St. Victor: A Medieval Guide to the Arts*. Translated by Jerome Taylor. Records of Civilization, Sources and Studies, 64. New York: Columbia University Press, 1961.

———. *Hugh of Saint Victor: Selected Spiritual Writings*. Translated by a Religious of C.S.M.V. New York: Harper and Row, 1968.

———. *Hugonis de Sancto Victore Didascalicon de studio legendi: A Critical Text*. Edited by Charles Henry Buttimer. Catholic University of America Studies in Medieval and Renaissance Latin, 10. Washington, D.C.: Catholic University of America Press, 1939.

———. *Hugonis de Sancto Victore opera Propaedeutica*. Edited by Roger Baron. Publications in Mediaeval Studies, The University of Notre Dame, 20. Notre Dame, Indiana: University of Notre Dame Press, 1966.

———. *In Ecclesiasten homiliae*. *PL* 175: 113–256.

Innocent III. *De contemptu mundi*. *PL* 217: 701–46.

Isidore of Seville. *Differentiae*. *PL* 83: 9 98

———. *Etymologiae*. Edited by W. M. Lindsay. Oxford: Clarendon Press, 1911.

———. *Liber numerorum*. *PL* 83: 179–200.

Isocrates. *Panegyrics*. Loeb Classical Library. London: Heinemann, 1928.

Jean of Antioch. *Notice sur la Rhétorique de Cicéron traduite par Maître Jean d'Antioche, ms. 590 de Musée Condé*. Edited by Léopold Delisle. Paris: Librairie C. Klincksieck, 1899.

Jerome. *Dialogus contra Pelagianus*. *PL* 23: 495–588.

John of Dacia. *Divisio scientiae*. In *Johannis Daci opera*, edited by Alfred Otto. Corpus philosophorum Danicorum Medii Aevi, 1. Hauriae: Apud Librarium G. E. C. Gad, 1955.

John of Salisbury. *Ioannis Saresberiensis episcopi Carnotensis Policraticus sive de nugis curialium et vestigiis philosophorum libri VIII*. 2 vols. Edited by Clemens C. I. Webb. Oxford: Oxford University Press, 1909.

John the Scot. *Annotationes in Marcianum*. Edited by Cora E. Lutz. Cambridge, Mass.: The Mediaeval Academy of America, 1939.

Kilwardby, Robert. *De ortu scientiarum*. Edited by Albert G. Judy. Oxford: Clarendon Press, 1976.

The Luttrell Psalter. Facsimile Edition. Edited by E. G. Millar. London: British Museum, 1932.

Martianus Capella. *The Marriage of Philology and Mercury*. Translated by William Harris Stahl. New York: Columbia University Press, 1971.

———. *Martianus Capella*. Edited by Adolfus Dick and Jean Preáux. Stuttgart: Teubner, 1978.

Neckham, Alexander. "The Treatise *De utensilibus* of Alexander Neckham." In *A Volume of Vocabularies*, edited by Thomas Wright. London: private printing, 1857–1873.

Nemesius of Emesa. *De natura hominis*. *PG* 40: 503–816.

———. *De natura hominis*. Translated by William Telfer. In *Cyril of Jerusalem and Nemesius of Emesa*. Library of Christian Classics, 4. Philadelphia: Westminster Press, 1955.

———. *Nemesii Episcopi Premnon physicon; sive περὶ φύσεος ἀνφρώπου liber an Alfano, Archiepiscopo Salerni in latinum translatus*. Edited by Carolus Burkhard. Leipzig: Teubner, 1917.

Peter Comestor. *Historia scholastica*. *PL* 198: 1055–1722.

Philostratus. *The Life of Apollonius of Tyana*. 2 vols. Loeb Classical Library. London: Heinemann, 1912.

———. *Über Gymnasik*. Edited and translated by Julius Jünthner. Leipzig: Teubner, 1909.

Plato. *Gorgias*. Edited by E. R. Dodds. Oxford: Clarendon Press, 1959.

———. *Philebus*. Loeb Classical Library. London: Heinemann, 1925.

———. *Platonis Opera*. Edited by Ioannes Burnet. 5 vols. Oxford: Clarendon Press, 1907.

———. *Politicus*. Loeb Classical Library. London: Heinemann, 1925.

———. *Protagoras*. Loeb Classical Library. London: Heinemann, 1924.

———. *Republic*. Loeb Classical Library. London: Heinemann, 1935.

Pliny. *Natural History*. 10 vols. Loeb Classical Library. London: Heinemann, 1938.

Plotinus. *Enneads*. In *Opera*, edited by Paul Henry and Hans-Rudolf Schwyzer. Museum Lessianum series philosophica, 34. Paris: Desclée de Brouwer et Cie, 1959.

———. *Enneads*. Translated by Stephen MacKenna. London: Faber and Faber, 1962.

Plutarch. *Lives*. Loeb Classical Library. London: Heinemann, 1916.

Proclus. *Commentary on the First Book of Euclid's Elements*. Translated by Glenn R. Morrow. Princeton: Princeton University Press, 1970.

———. *Procli Diadochi in primum Euclidis Elementorum librum Commentarii, ex recognitione Godofred Friedlein*. Edited by Gottfried Friedlein. Leipzig: Teubner, 1873.

Quintilian. *Institutio oratoria*. Loeb Classical Library. London: Heinemann, 1921.

Raoul de Longchamps. *Commentary on the Anticlaudianus of Alanus de Insulis*. Edited by Jan Sulovsky. Warsaw: Zaklad Narodowy im. Ossolinskitch, 1972.

Raymond Lull. *Arbre de ciència*. In *Obres essencials*, edited by Armand Llinarès. Barcelona: Éditorial Selecta, 1957.

Reisch, G. *Margarita philosophica*. Freiburg: Opera Joannis Schotti, 1504.

Remigius of Auxerre. *Remigii Autissiodorensis Commentum in Martianum Capellam*, Libri I–II. Edited by Cora E. Lutz. Leiden: E. J. Brill, 1965.

Rhabanus Maurus. *De institutione clericorum*. *PL* 107: 293–420.

———. *De universo*. *PL* 111: 9–614.

Richard of Saint Victor. *Liber exceptionum: Texte critique avec introduction, notes et tables*. Edited by Jean Chatillon. Textes philosophiques du moyen âge, 5. Paris: J. Vrin, 1958.

Robert de Melun. *Oeuvres de Robert de Melun*. 2 vols. Edited by Raymond M. Martin. Spicilegium Sacrum Lovaniense, Études et Documents, fasc. 21. Louvain: Spicilegium sacrum Lovaniense, 1947.

Rupert of Deutz. *De operibus Spiritus Sancti*. Edited by Hrabanus Haacke. Corpus christianorum continuatio mediaevalis, 24. Turnholt: Brepols Editores Pontificii, 1972.

Sanchez de Arevalo Ruy (Bishop Roderigo of Zamora). *Speculum vitae humanae*. Augsburg: Gunter Zainer, 1471.

Scholia ad Dionysius Thrac. In *Anecdota graeca*, vol. 2, edited by Immanuelis Bekker. Berlin: Apud G. Reimerum, 1816.

Selections illustrating the History of Greek Mathematics. Loeb Classical Library, London: Heinemann, 1941.

Seneca. *Ad Lucilium epistulae morales*. Loeb Classical Library. London: Heinemann, 1930.

Thomas Aquinas. *Commentary on the Metaphysics of Aristotle*. Translated by John P. Rowan. Chicago: Henry Regnery, 1969.

———. *Commentary on the Posterior Analytics of Aristotle*. Translated by F. R. Larcher. Albany, New York: Magi Books, 1970.

———. *The Division and Methods of the Sciences: Questions V and VI of his Commentary on the 'De Trinitate' of Boethius*. Translated by Armand Maurer. 3rd. rev. ed. Toronto: Pontifical Institute of Mediaeval Studies, 1963.

———. *Opera omnia*. Rome: Opera omnia iussu impensaque, Leonis XIII. P. M. edita. 1882–1918.

———. *Sancti Thomae de Aquino Expositio super librum Boethii De Trinitate*. Edited by Bruno Decker. Leiden: E. J. Brill, 1955.

———. *Summa theologiae. Latin text and English translation, introductions, notes, appendices and glossaries*. 41 vols. Cambridge, England: Blackfriars, 1964–76.

Victorinus, Maximus. *Ars Victorini grammatici*. In vol. 6 of *Grammatici Latini*, edited by Henrici Keil. Leipzig: Teubner, 1870. Reprint. Hildsheim: Georg Olms, 1961.

Vincent of Beauvais. *Speculum doctinale*. Vol. 2 of *Speculum quadruplex sive speculum maius*. Edited by Douai. Graz: Akademische Druck- u. Verlagsanstalt, 1965.

Vitruvius. *Ten Books on Architecture*. Loeb Classical Library. London: Heinemann, 1931.

William of Conches. *Glosae super Platonem: Texte critique*. Edited by Edouard Jeauneau. Paris: J. Vrin, 1938.

———. (?) *Un brano inedito della "Philosophia" di Guglielmo di Conches*. Edited by Carmelo Ottaviano. Naples: Alberto Morano Editore, 1935.

Wright, Thomas, ed. *The Anglo-Latin Satirical Poets and Epigrammatists*. London: Her Majesty's Stationery Office, 1872.

Zenophon. *Oeconomicus*. Loeb Classical Library. London: Heinemann, 1936.

Secondary Sources

Alessio, Franco. "La filosofia e le 'artes mechanicae' nel secolo XII." *Studi Medievali*, 3rd series, 6 (1965): 71–155.

Allard, Guy. "Réactions de trois penseurs du XIIIe siècle vis-à-vis de l'Alchimie." In *La science de la nature: Théories et pratiques*. Cahiers d'études médiévales, 2. Montreal: Bellarmin; Paris: J. Vrin, 1974.

———. "Les arts mécaniques aux yeux de l'idéologie médiévale." In *Les arts mécaniques au moyen âge*. Cahiers d'études médiévales, 7. Montreal: Bellarmin; Paris: J. Vrin, 1982.

Amundsen, Darrel W. "Medicine and Surgery as Art or Craft. The Role of Schematic Literature in the Separation of Medicine and Surgery in the Middle Ages." *Transactions and Studies of the College of Physicians of Philadelphia* 1 (1979): 43–57.

Attfield, Robin. "Christian Attitudes to Nature." *Journal of the History of Ideas* 44 (1983): 369–386.

Bachrach, Bernard S. "Charles Martel, Mounted Shock Combat, the Stirrup and Feudalism." *Studies in Medieval and Renaissance History* 7 (1970): 49–75.

Baker, Peter Harte. "Liberal Arts as Philosophical Liberation: St. Augustine's *De Magistro*." In *Arts libéraux et philosophie au moyen âge; Actes du quatrième Congrès International de Philosophie Médiévale*. Paris: J. Vrin, 1969.

Baldwin, John W. *Masters, Princes, and Merchants: The Social Views of Peter the Chanter and his Circle*. 2 vols. Princeton: Princeton University Press, 1970.

———. "The Medieval Theories of the Just Price: Romanists, Canonists, and Theologians in the Twelfth and Thirteenth Centuries." *Transactions of the American Philosophical Society*, n.s. 49, part 4. Philadelphia: The American Philosophical Society, 1959.

Bambrough, J. R. "Plato's Political Analogies." In *Philosophy, Politics and Society*, edited by Peter Laslett. Oxford: Basil Blackwell, 1963.

Barbour, Ian G., ed. *Western Man and Environmental Ethics: Attitudes toward Nature and Technology*. Reading, Mass.: Addison-Wesley Publishing Company, 1973.

Bark, William Carroll. *Origins of the Medieval World*. Stanford, Calif.: Stanford University Press, 1958.

Baron, Roger. *Études sur Hugues de Saint-Victor*. Bruges: Desclée de Brouwer, 1963.

———. *Science et sagesse chez Hugues de Saint-Victor*. Paris: P. Lethielleux, 1957.

Beaujouan, Guy. "L'interdépendence entre la science scolastique et les techniques utilitaires (XIIe, XIIIe et XIVe siècles)." In *Les Conférences du Palais de la Découverte*. Sér. D. Histoires des Sciences, 46. Paris: Université de Paris, 1957.

———. "Réflexions sur les rapports entre théorie et pratique au Moyen Âge." In *The Cultural Context of Medieval Learning*, edited by J. E. Murdoch and E. D. Sylla. Boston Studies in the Philosophy of Science, 24. Dordrecht and Boston: D. Reidel, 1975.

Beichner, Paul E. "The Medieval Representative of Music, Jubal or Tubalcain?" *Texts and Studies in the History of Medieval Education*, 2. Notre Dame: Medieval Institute, University of Notre Dame Press, 1954.

Benson, Robert L., Giles Constable, and Carol D. Lanham, eds. *Renaissance and Renewal in the Twelfth Century*. Cambridge, Mass.: Harvard University Press, 1982.

Benz, Ernst. "The Christian Expectation of the End of Time and the Ideal of Technical Progress." In *Evolution and Christian Hope: Man's Concept of the Future from the Early Fathers to Teilhard de Chardin*. Garden City, New York: Doubleday, 1966.

———. "Fundamenti cristiani della tecnica occidentale." In *Tecnica e casistica*, edited by Enrico Castelli. Paduo: Casa Editrice Dott. Antonio Milani, 1964.

Bischoff, Bernhard. "Eine verschollene Einteilung der Wissenschaften." *Archives d'histoire doctrinale et litteraire du Moyen Âge* 33 (1958): 5–20.

Bissen, J. M. *L'exemplairisme divin selon Saint Bonaventure*. Paris: J. Vrin, 1929.

Bloch, Marc. "Avènement et conquêtes du moulin à eau." *Annales d'histoire économique et sociale* 7 (1935): 538–563.

———. *Land and Work in Mediaeval Europe: Selected Papers by Marc Bloch*. Translated by J. E. Anderson. London: Routledge and Kegan Paul, 1967. Reprint. New York: Harper and Row, 1969.

———. "Les 'inventions' médiévales." *Annales d'histoire économique et sociale* 7 (1935): 634–643.

Boissonnade, P. *Land and Work in Medieval Europe: The Evolution of the Medieval Economy from the Fifth to the Fifteenth Century*. Translated by Eileen Power. New York: Harper and Row, 1964.

Burford, Alison. *Craftsmen in Greek and Roman Society*. Ithaca, New York: Cornell University Press, 1972.

The Cambridge Economic History of Europe. Edited by M. M. Poston and H. J. Habakkuk. Cambridge, England: Cambridge University Press, 1952–79.

Cappuyns, M. *Jean Scott Erigène: Sa vie, son oeuvre, sa pensée*. Brussels: Culture et Civilization, 1964.

Carus-Wilson, E. M. "An Industrial Revolution in the Thirteenth Century." *Economic History Review* 7 (1941): 39–55.

Catalogus translationum et commentariorum: Medieval and Renaissance Latin translations and commentaries. Edited by Paul O. Kristeller and F. Cranz. Washington, D.C.: Catholic University of America Press, 1971.

Caws, Peter. "Praxis and Techne." In *The History and Philosophy of Technology*, edited by George Bugliarello and Dean B. Doner. Urbana, Il.: University of Illinois Press, 1979.

Charlesworth, M. J. *Aristotle on Art and Nature*. Auckland University College Bulletin No. 50, Philosophy Series No. 2. Auckland: Auckland University Press, 1957.

Chenu, M.-D. "Arts 'mécaniques' et oeuvres serviles." *Revue des sciences philosophiques et théologiques* 29 (1940): 313–315.

———. "Civilisation urbaine et théologie: L'École de Saint-Victor au XIIe siècle." *Annales: Economies, sociétiés, civilisations* 29 (1974): 1253–1263.

———. *Nature, Man, and Society in the Twelfth Century: Essays in New Theological Perspectives in the Latin West*. Edited and translated by Jerome Taylor and Lester K. Little. Chicago: University of Chicago Press, 1968.

Clagett, Marshall. "King Alfred and the Elements of Euclid." *Isis* 45 (1954): 269–277.

———, and Edward Grant, eds. *A Source Book in Medieval Science*. Cambridge, Mass.: Harvard University Press, 1974.

Contreni, John J. *The Cathedral School of Laon from 850 to 930: Its Manuscripts and Masters*. Münchener Beiträge zur Mediavistik und Renaissance-Forschung, 29. Munich: Bei der Arbeo-Gesellschaft, 1978.

———. "Inharmonious Harmony: Education in the Carolingian World." *Annals of Scholarship* 1 (1980): 81–96.

———. "John Scottus, Martin Hiberniensis, The Liberal Arts, and Teaching." In *Insular Latin Studies: Papers on Latin Texts and Manuscripts of the British:* Pontifical Institute of Mediaeval Studies, 1981.

Conway, Pierre and Benedict Ashley. "The Liberal Arts in Thomas Aquinas." *Thomist* 22 (1959): 460–532.

Coperhaver, Brian P. "The Historiography of Discovery in the Renaissance: The Sources and Composition of Polydore Vergil's 'De inventoribus rerum,' vols. 1–3." *Journal of the Warburg and Courtauld Institutes* 41 (1978): 193–222.

Copleston, Frederick. *A History of Philosophy*. Vols. 1–3. Garden City, New York: Doubleday: Image Books, 1962.
Courcelle, Pierre. *Late Latin Writers and their Greek Sources*. Translated by Harry E. Wedeck. Cambridge, Mass.: Harvard University Press, 1969.
Crombie, A. C. *Medieval and Early Modern Science*. 2 vols. Garden City, New York: Doubleday, Anchor Books, 1959.
———. *Robert Grosseteste and the Origins of Experimental Science, 1100–1700*. Oxford: Clarendon Press, 1953.
———. "The Significance of Medieval Discussions of Scientific Method for the Scientific Revolution." In *Critical Problems in the History of Science*, edited by Marshall Clagett. Madison, Wisc.: University of Wisconsin Press, 1959.
Crouse, Robert Darwin. "Honorius Augustodunensis: The Arts as *via ad patriam*." In *Arts libéraux et philosophie au Moyen Âge: Actes du Quatrième Congrès International de Philosophie Médiévale*. Montreal: Institut d'Études Médiévales, 1969.
Curtius, Ernst Robert. *European Literature and the Latin Middle Ages*. Translated by Willard R. Trask. Bollingen Series, 36. Princeton: Princeton University Press, 1973.
Daumas, Maurice, ed. *Histoire générale des techniques*. Vol. 1. Paris: Presses Universitaires de France, 1962.
de Gandillac, Maurice. "Place et signification de la technique dans le monde médiéval." In *Tecnica e casistica*, edited by Enrico Castelli. Padua: Casa Editrice Dott. Antonio Milani, 1964.
de Rijk, L. M. "Some Notes on the Twelfth Century Topic of the Three (Four) Human Evils and of Science, Virtue, and Techniques as Their Remedies." *Vivarium* 5 (1967): 8–15.
Derr, Thomas Seiger. "Religious Responsibility for Ecological Crisis: An Argument Run Amok." *Worldview* 18, no. 1 (January, 1975): 39–45.
DeWald, Ernest. *The Illustrations of the Utrecht Psalter*. Princeton: Princeton University Press, 1932.
De Wulf, Maurice. *Histoire de la philosophie médiévale*. 2 vols. Louvain: Institut Supérieur de Philosophie, 1924.
Díaz y Díaz, Manuel. "Les arts libéraux d'après les écrivains espagnols et insulaires aux VIIe et VIIIe siècles." In *Arts libéraux et philosophie au Moyen Âge: Actes du Quatrième Congrès International de Philosophie Médiévale*. Montreal: Institut d'Études Médiévales, 1969.
Dijksterhuis, E. J. *The Mechanization of the World Picture*. Translated by C. Dikshoorn. Oxford: Clarendon Press, 1969.
Dresbeck, Leroy. "*Techne, Labor et Natura*: Ideas and Active Life in the Medieval Winter." *Studies in Medieval and Renaissance History* n.s. 2 (1979): 83–119.
Duby, Georges. *Rural Economy and Country Life in the Medieval West*. Translated by Cynthia Postan. Columbia, South Carolina: University of South Carolina Press, 1968.
———. *The Three Orders: Feudal Society Imagined*. Translated by Arthur Goldhammer. Chicago: The University of Chicago Press, 1980.
Duhem, Pierre. *Le système du monde: Histoire des doctrines cosmologiques de Platon à Copernic*. 10 vols. Paris: Hermann, 1913–54.
Easton, Stewart Copinger. *Roger Bacon and his Search for a Universal Science: A Reconsideration of the Life and Work of Roger Bacon in the Light of His Own Stated Purposes*. Oxford: Basil Blackwell, 1952. Reprint. New York: Russell and Russell, 1971.
Eastwood, Bruce Stansfield. "The Place of Medicine in a Hierarchy of Knowledge: The Illustration in Lyon Palais des Arts, ms. 22, f. lr, from the Eleventh Century." *Sudhoffs Archiv* 66 (1982): 20–37.
École Nationale des Chartes. Positions des thèses soutenues par les élèves de la promotion de 1951. Paris: École des Chartes, 1951.
Edelstein, Ludwig. "Recent Interpretations of Ancient Science." *Journal of the History of Ideas* 13 (1952): 579–585.
Ellul, Jacques. "Technique and the Opening Chapters of Genesis." In *Theology and Technology: Essays in Christian Analysis and Exegesis*, edited by Carl Mitcham and Jim Grote. New York: University Press of America, 1984.
———. *The Technological Society*. Translated by John Wilkinson. New York: Vintage-Knopf, 1964.
Evans, M. W. *Medieval Drawings*. Feltham, New York: Hamlyn, 1969.
Fakhry, Majid. "The Liberal Arts in the Mediaeval Arabic Tradition from the Seventh to the Twelfth Centuries." In *Arts libéraux et philosophie au Moyen Âge: Actes du Quatrième*

Congrès International de Philosophie Médiévale. Montreal: Institut d'Études Médiévales, 1969.

Farrington, Benjamin. *Greek Science*. London: Penguin Books, 1944.

Feldhaus, Franz Maria. *Die Technik der Antike und des Mittelalter*. Potsdam: Walter Bullert, 1931.

Finley, Moses I. "Technical Innovation and Economic Progress in the Ancient World." *Economic History Review* 2nd series 18 (1965): 29–45.

Fisher, N. W. and S. Unguru. "Experimental Science and Mathematics in Roger Bacon's Thought." *Traditio* 27 (1971): 353–378.

Flint, Robert. *Philosophy as Scientia Scientiarum, and A History of Classification of the Sciences*. Edinburgh: W. Blackwood, 1904.

Fontaine, Jacques. *Isidore de Séville et la culture classique dans l'Espagne wisigothique*. 2 vols. Paris: Études Augustiniennes, 1959.

———. "Isidore de Séville et l'astrologie." *Revue des études latines* 31 (1953): 271–300.

Forbes, Robert J. *Man the Maker: A History of Technology and Engineering*. New York: Schuman, 1950.

———. *Studies in Ancient Technology*. 9 vols. Leiden: E. J. Brill, 1964–66.

Fortin, Ernest L. "Augustine, the Arts and Human Progress." In *Technology and Theology: Essays in Christian Analysis and Exegesis*, edited by Carl Mitcham and Jim Grote. New York: University Press of America, 1984.

Fudpucker, Wilhelm E. "Through Christian Theology to Technological Christianity." In *Theology and Technology: Essays in Christian Analysis and Exegesis*, edited by Carl Mitcham and Jim Grote. New York: University Press of America, 1984.

Gagné, Jean. "Du *quadrivium* aux *scientiae mediae*." In *Arts libéraux et philosophie au Moyen Âge; Actes du quatrième Congrès International de Philosophie Médiévale*. Montreal: Institut d'Études Médiévales, 1969.

Gagnon, Claude. "Recherche bibliographique sur l'Alchimie médiévale occidentale." In *La science de la nature: Théories et pratiques*. Cahiers d'études médiévales, 2. Montreal: Bellarmin; Paris: J. Vrin, 1974.

Garin, Eugenio. "'La dignitas hominis' e la litteratura patristica." *La Rinascita* 1 (1938): 102–146.

Geoghegan, Arthur T. *The Attitudes towards Labor in Early Christianity and Ancient Culture*. The Catholic University of America Studies in Christian Antiquity, no. 6. Washington, D.C.: The Catholic University of America Press, 1945.

Gille, Bertrand. "Esprit et civilisation techniques au moyen âge." *Les Conférences du Palais de la Découverte*. Series D, no. 10, Paris: Université de Paris, 1965.

———. *Les mécaniciens grecs: La naissance de la technologie*. Paris: Éditions du Seuil, 1980.

Gimpel, Jean. *The Medieval Machine: The Industrial Revolution of the Middle Ages*. New York: Holt, Rinehart and Winston, 1976. Reprint. New York and London: Penguin Books, 1980.

Glacken, Clarence. *Traces on the Rhodian Shore: Nature and Culture in Western Thought from Ancient Time to the End of the Eighteenth Century*. Berkeley and Los Angeles: University of California Press, 1967.

Gompf, Ludwig. "Der Leipziger 'Ordo artium.'" *Mittellateinisches Jahrbuch* 3 (1966): 94–128.

Grabmann, Martin. *Die Geschichte der scholastischen Methode*. 2 vols. Freiburg: Herder'sche Verlag, 1909. Reprint. Graz: Akademische Druck- u. Verlagsanstalt, 1957.

———. *Mittelalterliches Geistesleben*. 2 vols. Munich: Max Hueber, 1926.

Grant, Edward. *Physical Science in the Middle Ages*. Cambridge, England: Cambridge University Press, 1977.

Gregory, Tullio. *Anima mundi: La filosofia di Guglielmo di Conches et la scuola di Chartres*. Florence. G. C. Sansoni, 1955.

———. "L'idea di natura nella filosofia medievale prima del'ingresso della fisica di Aristotele: il secolo xii." In *La filosofia della natura nel Medioevo: Atti del Terzo Congresso Internazionale di Filosofia Medievale, 1965*. Milan: Società editrice Vita e pensiero, 1966.

Grundel, Johannes. *Das "Speculum Universale" des Radulfus Ardens*. Munich: Max Hueber, 1961.

Hackett, Jeremiah M. "The Meaning of Experimental Science (*Scientia experimentalis*) in the Philosophy of Roger Bacon." Ph.D. diss., University of Toronto, 1983.

Hall, Bert. "Production et diffusion de certains traités de techniques au moyen âge." In

Les arts mécaniques au moyen âge. Cahiers d'études médiévales, 7. Montreal: Bellarmin; Paris: J. Vrin, 1982.

Hall, Rupert. "The Scholar and the Craftsman in the Scientific Revolution." In *Critical Problems in the History of Science*, edited by Marshall Clagett. Madison, Wis.: University of Wisconsin Press, 1959.

Haskins, Charles. "Michael Scot and Frederick II." *Isis* 4 (1921): 250–275.

———. *The Renaissance of the Twelfth Century*. Cambridge, Mass.: Harvard University Press, 1927.

———. *Studies in the History of Mediaeval Science*. Cambridge: Cambridge University Press, 1924.

Hillgarth, Jocelyn N. "A Critical Review of the Literature since 1935." In *Isidoriana: Estudios sobre San Isidore de Sevilla en el XIV centenario de su nacimiento*. Leon: Centro de Estudios "San Isidoro," 1961.

Hilton, R. H., and P. H. Sawyer. "Technical Determinism: The Stirrup and the Plough." *Past and Present* 24 (1963): 90–100.

Hinwood, Bonaventure. "The Division of Human Knowledge in the Writings of Saint Bonaventure." *Franciscan Studies* n.s. 38 (1978): 220–259.

Holdsworth, Christopher. "The Blessings of Work: the Cistercian View." In *Sanctity and Secularity: The Church and the World*, edited by Derek Baker. Studies in Church History, 10. New York: Harper and Row, 1973.

Hunt, Richard William Hunt. "The Introductions to the 'Artes' in the Twelfth Century." In *Studia mediaevalia in honorem R. J. Martin*. Bruges: De Tempel, 1948.

Jardine, Lisa. *Francis Bacon: Discovery and the Art of Discourse*. Cambridge: Cambridge University Press, 1974.

Javelet, Robert. *Image et resemblance au douzième siècle de Saint Anselme à Alain de Lille*. 2 vols. Paris: Éditiones Letouzey et Ané, 1967.

Jonas, Hans. "The Practical Uses of Theory." In *The Phenomenon of Life: Toward a Philosophical Biology*. New York: Dell Publishing Company, Delta Books, 1966.

Kahn, Arthur D. "'Every Art Possessed by Man Comes from Prometheus': The Greek Tragedians and Science and Technology." *Technology and Culture* 11 (1970): 133–162.

Katzenellenbogan, Adolf. *The Sculptural Programs of Chartres Cathedral*. Baltimore: Johns Hopkins University Press, 1968.

Kleinz, John Phillip. *The Theory of Knowledge of Hugh of St. Victor*. Catholic University of America Philosophical Studies, 87. Washington, D.C.: Catholic University of America Press, 1944.

Klemm, Friedrich. *A History of Western Technology*. Translated by Dorothea Waley Singer. Cambridge, Mass.: The Massachusetts Institute of Technology Press, 1964.

———. "Die sieben mechanischen Künste des Mittelalter." *Die BASF* 12 (1962): 46–51.

Knowles, David. *The Evolution of Medieval Thought*. Baltimore: Helicon Press, 1962.

Kovach, Francis J. "Divine Art in Saint Thomas Aquinas." In *Arts libéraux et philosophie au Moyen Âge: Actes du Quatrième Congrès International de Philosophie Médiévale*. Montreal: Institut d'Études Médiévales, 1969.

Kristeller, Paul Oskar. "The Modern System of the Arts." *Journal of the History of Ideas* 12 (1951): 496–527.

Ladner, Gerhart B. *The Idea of Reform: Its Impact on Christian Thought and Action in the Age of the Fathers*. Revised edition. Cambridge, Mass.: Harvard University Press, 1959. Reprint. New York: Harper and Row, 1967: 59–94.

———. "The Philosophical Anthropology of Saint Gregory of Nyssa." *Dumbarton Oaks Papers* 12 (1958): 61–94.

Laistner, M. L. W. "Notes on Greek from the Lectures of a Ninth Century Monastery Teacher." *Bulletin of the John Rylands Library* 7 (1922–23): 421–456.

———. *Thought and Letters in Western Europe A.D. 500 to 900*. Ithaca, New York: Cornell University Press, 1966.

———. "The Western Church and Astrology during the Early Middle Ages." In *The Intellectual Heritage of the Early Middle Ages*, edited by Chester G. Starr. New York: Octagon Books, 1966.

Landes, David. *Revolution in Time: Clocks and the Making of the Modern World*. Cambridge, Mass.: Harvard University Press, 1984.

Law, Vivien. *The Insular Latin Grammarians*. Woodbridge, Suffolk: The Boydell Press, 1982.

Le Blond, J. M. *Logique et méthode chez Aristote*. Paris: J. Vrin, 1939.

LeClercq, Jean. "Écrits monastiques sur la Bible aux XIe-XIIIe siècles." *Medieval Studies* 15 (1953): 45–106.
Lee, Desmond. "Science, Philosophy and Technology in the Greco-Roman World." *Greece and Rome* 20 (1973): 69–78.
Lefebvre des Noëttes, Richard. *L'attelage et le cheval de selle à travers les âges*. Paris: A. Picard, 1939.
———. *La force motrice animale à travers les âges*. Paris: Berger-Levrault, 1924.
———. "La force motrice animale et le rôle des inventions techniques." *Revue de synthèse historique* 43 (1927): 83–91.
———. "La 'nuit' du Moyen Age et son inventaire." *Mercure de France* 235 (1932): 572–599.
Le Goff, Jacques. *Time, Work, and Culture in the Middle Ages*. Translated by Arthur Goldhammer. Chicago: The University of Chicago Press, 1980.
Legowicz, Jan. "Le problème de la théorie dans les *artes illiberales* et la conception de la science au moyen âge." In *Arts libéraux et philosophie au moyen âge: Actes du quatrième Congrès International de Philosophie Médiévale*. Paris: J. Vrin, 1969.
Lemay, Richard. *Abu Ma'shar and Latin Aristotelianism in the Twelfth Century: The Recovery of Artistotle's Natural Philosophy through Arabic Astrology*. American University of Beirut Publication of the Faculty of Arts and Sciences, Oriental Series No. 38. Beirut: American University of Beirut, 1962.
Lindberg, David C., ed. *Science in the Middle Ages*. Chicago: The University of Chicago Press, 1978.
Little, A. G., ed. *Roger Bacon Essays*. Oxford: Clarendon Press, 1914.
Lloyd, G. R. E. *Polarity and Analogy: Two Types of Argumentation in Early Greek Thought*. Cambridge, England: Cambridge University Press, 1961.
Long, Pamela O., ed. *Science and Technology in Medieval Society*. Annals of the New York Academy of Sciences, 441. New York: New York Academy of Science, 1985.
Lovejoy, Arthur O. and George Boas. *Primitivism and Related Ideas in Antiquity*. Baltimore: Johns Hopkins Press, 1935.
Lubac, Henri de. *Exégèse médiévale; les quatre sens de l'Écriture*. 4 vols. Paris: Aubier, Éditiones Montaige, 1959.
Lusignan, Serge. "Les arts mécaniques dans le *Speculum Doctrinale* de Vincent de Beauvais." In *Les arts mécaniques au moyen âge*. Cahiers d'études médiévales, 7. Montreal: Bellarmin; Paris: J. Vrin, 1982.
———. "Préface au *Speculum Maius* de Vincent de Beauvais: Réfraction et diffraction." In *Cahiers d'études médiévales*, 5. Montreal: Bellarmin; Paris: J. Vrin, 1980.
Lutz, Cora E. "Remigius' Ideas on the Classification of the Liberal Arts." *Traditio* 12 (1956): 56–86.
———. "Remigius' Ideas on the Origin of the Seven Liberal Arts." *Medievalia et Humanistica* 10 (1956): 32–49.
McIlwain, C. H. "Mediaeval Institutions in the Modern World." *Speculum* 16 (1943): 275–283.
MacKinney, Loren C. *Early Medieval Medicine with special reference to France and Chartres*. Baltimore: The Johns Hopkins Press, 1937.
Magoulias, H. J. "Trades and Crafts in the Sixth and Seventh Centuries as Viewed in the Lives of the Saints." *Byzantinoslavica* 37 (1976): 11–35.
Mahdi, Muhsin. "Science, Philosophy, and Religion in Alfarabi's *Enumeration of the Sciences*." In *The Cultural Context of Medieval Learning*, edited by John E. Murdoch and Edith Sylla. Boston Studies in the Philosophy of Science, 26. Boston: D. Reidel, 1975.
Mâle, Emile. *The Gothic Image: Religious Art in France of the Thirteenth Century*. Translated by Dora Nussey. New York: Harper and Row, 1972.
Mariétan, Joseph. *Problème de la classification des sciences d'Aristote à s. Thomas*. Paris: F. Alcan, 1901.
Marle, R. van. *Iconographie de l'art profane au Moyen-Âge et à la Renaissance*. 2 vols. The Hague: Martines Nijhoff, 1931–32.
Marrone, Steven P. *William of Auvergne and Robert Grosseteste: New Ideas of Truth in the Early Thirteenth Century*. Princeton: Princeton University Press, 1983.
Marrou, Henri Irénée. "Les arts libéraux dans l'antiquité classique." In *Arts libéraux et philosophie au Moyen Âge: Actes du Quatrième Congrès International de Philosophie Médiévale*. Montreal: Institut d'Études Médiévales, 1969; Paris: J. Vrin, 1969.

———. *A History of Education in Antiquity*. Translated by George Lamb. New York: Mentor, 1964.

———. *Saint Augustin et la fin de la culture antique*. Bibliothèque des Écoles Françaises d'Athènes et de Rome, fasc. 145. Paris: Boccard, 1938.

Marx, Friedrich, ed. *Corpus medicorum latinorum*. Vol. 1. Leipzig: Teubner, 1915.

Merton, Robert K. *Science, Technology and Society in Seventeenth-Century England*. New Jersey: Humanities Press, 1978.

Mitcham, Carl. "Philosophy and the History of Technology." In *The History and Philosophy of Technology*, edited by George Bugliarello and Dean B. Doner. Urbana, Ill.: University of Illinois Press, 1979.

———. "The Religious and Political Origins of Modern Technology." In *Philosophy and Technology*, edited by Paul T. Durbin and Friedrich Rapp. Boston: D. Reidel, 1983.

———, and Jim Grote. "Aspects of Christian Exegesis: Hermeneutics, the Theological Virtues, and Technology." In *Theology and Technology: Essays in Christian Analysis and Exegesis*, edited by Carl Mitcham and Jim Grote. Lanham, Maryland: University Press of America, 1984.

Molland, A. G. "Medieval Ideas of Scientific Progress." *Journal of the History of Ideas* 39 (1978): 561–578.

Mondolfo, Rodolfo. "The Greek Attitude toward Manual Labor." *Past and Present* 6 (1954): 1–4.

Morrison, Karl F. *The Mimetic Tradition of Reform in the West*. Princeton: Princeton University Press, 1982.

Mumford, Lewis. *Technics and Civilization*. New York: Harcourt, Brace and Company, 1934.

Nascimento, Carlos A. Ribeiro do. "La statut épistemologique des 'sciences intermédiaires' selon S. Thomas d'Aquin." In *La Science de la nature: Théories et pratiques*. Cahiers d'études médiévales, 2. Montreal: Bellarmin; Paris: J. Vrin, 1974.

Nasr, Seyyed Hossein. *Science and Civilization in Islam*. Cambridge, Mass.: Harvard University Press, 1968.

Needham, J., L. Wang and Derek J. de Solla Price. *Heavenly Clockwork: The Great Astronomical Clock of Medieval China*. Cambridge, England: Cambridge University Press, 1959.

O'Donnell, J. Reginald. "The Sources and Meaning of Bernard Silvester's Commentary on the Aeneid." *Medieval Studies* 24 (1962): 233–249.

Ogilvy, J. D. A. *Books Known to Anglo-Latin Writers Aldhelm to Alcuin (670–804)*. Studies and Documents, 2. Cambridge, Mass.: The Mediaeval Academy of America, 1936.

Ovitt, George, Jr. *The Restoration of Perfection: Labor and Technology in Medieval Culture*. New Brunswick, N.J.: Rutgers University Press, 1987.

———. "The Status of the Mechanical Arts in Medieval Classifications of Learning." *Viator* 14 (1983): 89–105.

Pare, G. A. Brunet and P. Trembly. *La Renaissance du XIIe siècle: Les écoles et l'enseignement*. Paris: Libraire Philosophique J. Vrin, 1933.

Parent, J. M. *La doctrine de la création dans l'école de Chartes*. Paris: J. Vrin, 1938.

Parente, Margherita Isnardi. *Techne: Momenti del pensiero greco da Platone ad Epicuro*. Florence: La Nuova Italia, 1966.

Parker, H. "The Seven Liberal Arts." *English Historical Review* 5 (1890): 417–461.

Pascal, Paul. "The 'Institutionum disciplinae' of Isidore of Seville." *Traditio* 13 (1957): 425–431.

Passmore, John. *Man's Responsibility for Nature: Ecological Problems and Western Traditions*. New York: Charles Scribner's Sons, 1974.

Pedersen, Olaf. "Du quadrivium à la physique: Quelques aperçus de l'évolution scientifique au Moyen Âge." In *Artes Liberales von der Antiken Bildung zur Wissenschaft des Mittelalters*, edited by Josef Koch. Studien und Texte zur Geistesgeschichte des Mittelalters, no. 5. Leiden: E. J. Brill, 1959.

Peters, F. E. *Aristotle and the Arabs: The Aristotelian Tradition in Islam*. New York: New York University Press, 1968.

Price, Derek J. de Solla. *Gears from the Greeks: The Antikythera Mechanism*. Transactions of the American Philosophical Society, vol. 64, no. 7. Philadelphia, 1974. Reprint. New York: Science History Publications, 1975.

Quinn, John Francis. *The Historical Constitution of St. Bonaventure's Philosophy*. Studies and Texts, 23. Toronto: Pontifical Institute of Mediaeval Studies, 1973.

Riché, Pierre. *Education and Culture in the Barbarian West from the Sixth Through the Eighth*

Century. Translated by John J. Contreni. Columbia, South Carolina: University of South Carolina Press, 1978.

Riddle, John M. "Theory and Practice in Medieval Medicine." *Viator* 5 (1974): 161–184.

Robbins, F. E. *The Hexaemeral Literature: A Study of The Greek and Latin Commentaries on Genesis*. Chicago: University of Chicago Press, 1912.

Rosen, Edward. "The Invention of Eyeglasses." *Journal of the History of Medicine and Allied Sciences* 11 (1965): 13–46, 183–218.

———. "Renaissance Science as Seen by Burckhardt and His Successors." In *The Renaissance: A Reconsideration of the Theories and Interpretations of the Age*, edited by T. Helton. Madison, Wisc.: University of Wisconsin Press, 1961.

Rosenthal, Franz. *The Classical Heritage in Islam*. Translated by Emile and Jenny Marmorstein. Berkeley: University of California Press, 1975.

Rossi, Paolo. *Philosophy, Technology, and the Arts in the Early Modern Era*. Translated by Salvator Attanasio and edited by Benjamin Nelson. New York: Harper and Row, Harper Torchbooks, 1970.

Salmon, D. H. "The Medieval Latin Translations of Alfarabi's Works." *New Scholasticism* 13 (1939): 245–261.

Schadewaldt, Wolfgang. "The Concepts of Nature and Technique according to the Greeks." *Research in Philosophy and Technology* 2 (1979): 159–171.

Schaefer, Alexander. "The Position and Function of Man in the Created World according to Saint Bonaventure." *Franciscan Studies* n.s. 20 (1960): 261–316.

Schuhl, Maxime. "Remarques sur Platon et la technologie." *Revue des études grecques* 66 (1953): 465–472.

Sharp, D. E. "The *De ortu scientiarum* of Robert Kilwardby." *The New Scholasticism* 8 (1934): 1–30.

Shelby, Lon R. "The Geometrical Knowledge of Mediaeval Master Masons." *Speculum* 47 (1972): 395–421.

Silverstein, Theodore. "Guillaume de Conches and Nemesius of Emessa: On the Sources of the New Science of the Twelfth Century." In *Harry Austryn Wolfson Jubilee Volume*. Jerusalem: American Academy for Jewish Research, 1965.

Singer, Charles, E. J. Holmyard, and A. R. Hall, eds. *A History of Technology*. Vol. 2 Oxford: Clarendon Press, 1965.

Smalley, Beryl. *The Study of the Bible in the Middle Ages*. New York: Philosophical Library, 1952. Reprint. Notre Dame, Indiana: University of Notre Dame Press, 1970.

Snell, Bruno. *The Discovery of the Mind: The Origins of European Thought*. Cambridge, Mass.: Harvard University Press, 1953. Reprint. New York: Harper and Row, 1960.

Solmsen, Friedrich. "Nature as Craftsman in Greek Thought." *Journal of the History of Ideas* 24 (1963): 473–496.

Southern, R. W. *Medieval Humanism and Other Studies*. New York: Harper and Row, 1970.

Stahl, William Harris. *Roman Science: Origins, Development and Influence to the Later Middle Ages*. Madison, Wisconsin: University of Wisconsin Press, 1962.

Steneck, Nicholas H. "A Late Medieval *Abor scientiarum*." *Speculum* 50 (1975): 245–269.

Sternagel, Peter. *Die Artes Mechanicae im Mittelalter. Begriffs- und Bedeutungsgeschichte bis zum Ende des 13. Jahrhunderts*. Kallmung über Regensburg: Lassleben, 1966.

Stock, Brian. "Experience, Praxis, Work and Planning in Bernard of Clairvaux: Observations on the *Sermones in Cantica*." In *The Cultural Context of Medieval Learning*, edited by J. E. Murdoch and E. D. Sylla. Boston Studies in the Philosophy of Science, 24. Dordrecht and Boston: D. Reidel, 1975.

———. *The Implications of Literacy: Written Language and Models of Interpretation in the Eleventh and Twelfth Centuries*. Princeton: Princeton University Press, 1983.

———. *Myth and Science in the Twelfth Century: A Study of Bernard Silvester*. Princeton: Princeton University Press, 1972.

Tatķiewicz, W. "Classification of the Arts in Antiquity." *Journal of the History of Ideas* 24 (1963): 231–240.

Taylor, Jerome. *The Origin and Early Life of Hugh of St. Victor: An Evaluation of the Tradition*. Texts and Studies in the History of Medieval Education, 5. Notre Dame, Indiana: The Mediaeval Institute, 1957.

Temkin, Owsei. "Greek Medicine as Science and Craft." *Isis* 44 (1953): 213–225.

Testard, Maurice. *Saint Augustin et Cicéron*. Paris: Études Augustiniennes, 1958.

Thomas, Keith. *Man and the Natural World: A History of the Modern Sensibility*. New York: Pantheon Books, 1983.
Thorndike, Lynn. *A History of Magic and Experimental Science*. 8 vols. New York: Columbia University Press, 1923–58.
———. *Michael Scot*. London: Thomas Nelson and Sons, 1965.
———. "Renaissance or Prenaissance?" *Journal of the History of Ideas* 4 (1943): 65–74.
Trinkaus, Charles. *"In Our Image and Likeness": Humanity and Divinity in Italian Humanist Thought*. 2 vols. Chicago: University of Chicago Press, 1970.
Usher, Abbott Payson. *A History of Mechanical Inventions*. Revised ed. Cambridge, Mass.: Harvard University Press, 1966.
Van Engen, John. "Theophilus Presbyter and Rupert of Deutz: The Manual Arts and Benedictine Theology in the Early Twelfth Century." *Viator* 11 (1980): 147–163.
Van Steenberghen, Fernand. *Aristotle in the West: The Origins of Latin Aristotelianism*. Translated by Leonard Johnston, 2nd ed. Louvain: Nauwelaerts Publishing House, 1970.
Vermeirre, Andre. "La navigation d'après Hugues de Saint-Victor et d'après la pratique au XIe siècle." In *Les arts mécaniques au moyen âge*. Cahiers d'études médiévales, 7. Montreal: Bellarmin; Paris: J. Vrin, 1982.
Vernant, Jean-Pierre. *Myth et pensée chez les grecs: Études de psychologie historique*. Paris: François Maspero, 1965.
Vicaire, P. H. "Les Porrétains et l'Avicennisme avant 1215." *Revue des sciences philosophiques et théologiques* 26 (1937): 449–482.
Wallace-Hadrill, D. S. *The Greek Patristic View of Nature*. Manchester: Manchester University Press, 1968.
Webster, J. C. *The Labors of the Months in Antique and Mediaeval Art to the End of the XIIth Century*. Chicago: Northwestern University Press, 1938.
Weisheipl, James, ed. *Albertus Magnus and the Sciences: Commemorative Essays, 1980*. Toronto: Pontifical Institute of Mediaeval Studies, 1980.
———. "Classification of the Sciences in Medieval Thought." *Mediaeval Studies* 27 (1965): 54–90.
Weiswurm, Alcuin A. *The Nature of Human Knowledge According to Saint Gregory of Nyssa*. The Catholic University of America Philosophical Studies, 136. Washington, D.C.: The Catholic University of America Press, 1952.
Wetherbee, Winthrop. *Platonism and Poetry in the Twelfth Century: The Literary Influence of the School of Chartres*. Princeton: Princeton University Press, 1972.
White, Lynn, jr. "Cultural Climates and Technological Advance in the Middle Ages." *Viator* 2 (1971): 171–201.
———. "Eilmer of Malmesbury, an 11th Century Aviator: A Case Study of Technological Innovation, Its Context and Tradition." *Technology and Culture* 2 (1961): 97–111.
———. "The Historical Roots of Our Ecologic Crisis." *Science* 155, whole no. 3767 (March 10, 1967): 1203–12.
———. "The Iconography of *Temperantia* and the Virtuousness of Technology." In *Action and Conviction in Early Modern Europe: Essays in Memory of E. Harris Harbison*, edited by T. K. Rabb and J. E. Seigel. Princeton: Princeton University Press, 1969.
———. "Medical Astrologers and Late Medieval Technology." *Viator* 6 (1975): 295–308.
———. "Medieval Engineering and the Sociology of Knowledge." *Pacific Historical Review* 44 (1975): 1–21.
———. *Medieval Religion and Technology: Collected Essays*. Berkeley and Los Angeles: University of California Press, 1978.
———. *Medieval Technology and Social Change*. London: Oxford University Press, 1964.
———. "Natural Science and Naturalistic Art in the Middle Ages." *American Historical Review* 52 (1947): 421–435.
———. "What Accelerated Technological Progress in the Western Middle Ages?" In *Creation: The Impact of an Idea*, edited by Daniel O'Conner and Francis Oakley. New York: Scribner, 1969.
Whitehead, Alfred North. *Science and the Modern World*. New York: Macmillan Company, 1925. Reprint: New York: Free Press, 1967.
Whitney, Elspeth. "Crafts, Philosophy, and the Liberal Arts in the Early Middle Ages." *Annals of Scholarship* 4 (1987): 11–27.
Winner, Langdon. *Autonomous Technology: Technics-out-of-Control as a Theme in Political Thought*. Cambridge: Mass.: The MIT Press, 1971.
Wolfson, Harry A. "The Classification of the Sciences in Medieval Jewish Philosophy." In *Hebrew Union College Jubilee Volume (1875–1925)*. Vols. 2 and 3. Philadelphia: Jewish Publication Society Press, 1925–26.

Index

PUBLICATIONS

OF

The American Philosophical Society

The publications of the American Philosophical Society consist of PROCEEDINGS, TRANSACTIONS, MEMOIRS, and YEAR BOOK.

THE PROCEEDINGS contains papers which have been read before the Society in addition to other papers which have been accepted for publication by the Committee on Publications. In accordance with the present policy one volume is issued each year, consisting of four quarterly numbers, and the price is $24.00 net per volume. Individual copies may be purchased at $10.00 per copy.

THE TRANSACTIONS, the oldest scholarly journal in America, was started in 1769. In accordance with the present policy each annual volume is a collection of monographs, each issued as a part. The current annual subscription price is $70.00 net per volume. Individual copies of the TRANSACTIONS are offered for sale.

Each volume of the MEMOIRS is published as a book. The titles cover the various fields of learning; most of the recent volumes have been historical. The price of each volume is determined by its size and character, but subscribers are offered a 20 per cent discount.

The YEAR BOOK is of considerable interest to scholars because of the reports on grants for research and to libraries for this reason and because of the section dealing with the acquisitions of the Library. In addition it contains the Charter and Laws, and lists of members, and reports of committees and meetings. The YEAR BOOK is published about April 1 for the preceding calendar year. The current price is $12.00. A separate volume of GRANTEES' REPORTS is published annually. The listed price is $10.00.

An author desiring to submit a manuscript for publication should send it to the Editor, American Philosophical Society, 104 South Fifth Street, Philadelphia, Pa. 19106.

www.ingramcontent.com/pod-product-compliance
Lightning Source LLC
LaVergne TN
LVHW081602100826
845153LV00004B/439

* 9 7 8 1 4 2 2 3 7 4 1 9 1 *